# TEDDY'S TANTRUM
JOHN D. WEAVER AND THE EXONERATION OF THE 25TH INFANTRY

TOM DURWOOD

Copyright 2021 Tom Durwood.

Originally published as an eBook in 2012.

ISBNs 978-1-952520-08-2 Paperback

978-1-952520-09-9 eBook

Book design by Kelley Creative.

# Table of Contents

| | |
|---|---:|
| Abstract | V |
| Introduction | VII |
| Prologue | 3 |
| **PART ONE: THE TANTRUM** | **11** |
| CHAPTER 1 \| Bonus March | 13 |
| CHAPTER 2 \| The World's Work | 23 |
| CHAPTER 3 \| Harriett | 33 |
| CHAPTER 4 \| A Quasi Battleground | 37 |
| CHAPTER 5 \| Forward Observer | 51 |
| CHAPTER 6 \| Justice or Death | 59 |
| CHAPTER 7 \| Studio 55 | 73 |
| CHAPTER 8 \| Einen Wilden Baren | 89 |
| CHAPTER 9 \| Fire in the Hills | 109 |
| CHAPTER 10 \| Special Order 266 | 119 |
| CHAPTER 11 \| A Stray Remark | 131 |
| **PART TWO: THE DETECTIVE** | **133** |
| CHAPTER 12 \| Aftermath | 135 |
| CHAPTER 13 \| Weaver Investigates | 169 |
| CHAPTER 14 \| A Reputation Cleared | 187 |
| CHAPTER 15 \| Jalester Lincoln | 203 |
| CHAPTER 16 \| A Second Book | 207 |
| CHAPTER 17 \| More Lost Stories | 221 |

| | |
|---|---:|
| **PART THREE: HISTORY AND LITERATURE** | **231** |
| CHAPTER 18 \| The Anger of the Legions | 233 |
| CHAPTER 19 \| Mosaic | 243 |
| CHAPTER 20 \| Imperial Grunts | 255 |
| CHAPTER 21 \| Tribal Loyalties | 265 |
| CHAPTER 22 \| A Twitch on the Right Side | 269 |
| EPILOGUE \| Centennial | 275 |
| Endnotes | 307 |
| Select Bibliography | 342 |

# Abstract

IN 1967, A JOURNEYMAN WRITER named John Weaver pointed to a photograph in the family album. "Where was that taken?" Weaver asked his mother. "Texas, dear," answered John's mother. "And what were we doing in Texas, Mother?"

"Some Negro soldiers shot up the town," she explained, "and Teddy Roosevelt kicked them out of the Army."

His curiosity sparked by this stray remark, Weaver investigated. He found a story long buried by the giant reputation of "TR." One hundred and sixty-seven men of the all-black 25th Infantry had indeed been dismissed without a trial after a midnight raid in the border town of Brownsville. What is more, Weaver found that Roosevelt carried out a vendetta against the troops of the 25th Infantry, alongside of whom he had fought in Cuba, hiring private investigators to coerce "confessions" and gather the flimsiest evidence against them. He drummed their champion, Senator Joseph Foraker of Ohio, out of office.

With the support of his wife, Harriett, Weaver uncovered all aspects of the entire episode and published a book which exonerated the soldiers. In February of 1973, the U.S. Army issued an apology to the men of the 25th Infantry and awarded the sole surviving battalion member (Dorsie Willis) back pay. Historian Lewis Gould called it a correction of "one of the most glaring miscarriages of justice in American history."

*Teddy's Tantrum* is the first chronicle of the entire Brownsville story, treating Weaver's work and the troops' exoneration as an equal part of the narrative. Original scholarship provides an account of John D. Weaver's early career and his two-decade campaign on behalf of the 25th. In the manuscript's first sections, the author follows three separate storylines – John Weaver, Theodore Roosevelt, and the men of the 25$^{th}$ Infantry – until the three merge, and Weaver's detective work uncovers the truth of the buried episode. In the book's third section, the author enlists several leading scholars to help interpret the many aspects, roots and consequences of the tantrum.

# Introduction

IN THE FALL OF 1906, Theodore Roosevelt lost his temper.

Someone had shot up the border town of Brownsville, Texas, where the all-black 25th Infantry had recently been stationed. Multiple hearings into the incident dragged on for months, without resolution, so Roosevelt impulsively settled the matter himself.

This epic outburst turned into a national drama that would last over four years and ruin over a hundred lives, generating tens of thousands of words of controversy in newspapers, in Congress, and in churches and communities across America. It ended the political career of the Senator who opposed Roosevelt, who compounded the tantrum by refusing to make amends, going to extraordinary ends to avoid doing so. It was a very bad hour in the career of one of our very best presidents.

One of the drama's minor players was a court reporter named Henry Weaver. Like many observers of the nine hearings which would fail to resolve the Brownsville matter, Weaver thought the men of the 25th Infantry were being denied justice, but there was little he or anyone else could do to slow Theodore Roosevelt once he had made up his mind.

In 1967, Henry Weaver's son, John, pointed to a photograph in the family album and asked where it had been taken. That idle question set him on a quest over two decades long to dig up the truth about what had happened in 1906 and bring justice to the 25th Infantry.

# Teddy's Tantrum

The historian and literary theorist Dominic LaCapra writes that it takes one hundred years to fully understand history. This book takes the 100-year arc of the Brownsville episode -- that is, both the original raid and its retelling -- and sets out to answer five questions:

a) Why did the original Raid break out?
b) Why did "TR" dismiss the soldiers?
c) How could he get away with it?
d) How did it get buried in history?
e) How and why was it resurrected?

I am not a scholar, so in the book's third section I have turned to experts in several fields to help understand the many aspects of this episode.

One of my early readers called this a minor event. It may be minor in its immediate effects, but the Brownsville Raid episode and, perhaps equally significantly, its resurrection and retelling, touch on some of the most powerful themes of the modern age. I hope my readers will follow the thread of my narrative into all the nooks and crannies where the investigation takes it.

Teddy had lost his temper before.

There was the time on the floor of the 1884 Republican National Convention when he stood on a chair about ten feet from a delegate named George William Curtis, engaged in a "blisteringly personal debate." Delegate J.S.Whipple called the image of Roosevelt pointing, bristling with anger, every bit the "human fighting machine … a picture never to be forgotten."

# Introduction

There was the time when young Theodore "let the wolf rise in him" as he was boxing his younger brother Eliot and started beating him senseless, hitting him in the head over and over until big sister Bamie stopped him.

"Each one of us has in him certain passions and instincts," Roosevelt warned a YMCA audience in 1900, "which if they gained the upper hand in his soul would mean that the wild beast had come uppermost in him."

There was the incident in a Wyoming bar, when he encountered a drunken saloon bully and knocked him unconscious. "Don't hit a man at all if you can help it," Roosevelt advised. "Don't hit a man if you can possibly avoid it; but if you do hit him, put him to sleep."

There was the time his son Quentin and his friends used Andrew Jackson's portrait as a spitball target, covering Old Hickory with gobs of masticated paper. That night, the boys were awakened by the apparition of an angry President.

"Who stuck the first spitball?" he asked fiercely.

Quentin, Charlie, and Dick all voiced confession together.

"Impossible!" TR said, his voice ringing harshly down the hall. "It's all very sporting to try and take the blame from one another but I – want – the – truth!"

"I think I did," Quentin said.

"You think!"

"Yessir –"

"I—I—[ he pronounced it 'Aiee'] don't like this!" TR said. [1]

He sentenced Quentin to seven days alone in the White House, banishing his friends for that time. "We felt the justice of the reproof and the weight of the punishment," wrote Quentin's boyhood friend many years later.

Roosevelt lost his temper with his childhood sweetheart Edith Carow in an exchange hidden to history. The two strong-willed sweethearts exchanged heated words in the gazebo of the Oyster Bay house. From the porch, his sister Bamie could see Theodore's flushed features, but could not hear the words being spoken. The two parted angrily, not to speak for seven years, during which time Roosevelt would meet and marry Alice Hathaway Lee, a very different type of woman. Only after Alice's death did Theodore mend the rift caused by the tantrum and make Edith his second wife, a happy union that lasted the rest of his life.

Them there was perhaps his most epic temper tantrum, the one against Taft, which erupted in 1910 after years of simmering and turned into the Bullmoose Party and the botched election of 1912.

Roosevelt took pride in his temper, since it reflected a properly "savage" heart. He wrote admiringly in *The Winning of the West* of a settler named William Campbell, a "true type" of the "earnest, eager men who pushed the border ever farther westward." While a "firm friend, staunch patriot, and tender loving husband," Campbell was subject to "fits of raging wrath that impelled him to any deed of violence." He hunted down horse thieves with "furious zest' and "a relentless and undying hatred."[2] Roosevelt's own slaughtering of animals in the wake of his first wife's death fits this pattern. He also admired a Revolutionary War militia commander named Benjamin Cleavland, a man who was famous for the brutality in his character" and for "persecut[ing] his foes

# Introduction

with ruthless ferocity, hanging and mutilating any Tories."[3] "If such men failed to learn mercy … Roosevelt wrote, 'at least they knew that it is still better to be just and strong and brave.'"[4] Describing his Dakota ranch hands, Roosevelt writes that "they become more furiously angry and excited than I do."[5] To Roosevelt, it was sometimes better to be strong and brave than to be just.

Roosevelt spent his lifetime keeping his temper in check. "I keep my good health by having a very bad temper, kept under good control," he was fond of saying, and if any of his listeners thought he was making a pleasant aphorism, they were mistaken. It was a very, very bad temper.

Roosevelt did not lose his temper in this single instance, but was wrestling with it throughout his life and career. The few times he lost his temper may be more revealing than any of the thousand times he held it in check.

This book concerns his worst tantrum.

The story of the incident's rediscovery and the eventual redressing of the tantrum's wounds is one of the unusual and little-known revisions in America's history of, well, history. As Lewis Gould declared, "it is rare that a single book changes the way that a past event is seen and interpreted," as happened in this case.

I have tried to set the events between June, 1906 and December, 1907 in their fullest context. I have tried to show the various forces which acted upon Roosevelt at the time. I have tried to let the characters and events speak for themselves. Roosevelt has attracted some of the century's best historians; I have mined their works wherever possible, and quote them directly rather than try to re-phrase them.

Special thanks to Chica Weaver for her help and insight into her late husband's personality, motivations, and three-decade mission to exonerate the men of the 25th Infantry. Pamela Fiore, John's long-time friend and editor at *Travel and Leisure* provided letters and insights into his working habits and his close relationship with Harriett, who in effect subsidized the first two decades of the Brownsville work with her real estate investments and emotional support. Carl Reiner, dinner companion to the Weavers on many occasions, contributed the Untermeyer and Passover anecdotes. Thanks also to Harriett Weaver's niece, Nancy Krupa, for her memories of the couple and their habits. Simon Elliot of the UCLA Special Collections not guided me through the extensive collection and shared his experiences with John and Harriett Weaver. Jim Perry knew the couple through their long involvement with the Los Angeles Fire Department and added a perspective on their non-Brownsville involvements.

I am indebted to a talented group of historians and Roosevelt scholars whose vigorous and sometimes downright rude comments early in the project set me on what I hope is the right path. Prof. John Milton Cooper of the University of Wisconsin correctly advised me to start with Weaver as the entry point into the story. Prof. John David Smith of The University of North Carolina Charlotte After Prof. Smith suggested I try and illuminate empire as a factor in the Raid, I began to see the elements of rising and falling empires (the Russo-Japanese War, the building of the

# Introduction

Panama Canal, J.P. Morgan, discord in the military, the battered world financial markets) everywhere in TR's letters and in concurrent events during the time period covered by the Raid. I have attempted to show these elements not in a lump at the end of the narrative but throughout the story. Dennis Showalter of Colorado College suggested I alternate between Weaver and the original cycle of events (it took me two drafts to comprehend the wisdom of that particular suggestion). It was also Dennis who recommended that I needed to address the theme of presidential powers and the constitution. Roosevelt biographer and Executive Director of The Theodore Roosevelt Society, Ed Renehan made extensive comments on the early version, and remembered the date of Tyler Dennett's discovery of the Perdicaris telegram. Thanks also to G. Edward White of the University of Virginia; Tim Pritchard; Prof. Robert B. Edgerton of UCLA; Digby Diehl for his support of the project, and Lewis Gould, who championed John D. Weaver all the way through.

The men of the 25th Infantry were the most difficult thread of this story to get hold of. Two researchers and I tried and failed to track the Raid survivors, so Dorsie Willis will have to represent the entire regiment. I felt I could not tell their story without also telling the story of their successors, men like Jalester Lincoln, the amazing John Fox, and mighty Dwight Johnson of the 4th Infantry; men like Colin Powell and young Lt. Reginald Allen, who wears the colors as I write this, leading our own Buffalo Soldiers as they patrol the new borderlands of Iraq and Afghanistan.

*-- Tom Durwood, Greenville, North Carolina*

# Teddy's Tantrum

"Father wrote a book about Oliver [Cromwell]. He says he was a very great man and that he hates him for some things, and loves him for others. He says, too, that's one way you know a man is great – when everything is all mixed up, in him, and about him …"

-- *Young Quentin Roosevelt to his friends as they regarded Cromwell's framed autograph hanging on a wall in the White House*

# Prologue

> The welfare of each of us is dependent fundamentally upon the welfare of all of us.
>
> -- *Theodore Roosevelt, New York State Fair, Syracuse, September 7, 1903*

### July, 1898

"General, if you will order a charge," said the young officer, "I will lead it."

The Americans were doomed if they did not move.

The general, thinking of the last war, was making the mistake of waiting. At the base of Kettle Hill, outside the fortified city of Santiago, in the disease-ridden swamps of Cuba, surrounded as they were by ever-increasing hostile fire, this was a terrible mistake. The enlisted men knew it. Only storming the heights would silence the Spanish guns, and give them an approach to the city. The Spaniards were so entrenched that simply returning the fire did no good.

"If you do not wish to order a charge, General, I should like to volunteer."

Brigadier General Hamilton S. Hawkins was paralyzed by indecision. He was waiting for the $2^{nd}$ Division, under the command of Henry Lawton, to arrive, and for the howitzers battery under the command of George Grimes to line up to their right. But there was no sign of Lawton, or Grimes. Hawkins hesitated. In the Civil War, Union troops had rushed in heedlessly on entrenched enemy positions and paid heavy prices for it. That was in Virginia, forty years earlier. Here, now, in Cuba, at the base of Kettle Hill, Hawkins could not make a decision. He did not fully understand the third rule of warfare: advance or die.[1]

Lieutenant Jules Ord of the 6th Infantry understood. He had risen from private to Quartermaster Sergeant to Second Lieutenant and now First Lieutenant, and understood that if they stayed where they were, the Americans had no chance.

"May I?"

The key to taking Santiago lay in the heights overlooking the city to the east, near a little town called San Juan. Rising up from the jungle were Kettle and San Juan Hills: Kettle Hill was well-defended by seven hundred Spanish soldiers in fortified, entrenched positions. The Americans were camped at the foot of the hill while armaments were brought into position. But there was no sign of the American armaments, and the Spanish guns were cutting the Americans to pieces.

"*May I volunteer?*"

"I would not ask any man to volunteer," demurred Hawkins.

"If you do not forbid it, I will start it," said Lieutenant Ord.

Still, Hawkins said nothing.

So far, it had been one of the least-organized wars in modern history. Some 16,000 American troops had landed at Daiquiri over four haphazard days, regular and volunteer brigades from New York and Minnesota and a dozen other places. Half of the

# Prologue

volunteers and all their horses had been left behind at Tampa. Regulars had been left to forage for food and water on their own. Meanwhile, the Spanish force of over 10,000 was well-entrenched at Santiago under Garcia Iniguez, one of the most competent of the Spanish generals. The heat of the Cuban jungle was humid, oppressive and deadly: the Americans were uneasy and anxious to press the battle, well aware that yellow fever had wiped out the British forces in a similar engagement a century earlier.

"We can't stay here, can we?"

Young Lieutenant Ord pressed the issue. "Undaunted by the silence"[2] emanating from Hawkins, Ord raised the stakes.

*"I only ask you not to refuse permission,"* he said.[3]

The enterprising men of the Signal Corps had sent up an observation balloon about fifty feet above the American position. This of course served as a perfect marker for Spanish artillery, which rained fire upon the American troops and the two "hapless occupants" of the balloon, Lieutenant George M. Derby and Lieutenant Joseph Maxfield. "Every gun, both great and small, was playing upon"[4] the observation balloon and on the men gathering below them. It was only a matter of time until the Americans were decimated.

Hawkins turned to look at his young officer.

"I will not ask for volunteers," he said. "I will not give permission and I will not refuse it. God bless you and good luck."

Lieutenant Jules Ord of the 6th Infantry smiled.

With a pistol in one hand and a sword in the other, he ran forward.

# Teddy's Tantrum

"Come on – come on you fellows!" he shouted. "Come on – we can't stop here!"

Ord advanced up Kettle Hill. The other American regiments saw him, and heard his shout, and the shout turned into a roar. A wave of young American men climbed up the slope. The United States Army had come to liberate Cuba from Spanish rule.

"Come on, boys!" yelled a sergeant in the 24th Infantry. "Let's knock the hell out of those sons of bitches."

The 24th advanced.

Sergeant George Barry of the 10th Cavalry grasped the colors and raised them, running up the hill. "Dress on the colors, boys, dress on the colors!"

Mingo Sanders of the 10th Cavalry heard the roar.

Tall, broad-shouldered, young everywhere but in the eyes, Mingo Sanders was all high cheeks, bow legs, and sinewy arms. Sanders was a veteran who had seen service all across the Great Plains. The troops under his command were mostly boys, barely young men, these black soldiers of the U.S. Army's 10th Cavalry, and they were used to patrolling badlands. The Army had chosen the all-black 24th and 25th regiments (of which the 9th and 10th Cavalry were regiments) for the Cuban mission partly out of a belief that the black troops would prove immune to tropical heat and disease.[5] Many of them had come into the service never having seen a gun or a horse; now they were competent soldiers, armed black warriors defending their country as free men. And in the deadly chaos of this cursed campaign, the black regiment understood that they would have to advance, and advance

## Prologue

together, in order to survive. They had learned the hard way that help would not be arriving, not now, not ever.

Sanders had grown up on a farm near Stillwell, Oklahoma and joined the Army for the promise of twenty U.S. dollars each month, since his father had six other children and could not keep food on the table. In exchange for those twenty dollars, the U.S. Army had requested that he lead a squadron to invade the fever-ridden island republic of Cuba, defeat the Spanish forces, and free the local populace.

The passage from Florida to Cuba was described by one of the soldiers: "We were huddled together below two other regiments and under the water line, in the dirtiest, closest, most sickening place imaginable."[6] As Theophilas Steward, a chaplain who traveled with them, put it, "Before them were the mountains with their almost impassable roads, the jungles filled with poisonous plants and the terrible prickly underbrush and pointed grass, in which skulked the land crab and various reptiles who bite or sting was dangerous ... and somewhere on the road ... they knew they were destined to meet a well-trained foe, skilled in all the arts of modern warfare, who would contest their advance."[7]

The young black men of the 10th Cavalry had now met the foe, and he was indeed skilled in the arts of warfare. They gripped their Jorgensen rifles close to their chests and began climbing the slope.

The 10th Cavalry advanced.

Half a mile away, Colonel Theodore Roosevelt, a man as responsible for the war as any, heard the roar of Jules Ord's reckless charge with relief.

# Teddy's Tantrum

Roosevelt and his squadron of volunteers, the "Rough Riders," had been pinned down by Spanish fire for hours, taking heavy casualties. Only hours earlier, his fellow officer, Bucky O'Neill, "… was strolling in front of his men, smoking a cigarette, for he was inveterately addicted to the habit …his men begged him to lie down … As he turned on his heel a bullet struck him in the mouth and came out at the back of his head; so that even before he fell his wild and gallant soul had gone out into the darkness."[8]

Roosevelt, the formidable Rough Rider who a month earlier had been Assistant Secretary of the Navy had seen several of his comrades die already. "My orderly was a brave young Harvard boy, Sanders, from that quant old Massachusetts town of Salem," he later wrote of that decisive hour. "The work of an orderly on foot, under the blazing sun, through the hot and matted jungle, was very severe, and finally the heat overcame him. He dropped; nor did he ever recover fully, and later he died from fever. In his place I summoned a trooper whose name I did not know… I directed him to go back and ask whatever general he came across if I could not advance, as my men were being much cut up. He stood up to salute and then pitched forward across my knees, a bullet having gone through his throat, cutting the carotid."[9]

At the sound of Ord's bold charge, Teddy Roosevelt found a horse, mounted it and led his men up the hill.

The engagement started erratically, seeming to meander and falter as the ragged line of American soldiers advanced towards the crest of the hill in an ungainly, arrhythmic pattern. It looked to observers like a terrible mistake, not a charge at all. The troops slipped on the muddy slope and stepped heavily through

# Prologue

the long grass. They struggled to get footing among thick shrubs and ground cover: the line bunched together here, strung out there. Scattered shouts rang out as the Spaniards saw them and fired from their hiding places behind the giant iron kettles of the sugar refinery and in the wooden mill-houses.

The muttered protests *("Gallant but foolish!")* of the foreign correspondents became urgent shouts, in several languages. A rolling undercurrent of deadly concussions joined the pinging and popping of rifle fire: the Spanish artillery found the range. The Americans roared in response and gained momentum.

The separate battalions merged into a stream of American soldiers charging up the slope, fanning out across the hilltop, overrunning the Spanish positions, jumping into the rifle pits to fight the enemy hand-to-hand. By the end of the afternoon, the Spaniards had abandoned Kettle Hill, retreating to the city of Santiago. A Signal Corps pilot from Milwaukee, riding the breeze in a second balloon, reported that afternoon that he saw the black men charge up the Cuban hill against the assembled host. "As Roosevelt stood on the crest of San Juan Hill, a moment he would always regard as the greatest in his life, he saw black Americans everywhere. They belonged to the Ninth and Tenth Cavalries and the twenty-fourth Infantry; they were among the finest regular soldiers in the U.S. Army, and Roosevelt knew this."[10]

The Americans swarmed over the Spanish positions and won Kettle Hill, moving quickly to take San Juan Hill. By the end of the week, the Americans had taken Santiago, and within the month Spain had ceded the Spanish American War.

# Teddy's Tantrum

"No men were any more brave or more daring, or showed greater courage in that slow, stubborn advance."[11] As Colonel Roosevelt himself would later write, "White regiments, black regiments, regulars and Rough Riders representing the young manhood of the North and South, fought shoulder to shoulder, unmindful of race or color, unmindful of whether commanded by ex-Confederates or not, and mindful of only their common duty as Americans."[12]

# PART ONE

# THE TANTRUM

We have been told, on leaving our native soil, that we were going to defend the sacred rights conferred on us by so many of our citizens settled overseas, so many years of our presence, so many benefits brought by us to populations in need of our assistance and our civilization.

I am told that in Rome, factions and conspiracies are rife, that treachery flourishes, and that many people in their uncertainty and confusion lend a ready ear to the dire temptations of relinquishment and vilify our action.

Make haste to reassure me, I beg you, and tell me that our fellow citizens understand us, support us and protect us as we ourselves are protecting the glory of the Empire.

If it should be otherwise, if we should have to leave our bleached bones on these desert sands in vain, then beware of the anger of the legions!

*-- Marcus Flavinius, Centurion in the 2nd Cohort of the Augusta Legion, to his cousin Tertulus in Rome (about 20 B.C.)*

# CHAPTER 1

# Bonus March

*"John loved standing up for things he believed in."*

*-- Pamela Fiore, John D. Weaver's editor*

JULY, 1932, WASHINGTON D.C.

In the summer of 1932, American men who had fought in World War I began to gather in the nation's capital. Small groups of veterans, men in their thirties and early forties who had fought in hellish battles at Cantigny and Belleau Wood and The Second Battle of the Marne, where twelve thousand American soldiers died in less than two weeks, rode in empty freight cars and on the backs of trucks. Many walked.

This small army of angry veterans began arriving in Washington D.C., some with their families, until 17,000 of them were camped out in tents and shacks. They gathered on the Anacostia Flats, a swamp across the river from the federal precincts of Washington, near the Eleventh Street Bridge, and took for shelter any object they could drag from junk piles. "There are shelters built of egg crates, of paper boxes, of rusty bed springs, of O. D. blankets, of newspapers, of scraps of junked automobiles, of old wall-paper, of pieces of corrugated iron rooting, of tin and bed ticking, of the rusty frames of beds, of tin cans, of rusty fence wire, of straw, of parts of baby carriages, of fence stakes, of auto seats. The man who can salvage an auto top from the dump has a mansion in this strange city … one man lived in a barrel filled with grass, another in a casket set on trestles, still another in a piano box which he labeled 'Academy of Music.'"[1]

These former soldiers called themselves the "Bonus Expeditionary Force," and their expedition had a single mission: to receive fair payment. At the conclusion of their service, the young soldiers had been given certificates in the place of cash: each Service Certificate held specific dollar values, and promised to pay interest as well … but they were not payable until 1945. The men and their families needed the money now. The House had passed a law agreeing to an immediate payment, but the Senate had defeated the bill. So these ex-soldiers had come to force the government's hand.

The Bonus Marchers made a vivid and lasting impression on a young man named John Weaver.

John Dowling Weaver, a small, slim, smart child of Washington, had just graduated from college. He had attended William & Mary College. Weaver's college thesis (eighty thousand words) topic was Henry Fielding, the 18th century British novelist (*Tom Jones*) and playwright who devoted himself to his writing in order "to promote the cause of virtue and to expose some of the most glaring evils, as well public as private, which at present infect the country …" Suffering for his political principles, Fielding lived in poverty for considerable periods of his life.

# Bonus March

The Weaver clan was a somewhat eccentric family with a healthy mistrust of the modern world. "If a fuse blew out ... we called an electrician. None of us knew where the fuse box was, and even if we'd known, we would never have dared touch it. Our aboriginal fear of electricity was so deep-seated that we were the last family in our section of Washington to install an electric refrigerator."[2] The family's "ineptitude with all mechanical devices" prompted a visit from the telephone company in the months after dial telephones were installed. It seems the Weavers had "dialed twice as many wrong numbers as any other subscriber in Washington." Weaver would recall that a vice president from the telephone company informed them that the Weaver misdialings "had even surpassed a national record set the preceding winter by an immigrant family in Brooklyn who had somehow confused the dial phone with the gas meter."[3]

John Weaver was born in Washington D.C. and grew up in the nation's capital, "testing the slickness of the floors in the Library of Congress." The topic at family dinner table discussion was usually civics. "I could find my way from blindfolded from the House to the Senate, from the Senate to the Supreme Court," Weaver would later write. "I used to see Presidents other children knew only from photographs. Woodrow Wilson was a gaunt, friendly man huddled in a lap robe in the back of his long dark car ... Teddy Roosevelt was Mother turning out the lights one night and sobbing softly, not that she had ever voted for him, but he was an era ..."[4] Every summer the family retreated to a home in the Virginia hills. "I fished and hunted with men who probably never turned over as much as a hundred dollars a year, but lived a life I envied ..."[5]

# Teddy's Tantrum

Young Weaver had seen the effects of the Depression, both on his own family and on the men of the Bonus March. He had clear memories of the struggles of working class families, including his own mother "hunched over the kitchen table with bills and a checkbook, deciding which creditors could be safely stalled another thirty days." At the time the Bonus Marchers were gathering, John Weaver was studying shorthand and typing to sharpen his job skills to follow his father, Henry, into the federal clerical bureaucracy. Henry Weaver, trained as a lawyer, worked as a Congressional Record court reporter, one of the six men who chronicled for posterity the speeches and debates which took place in the House of Representatives.

Young Weaver would never forget the Bonus Marchers, the veteran soldiers who "came shambling into Washington, not with the clenched fists of rebellion but with the slumped shoulders of helpless acquiescence."[6] Weaver went down to the river flats and talked to the ex-soldiers about their lives and their concerns, and their anger at a President who, for political reasons, was denying them their just due.

For months, the men "in frayed shirts, faded jeans, and overseas caps half-covering their thinning hair"[7] spoke out and demonstrated and did everything they could think of to get fair treatment from the nation they had served. In the end, the Bonus Marchers failed: the government refused to give them cash for their Service Certificates. Congress opposed them. Presidents Herbert Hoover and Franklin Delano Roosevelt opposed them. On July 29, federal forces set their tents on fire. Their cause faded from the news. Roosevelt offered the veterans the chance to enroll in the Conservation Corps, a forest work program. Eventually the city on the river flats dissipated, and the men who had once fought in their country's uniform returned to their homes, their honor denied, their spirits broken.

In 1933, Tyler Dennett found a telegram.

He was not looking for it, not in particular. Tyler Dennett was looking for documents that would make John Hay look good.

A scholar of United States policy toward China, Japan, and Korea in the nineteenth century, Dennett was a lecturer in American history at Johns Hopkins, which awarded him a Ph.D. degree in 1924. His 1925 book *Roosevelt and the Russo-Japanese War* uncovered the true account of this lesser-known chapter in U.S. – Asian relations.

For his new book on Hays, Dennett had gained access to the stored records of Theodore Roosevelt's administration. A "solid, square man with a massive head set on heavy shoulders" whose nickname was Tiger, Dennett wanted to correct the historical record on John Hay. He felt that Hay, Roosevelt's charming Secretary of State, had been overlooked by historians as a man of influence on America's foreign policy, particularly as it related to the Orient.

Dennett was searching through the dusty papers of Theodore Roosevelt's tenure in the White House, which had begun three decades earlier. In particular, he was sorting through boxes of documents regarding the famous Perdicaris incident. The Perdicaris matter had dramatically established both Theodore

# Teddy's Tantrum

Roosevelt's and the American nation's presence on the world stage. In the Spring of 1904, an American citizen named Ion Perdicaris was dining with his stepson in the terrace of their sumptuous compound in Tangiers when a band of Berber bandits led by Mulai Ahmed er Raisuli rushed in. Curved daggers to their throats, the two Americans were carried off on horseback and held for ransom. Raisuli's demands were high: $70,000 in gold, safe-conduct for all his tribesmen and, most outrageous of all, recognition as the sultan's *bashaw*, or governor, over two districts around Tangier.

Roosevelt's response was clear and simple:

*"Perdicaris free or Raisuli dead,"* he shouted to the Republican convention, and he heard roars of approval in response. America would not be blackmailed by some Moroccan bandit. No band of thieves could kidnap a United States citizen and get away with it.

Seven battleships from the Atlantic fleet were dispatched to North Africa.

Mulai Ahmed er Raisuli freed Ion Perdicaris and his stepson within the week.

But now, twenty-five years later, Tyler Dennett came across a curious paper. It was a telegram which was marked *"Confidential"* and dated "Tangier, July 22, 1904." It was written by S.R. Gummere, consul at Tangiers, addressed to the Honorable Francis Loomis, Assistant Secretary of State. This was the paragraph which caught Tyler Dennett's attention:

> *I beg further to report that I have today received a reply from Mr. Perdicaris, which admits the fact that he did assume Greek citizenship some forty years ago and has*

> *never taken steps to revive his citizenship in the United States, who protection he has enjoyed all these years without being entitled thereto.*

So Ion Perdicaris had not in fact been an American citizen. The bandits had kidnapped a Greek citizen. Gummere's note went on to say that the State Department will understand that "I am overwhelmed with amazement at this admission by Mr. Perdicaris, realizing its special seriousness at the present moment," surely a reference to the *USS Lousiana* and the six other American battleships which were at the time descending upon the Moroccan ports, "after the great efforts made in his behalf." S.R. Gummere ends with the cryptic, "His admission speaks for itself without comment of mine," a show of diplomatic restraint which no doubt the Honorable Francis Loomis, and his boss John Hay, and *his* boss Theodore Roosevelt, well appreciated.

Dennett found another half-dozen similarly worded telegrams delineating the movement upward in the chain of command the unhappy realization that America was rushing to save a Greek citizen. Almost two months before the Gummere telegram, one A.H. Slocomb of Fayetteville, North Carolina, had written to John Hay questioning Perdicaris' citizenship. In his letter, Slocomb recounted a discussion in Athens in 1862 in which Perdicaris had made it clear that he was in Athens to establish citizenship and thereby "save from confiscation by the Confederate States some valuable property inherited from his mother in South Carolina."

So Theodore Roosevelt had mobilized the nation's moral and military might in order to rescue an ex-patriot who had fled

America to save family holdings from confiscation during the Civil War. The discovery of this telegram meant that Roosevelt had known, even as the ships sailed across the Atlantic to the shores of Morocco, that he was not rescuing an American citizen at all, but a Greek citizen. How embarrassing: he had just announced to the Republican convention:

*"We want either Perdicaris alive or Raisuli dead!"*

"It is a bad business," Hay wrote. The President had kept the truth from the American public, for the American public's own good. "We must keep it excessively confidential."

And excessively confidential it had stayed, for almost three decades.

"No man was ever better served than President Roosevelt by his friends," concluded Dennett. The President's private papers had remained secret for thirty years, despite in many cases being circulated by Roosevelt to a wide circle of friends, many of whom were newspapermen.

John D. Weaver's moment of reckoning came early. John had followed his father into civil service. He began as an office boy in "one of the burgeoning bureaus of the New Deal," filing papers.[8]

"One afternoon I was summoned to the paneled office of my department head, a man who had fed long and well at the public trough. He'd had his eye on me. Yes sir, liked the way I firmed up the new procedural routines he was implementing. By George, I had my feet on the ground, eye on the ball. In short, God help me,

# Bonus March

I was being promoted. An extra twenty-five dollars a month went with the new rating.

"My department head swiveled back, waiting for my eyes to fill with grateful moisture, but in that instant I saw Old Weaver hobbling down the hall in his black alpaca coat. Yes sir, been with us forty years now, always the first to show up in the morning, the last to leave at night, and never missed a day in forty years. By George, you don't find 'em like that any more. Feet on the ground, eye on the ball. Must get around to giving him a gold watch one of these days.

"I got promoted," I announced at dinner that night.

"Fine," Dad said.

"I also handed in my resignation."

Dad hesitated. "Why?"

"I don't want to get trapped."

This time there was no hesitation. "You're absolutely right."

Young Weaver did not yet know where his place in the world might be, but he knew where it was not.

That same year, a South Dakota historian, Doane Robinson, had the idea to create a state monument in the Black Hills. He invited a sculptor he had read about to visit and give his opinion on such a project: Gutzon Borglum. Borglum was a Danish American sculptor with strong convictions about American monument art. It should, he felt, quit aping European works and create art that was drawn from American sources, memorializing American achievement. In 1908, at the unveiling of Borglum's

Civil War memorial in Sheridan Square, the sculptor had met President Theodore Roosevelt, who called the statue "first rate." That such a great man would bother to notice a young artist, much less take the time to compliment his work, had deeply impressed Borglum.

In South Dakota, Borglum suggested to Robinson that they create a national monument, something grand that would celebrate not only the Black Hills but the entire expansion of America westward. Such a monument, he argued, could feature the four greatest American presidents: George Washington, Thomas Jefferson, Abraham Lincoln, and Theodore Roosevelt.

# CHAPTER 2

# The World's Work

"As long as England succeeds in keeping the balance of power in Europe ... well and good; should she, however, for some reason or other fail in doing so, the United States would be obliged to step in . . ."

-- *TR to Baron Eckardstein (1911)*

**MAY, 1905**

Captain Vladimir Semenov saw the Japanese ships, but he did not understand, at least not at first.

The Japanese ships were reversing course. They were crossing directly in front of the Russian convoy, willing to expose themselves to lethal fire in order to gain a favorable striking position.

"How rash!" exclaimed his colleague, Lieutenant Reydkin. "Why, in a minute we'll be able to roll up the leading ships!"

At 13:49, the *Suvoroff* opened fire on the first two Japanese ships, the *Mikasa* and the *Shikisima*, at a range of 6400 yards. The entire Russian fleet followed suit. Their barrage would not have the desired effect.

On the night of May 27, 1905, Captain Semenov was watching the start of a climactic battle in the largest war ever waged. A gigantic, dysfunctional Russian force had moved across half of Asia to confront Japan. Both nations sought control of the coastal ports connecting Manchuria to the Sea of Japan. Both nations sought control of Manchuria.

Russia had staked everything on victory. The war against Japan was costing the Tsar a staggering 6 billion rubles, half of which was interest on debt to French and German lenders.[1] The borrowing was placing a huge strain on the European banks. The giant war had gone on too long, and Russia's very solvency "soon became the object of steady attention in the press."[2] Finance Minister Sergei Witte had bet Tsarist Russian economic hopes on the eastern markets to help repay its gigantic debts. Japan had borrowed, but not nearly so heavily. Japan's financial envoy, Viscount Takahashi Korekiyo, had been in deep trouble before he chose the right seat at dinner. When skeptical bankers along Wall Street and in London doubted that Japan could win such a campaign, they would not even enter loan negotiations. Then, one evening while in London making the rounds, Takahashi "was seated at dinner next to an unknown gentleman who expressed an 'uncommon interest' in Japan's plight."[3] It was Jacob Schiff, head of the banking firm Kuhn, Loeb & Co. Jacob Schiff, son of a family of distinguished German rabbis, had migrated from Frankfort to New York at the age of 18. He had no love for the Tsar and his virulent anti-Semitism, evidenced so recently in a purge in the province of Kishinev. That evening at dinner, Schiff agreed to take a look at Takahashi's proposal for a loan to Japan. Over the next two years, Kuhn Loeb would extend a series of loans amounting to $200 million, with "burdensome" interest rates.

The question of Russian solvency was causing ripples in the Paris Bourse and London financial markets: should the Tsar fail on his debts, world markets would suffer. Europe feared a broader revolt: Russia's vast peasant class, so long enslaved by this Tsar and this Tsar's predecessors, had begun agitating for a national revolution.

Two hundred thousand men had clashed at the land battle of Mukden two months earlier, and half a million were gathered on the Sakhalin peninsula for more combat. The Japanese had raised an army of 300,000 field troops, with a reserve of 400,000 trained reservists. Tsarist Russia's conscript army in the Far East, ill-trained and low in morale, was 80,000 at the beginning of 1904 and was reinforced to 250,000. And now the entire Russian fleet, having made its way halfway across the world, was being out maneuvered. The Russian Naval Ministry had sent eight battleships, three coastal cruisers, and eight cruisers from its Baltic Fleet through the North Sea (where they attacked the British fishing fleet), around the tip of Africa and through the Indian Ocean, stopping in Indonesia, to fight Japan. The ships had traveled 18,000 miles without repair and without maintenance. The steam boilers were badly in need of cleaning and broke down intermittently. The Russian forces were raw and, worse, internally fractured. The Russian military commander, Colonel Akashi, did not have the luxury of choosing troops that liked one another and so assembled a fighting force that fought conscripted Finnish troops and Poles, and Estonians who hated one another and hated the Russians who led them.

The fleet was headed to Vladivostok. Of the three routes, they had chosen to go through the straits of Tsushima, the most direct route.

The Japanese had been waiting.

They had seen the lights of the last two ships in the gigantic convoy.

Now the Japanese were crossing in front of the Russian convoy in order to bring their guns to bear from the port side.

Semenov's heart raced. *If we can sink even one of the Japanese ships --*

He watched through his binoculars as the Russian shells burst in the waters close to the two Japanese ships. He could not see any direct hits.

Semonov cursed Nebogatov, the Rear Admiral who was third in command. *Could they not aim properly?* There was so little time –

A Japanese shell whined. It "flew over us, making a sort of wail, different from the ordinary roar," as Semenov later described it. The shell exploded the moment it touched the water's surface. "After them came others ... Splinters whistled through the air, jingled against the side and superstructure"[4] of the Russian ship.

Two more Japanese ships, the *Fuji* and the *Asahi*, crossed in front of the Russians.

"The next shell," wrote Semenov in his memoir, "struck the side by the centre of six-inch turret, and there was a tremendous noise behind and below me on the port quarter ... a shell having fallen into the captain's cabin, and having penetrated the deck, had burst in the officers' quarters, setting them on fire."

Semenov ran to the conning tower. The Japanese shells had created havoc – burning bridges, smoldering debris, dead bodies, the decks decorated with blood and plumes of smoke. The chief signalman and the officer at the wheel were dead.

He looked out from the *Suvoroff*'s tower.

"The enemy had finished turning. His twelve ships were in perfect order at close intervals, steaming parallel to us ... forging ahead." He saw no fires, no falling bridges, no heeling over of wounded ships.

The Russian ships had trouble maneuvering in heavy seas and stormy southwest winds. The Japanese small craft "pressed furiously on them, with such determination and disregard for danger that there were several collisions. *Navarin* took four torpedo hits before sinking with 622 men on board ... *Sisoi Veliki* was torpedoed in the stern and began to sink very slowly; early the next morning she went to the bottom off Tsushima Island ... *Nakhimov* was torpedoed forward and, taking in tons of water, made for Tsushima, she went down the next morning ..."[5]

A Japanese woodcut of the sinking made it look almost pretty. The reality was grim and shocking. Over the next ten hours, the Japanese bombed the Russian fleet out of existence. All eight battleships were destroyed. At the end of the Battle of Tsushima, the Japanese dead numbered 117. They had lost three torpedo boats. The Russians had 4,380 men dead and twenty-one ships sunk, seven ships captured, and six disarmed.

# Teddy's Tantrum

Two thousand miles west of the Straits of Tsushima waited the one man who could end the war. All third-party attempts to negotiate an end the war had fallen through. There stood a man conversant with the necessary skills and principles, a man who closely followed each battle on maps mounted on his office wall, a man with no stake in the conflict, a fair man trusted by both nations to be impartial, the one man who could hope to broker a peace between these two deeply entrenched foes.

*The American President. Roosevelt.*

John Findley Wallace saw now that it was impossible.

It was one of the riskiest, most daunting enterprise ever undertaken. Wallace, a brilliant engineer and a stubborn, forceful man, saw now that the obstacles which had defeated the French would also defeat America.

A trans-isthmus canal could never be dug.

"I see only jungle and chaos from one end of the Isthmus to the other," he wrote his wife.

It was the greatest civil engineering feat in the history of mankind. It was the cleaving of a continent. The great campaign had been teetering: now it was collapsing

Wallace could not see how to actually dig the Panama Canal. He needed at least a year to test the French equipment, to gauge the diggers' capacities for attacking the principal gorge, the spine of a land bridge which connected North and South. He had yet to devise an overall system for hauling away the dirt and rubble, and a plan for feeding and housing the army of 10,000 workers, and a scheme for coordinating machines, dynamite, for mapping the gouging and exploding so many sites simultaneously. The hydraulics were not yet functional. The electric generators had yet to be tested.

The Canal, as currently conceived, was "a vast mistake."[6] Wallace was keeping the unpleasant news to himself that recent tests had uncovered bedrock as deep as 168 feet below sea level -- far deeper than assumed – under the site where the proposed *Bohio* dam was to be built.

The city of Colon was ugly and "unspeakably dirty,"[7] lacking a sewage system. Many of the Americans who came down were drunks and "tropical tramps" who had neither experience nor useful skills. The railroad was worn out and filthy, far too small for the massive job at hand. Sections of the rail ran across rickety bridges. Hygiene in the vermin-infested work camps was atrocious. The unskilled black workers who broke the rock and worked the dynamite – particularly those from the Indies -- were sullen and balky; the Chinese workers were better, but only because they were addicted to opium, shipments of which had recently been perilously late. There was no ice, no milk, few vegetables to eat. The water was foul. And the most common response among Commission members to Gorgas's insistence on clearing away the garbage and paving the streets was, "What's that got to do with digging the Canal?"

But worst of all was the red tape. The entire five-man Commission charged with overseeing the gargantuan construction insisted on vouching for every transaction, no matter how petty. As a result, the simple act of ordering and receiving equipment took on absurd difficulties. Wallace's chief architect had ordered 15,000 doors and 15,000 pairs of hinges to hang them. Twelve thousand doors and 240,000 pairs of hinges were delivered. "To hire a single handcart for an hour required six separate vouchers. Carpenters were forbidden to saw boards over ten feet in length without a signed permit."[8] Colonel Gorgas begged for screen wire to shut out the mosquitoes, but could get none because the Commission could not perform its function to approve it. In disgust, Wallace declared that the bureaucracy constraining all his efforts was a "system gone to seed." He said a child could break a single hemp fiber, but many strands woven together would hold in leash the biggest ship that floats; and, by the same token, enough red tape could prevent the building of the Panama Canal.[9]

All this was as nothing compared to the disease. It lurked everywhere, and brought the same fever-ridden, miserable death to the brightest young engineers, the strongest workers, and the most innocent wives, daughters, sons and infants. No matter what Gorgas and his roving squads of hygiene men did, they could not seem to extinguish the plague.

Within John Findley Wallace's little kingdom, ten thousand black men labored at the digging. Within twenty square miles of Wallace's office lay the rusting ruins of the French effort, giant dredging machines toppled over in the swamps, overgrown by vines. North of that lay thick, snake-ridden jungle and beyond that the dusty plains of the Mexican *bajio*. A thousand miles north and well east of that, resided the one man with the zeal, moral courage, vision, and sheer animal energy to prevent this most ambitious enterprise from collapsing.

# The World's Work

*The American President. Roosevelt.*

Theodore Roosevelt had a great deal on his mind during the month of May, 1906.

First, the new dog, Skip, was "not as yet entirely at home in the White House and rather clings to my companionship," he wrote to his son Kermit. "He seems to be fond of Archie, who loves him dearly. Mother is kind to Skip, but she does not think he is an aristocrat as Jack is. He is a very cunning little dog all the same."

Secondly, he could not find a way to defeat the Japanese wrestlers. Roosevelt had tried to choke one of them, but his clever Oriental foe had found a way to choke the President instead. As he described it in a letter:

> *DEAR KERMIT:*
>
> *I am wrestling with two Japanese wrestlers three times a week. I am not the age or the build one would think to be whirled lightly over an opponent's head and batted down on a mattress without damage. But they are so skilful that I have not been hurt at all. My throat is a little sore, because once when one of them had a strangle hold I also got hold of his windpipe and thought I could perhaps choke him off before he could choke me. However, he got ahead.*

Thirdly, he wanted to make sure he kept control over the White House while the First Lady, Edith, was away. The President failed to conquer his son Ted on the tennis court ("Yesterday

# Teddy's Tantrum

Ted and one of his friends played seven sets of tennis against Mr. Cooley and me and beat us four to three"). There was some distraction from the labor union men ("They made what I regarded as a rather insolent demand upon me, and I gave them some perfectly straight talk about their duty and about the preservation of law and order.") His younger sons, Quentin and Archie, proved more difficult to handle than the labor union men. "One night I came up-stairs and found Quentin playing the pianola as hard as he could, while Archie would suddenly start from the end of the hall where the pianola was, and, accompanied by both the dogs, race as hard as he could the whole length of the White House clean to the other end of the hall and then tear back again."

In the end, President Roosevelt was able to preserve order. The boys settled down to read a good book, "The Legend of Montrose," after "a vigorous pillow-fight," and, with Edith's return, the dog Skip seemed to have acclimated to his new home. "Both Skip and Jack have welcomed Mother back with frantic joy, and this morning came in and lay on her bed as soon as she had finished breakfast."

CHAPTER 3

# Harriett

> "Harriett is one of the wonders of our day," John (Cheever) once wrote, and on his deathbed he recalled a chicken dinner she had served him nearly forty years earlier.
>
> -- *John D. Weaver, Glad Tidings*

AFTER QUITTING THE CIVIL SERVICE in a moment of clarity in 1933, young John Weaver set off across country to find his place in the world. He "blew my savings on a trip to California" and took a job at the *Kansas City Star*. He wrote the most minor assignments washing his "only seersucker suit in the bathtub of a rented apartment."

A mutual friend introduced him to Harriett Sherwood, a bookish young woman who was working as a clerk and assistant to the poet Louis Untermeyer as he compiled an anthology called *Stars to Steer By*. Here is John's description of their first date. "When she first walked into the room, all I seemed to see was a pair of large, dark-brown eyes, at once lively curious and sad... I had never seen someone so lovely or so shy."[1] The two spent an awkward evening together, climbing the stairs to the roof to look down on the lights of the Plaza. Weaver "spun anecdote after anecdote" for the quiet Harriett. John walked her home at the end of the evening.

In some ways, it was a case of opposites attracting. Harriett Sherwood was a most pragmatic young woman, who sewed her own clothes, fixed the plumbing and broken furniture, and kept a strict budget. She was an only child whose father had died when she was five. Her mother ran a boarding house, a "big, old-fashioned, three-story house of gray stone and dark wood." Harriett, as described by John, was a delicate, inquisitive child, solitary and prone both to injuries (five broken arms in three years) and bouts of illness. Her father had died when she was four, leaving Harriett and her mother to move from a boarding house in Nebraska to an apartment in Kansas City, where they repaired their own light sockets, refinished their own chairs, and replaced their own washers on leaky faucets. Her mother worked long hours, despite her doctor's warnings of overwork. She and Harriett ran a boarding house until she took an office job and moved with her daughter into a series of apartments. In high school, the solitary girl had found friends among bookish peers. "The truth seekers of Central High debated capitalism and Cubism, Marx and Freud, Sacco-Venzetti and the Teapot Dome scandals. They listened to Stravinsky records, discovered Joyce, devoured *The American Mercury* …"[2] Weaver contrasted Harriett's "respectable Republican" upbringing with his own "large, boisterous family of whisky-drinking, poker-playing Democrats … We were a feast-or-famine family, and when we feasted, we went all the way. One year, when my father came into a bundle, we

# Harriett

tooled around Washington in a white Auburn convertible with red upholstery. Two years later we were living on mustard greens and trying frantically to peddle the car."[3]

John managed to "accidentally" meet Harriet at the bus stop in the weeks after their first date. They spent time with friends like Untermeyer, an engaging man of wide-ranging knowledge whom the playwright Arthur Miller described as "a distinguished-looking old New York type with a large aristocratic nose and a passion for conversation, especially about writers."[4]

Less than a year later, they were a couple. "'I'm due for a raise,' I told her, which was one way of asking her to marry me, and a few nights later she said, 'Mother's found a single apartment, so we can have this one,' which was her way of saying Yes."[5]

"I woke up with a way of life," is how Weaver describes meeting and marrying Harriett.

# CHAPTER 4

# A Quasi Battleground

"Fight, did you say? Why, they would charge into hell, fight their way out, and drag the devil out by the tail."

-- *Brigadier General Andrew Burt, who commanded the 25th Infantry for ten years*

JULY, **1906**

In Nebraska, Mingo Sanders and the men of the 9th Cavalry received the order in late Spring: they were being transferred to Fort Brown, Texas.

Their Chaplain, Theophilus Steward, for one, had a bad feeling.

"Texas, I fear, means a quasi battle ground for the Twenty-fifth Infantry," he wrote in a letter to the regiment's adjutant.

The men of the 25th had been living in a quasi battle ground as long as they could remember.

After the widely reported action at Kettle Hill, the black troops had become heroes. "Negroes had little, at the turn of the century, to help sustain our faith in ourselves except the pride that we took in the 9th and 10th Cavalry, the 24th and 25th Infantry," wrote historian Rayford Logan many years later. "Many Negro homes had prints of the famous charge of the colored troops up San Juan Hill. They were our Ralph Bunche, Marian Anderson, Joe Louis and Jackie Robinson." Since Kettle Hill, the 9th had engaged America's enemies at Ojo Caliente, where the Sioux warrior Lone Wolf stole 46 horses and staked five members of the 9th Cavalry to the ground to die. They had fought in the steaming jungles of the Philippines, leading a punitive expedition into the Lake Lano region, driving the Moro tribesmen out of Fort Gadungan for Taft, the Philippines Governor.

Now they had then had been drawn into an ill-defined, in-between military campaign against the Indians of the West. After the Civil War, the battle-weary nation was tired of maintaining an army. Military assets were released. "For even though the country during the Indian campaigns could not be said to be at peace, neither Congress nor the war-weary citizens in the populous Atlantic states were prepared to consider it in a state of war."[1] And in any case, there was strong sentiment against a large standing army as well as a widely held belief that the Indian problem could be settled by other than military means. The postwar Army began decades of decline, dropping from an 1867 level of about 57,000 to half that in the year that General Custer was killed,[2] then leveling off at an average of about 26,000.

So the black men of the 9th and 10th Cavalry, the 24th and 25th Infantries -- the buffalo soldiers -- were assigned to protect a million square miles of territory, making it safe for any settlers.

# A Quasi Battleground

There was no plan. The U.S. Army "lacked a formal body of doctrine for unconventional war" like this. "Heavy columns of infantry and cavalry, locked to slow-moving supply trains, crawled about the vast wilderness in search of the enemy. The goal was to surprise the Indians in their villages or, better yet, bring their fighting men into open combat on the battlefield. The ideal ... was the same for Indians as for British, Mexicans, or Confederates -- to entice them into assaulting fixed defenses or into standing against a mounted charge by cavalry or a bayonet charge by infantry."[3] In 1876, Major General Winfield Scott Hancock had assured a congressional committee that "the Army's Indian mission merited no consideration whatever in determining the proper strength, organization, and composition of the army ... Tomorrow's conventional war, not today's unconventional war, preoccupied the generals."[4]

In the Civil War, some tribes had fought for the South (the Cherokees) while others assisted the North (the Seminoles). The tribes were all pushed westward as new enterprises like the Bozeman Trail and the railroads broke up their lands. The Osage signed a treaty to live on a reservation in Missouri, then Oklahmoa; the Sioux in South Dakota; the Kickapoo in Illinois.

To help protect the white settlers from the red man, a string of tiny border outposts was built, forts which were erratically placed in response to demands by pioneer communities. The appearance of outposts like Fort Leavenworth in Kansas and Fort Niobrara in Nebraska and Fort Brown in Texas encouraged more settlers to move west, beyond the limit of military protection, "stirring up the

Indians and prompting the establishment of still more forts, often beyond effective logistical support."[5]

"Little ... in U.S. military practice represented a concession to the enemy's peculiar style of fighting ...Military leaders looked upon Indian warfare as a fleeting irritant."[6] The senior American officers fighting the Plains Indians had a mindset shaped by the experience commanding large armies during the Civil War. Frontier skirmishes had little in common with battles like Manassas and Gettysburg.

The soldiers of the 25th Infantry had mixed feelings about their adversaries. Once a 9th Cavalry patrol of fifty had followed Chief Victorio and his band of Apaches from the Gila River, near its junction with West Diamond Creek. The Apache set the forest and underbrush on fire to dissuade their pursuers, and Captain Beyer had led his men through the burning landscape. On May 29, they caught up with the Apache band. When Beyer went into the camp under a truce to talk with the Apache leader, he saw only sixteen braves, bedraggled women and children, ten horses, two mules, two burros, and "makeshift fortifications." Victorio went into "a harangue ... to the effect that he, Victorio, and his people were poor, that they did not want to fight ... that all they wanted was to be let alone."[7] These were far from the bloodthirsty savages portrayed by the dime novels.

Similarly, some of the Indian tribes had mixed feelings about the black men against whom they fought. When Captain Dodge led an expedition including Buffalo Soldiers against the Ute in 1878 on Colorado's Milk River, "not one Ute raised his rifle" when the black soldiers rode through their entrenchments. Several

## A Quasi Battleground

warriors called out *"To-Maricat'z*! The black-whitemen!" The Utes took note that the black men ride behind the white.[8] The black troops acted as mapmakers, contractors, and policemen, guarding payroll shipments from outlaws. "The Buffalo Soldiers also explored and mapped large areas of the southwest and strung thousands of miles of telegraph lines. The Black Soldiers built and fixed frontier outposts where towns and even cities would begin. Without the protection provided by the 9th and 10th Cavalries, crews building the ever expanding railroads were at the mercy of outlaws and hostile Indians."[9]

The following account of an encounter with bandits in 1889 is typical. It was written by the paymaster who accompanied a payroll wagon which outlaws tried to rob.

> *A small detachment from the 24th Infantry and the Ninth Cavalry were ambushed by bandits in Arizona as they guarded an army payroll wagon and its driver. From a promontory a band of outlaws pinned the men down…*
>
> *They were nearly all at the boulder when a signal shot was fired from the ledge of rocks about fifty feet above to the right, which was instantly followed by a volley, believed by myself and the entire party to be fifteen or twenty shots.*
>
> *A sharp, short fight, lasting something over thirty minutes, ensued during which time the … officers and privates, eight of whom were*

*wounded, two being shot twice, behaved in the most courageous and heroic manner …*

*Sergeant Brown, though shot the abdomen did not quit the field until again wounded, this time through the arm.*

*Private Burge who was to my immediate right, received a bad wound in the hand but gallantly held his post, resting his rifle on his fore-arm and continuing to fire with much coolness, until shot through the thigh and twice through the hat.*

*Private Arrington was shot through the shoulder, while fighting from this same position.*

*Privates Hames, Wheeler, and Harrison were also wounded, to my immediate left, while bravely doing their duty under a murderous cross-fire …*

*The brigands fought from six well-constructed, stone forts; the arrangements seemed thorough, the surprise complete …*

*I was a soldier in Grant's old regiment, and during the entire war it was justly proud of its record of sixteen battles and of the reflected glory of its old Colonel, the "Great Commander," but I never witnessed better courage or better fighting than shown by these colored soldiers, on May 11, 1889,*

# A Quasi Battleground

> *as the bullet marks on the robber positions to-day abundantly attest.*
>
> *-- Letter written by J.W. Wham, from the Medal of Honor File of Sergeant Benjamin Brown*[10]

Nonetheless, the black troops served proudly, for the most part. The steady pay was a help to their families, for whom economic prospects were bleak. The pensions they earned would help them advance their children and grandchildren.

Theodore Roosevelt's friend, the artist Frederic Remington, who rode with the Tenth Cavalry in the summer of 1888 and on another, later occasion, reported of the outfit that "They are charming men with whom to serve" despite never having a soft detail ..." He described them in admiring terms: "The physique of the black soldiers must be admired – great chests, broad-shouldered, upstanding fellows ..."[11] He found the 10th to be a regiment "full of soldiers who know what it is all about, this soldiering."

The townspeople of Fort Niobrara had appreciated the services of the 9th Cavalry. They spent money in the saloons and paid their bills on time. For four years, the men of the 9th had coexisted with the citizens of Nebraska, and not a single incident of conflict or disharmony.

Haroun Al-Roosevelt was mighty angry.

## Teddy's Tantrum

North Africa was behaving very badly. The Arab races in general, and one of their leaders in particular -- Mulai Abd-al-Aziz IV, the Sultan of Morocco -- were refusing to cooperate.

Theodore Roosevelt had earned the nickname Haroun Al-Roosevelt while Police Commissioner of New York. He and the reformer Jacob Riis habitually made forays into the netherworld of New York, visiting the paupers and prostitutes and denizens of "the other half" so they could more astutely address the problems of urbanization.

Now firmly entrenched in the White House, Theodore Roosevelt believed in "the material redemption of unimproved properties to the benefit of mankind at large."[12] By "unimproved properties" he meant northern Africa, or Panama's canal zone, or China in its entirety.

At the moment, Roosevelt was trying earnestly to redeem the uncivilized lands of Northern Africa for the benefit of mankind, yet the Arab tribes, heedless, continued in their random and barbaric ways. This was region of the world, which his friend and mentor Alfred Thayer Mahon had termed "the Middle East," was inhabited by a race of people who were unreliable. "Of course the best that can happen to any people that has not already a high civilization of its own is to assimilate and profit by American or European ideas, the ideas of civilization and Christianity."[13]

In 1905, it was felt that "the powers that border the Persian Gulf, Persia itself, Turkey, and some minor Arabian communities, are unable to give either the commercial or the military security that the situation will require."[14] So America had intervened – well, Roosevelt had intervened.

# A Quasi Battleground

The situation was this: Kaiser Wilhelm II of Germany, sick and tired of watching France colonize the entire African continent, made certain comments during a visit to Morocco. These comments encouraged Moroccan independence. France and her *Entente Cordiale* (England and Spain) quickly rebuffed this idea. Germany escalated its rhetoric and called for a pan-European conference to review France's ambitions. Troop movements brought all the free world's attention. A conference was arranged to settle the "Morocco crisis" by the one party who held the trust of all parties and exhibited a bottomless capacity for the issues, large and small, and personalities involved: the American president.

From January to April, representatives of five nations met in the city of Algeciras; while the crisis took place in Morocco its true center was somewhere between Paris, Berlin, and London. Roosevelt took to the diplomacy with relish. "There are plenty of jobs for which I am not competent, but I must say, I should greatly like to handle Egypt and India for a few months," he wrote to Whitelaw Reid, U.S. Ambassador to Britain. He sent a forty-two page letter to the English, reminding Britain that she needed to secure its communications with its own empire by securing peace in North Africa. He took the greatest pains to reassure each party that their best interests were being served, reiterating his philosophy over and over. The British sailed their North Sea Navy to the Strait of Gibralte to intimidate the German diplomats who were attending the conference.

At length, an agreement had been finalized. France ceded certain domestic issues to the Moroccans but retained control of the country.

But now it had been sixty days since the delicate truce had been agreed upon, an artful agreement that balanced all interests fairly. As Spring had turned to summer, Morocco's Sultan, Abdelaziz, also known as Mulai Abd-al-Aziz IV, would not sign the treaty settling the matter. Roosevelt was furious.

It was difficult dealing with the Oriental mind. As to direct dealings with the Arab, Lord Cromer, Britain's longtime Viceroy of Egypt, put it plainly: "Accuracy is abhorrent to the Oriental mind," Cromer pointed out. "Want of accuracy, which easily degenerates into untruthfulness, is in fact the main characteristic of the Oriental mind." He went on to explain that, while the Arab's ancestors might have displayed some higher reasoning skills, "their descendants are singularly deficient in the logical faculty ... Endeavor to explain a statement of plain fact from any Egyptian. His explanation will generally be lengthy, and wanting in lucidity. He will probably contradict himself half-a-dozen times before he has finished his story."[15]

Did Abdekaziz not see what was at stake? Without European intervention, Africa could quickly fall into the abyss. "The white man rules; but there is only one white man on the continent to one hundred others, who are either barbaric black heathen or fanatical Mohammedans."[16] Referring darkly to "Levantine agitators and the fanatics of the seventh-century type," Roosevelt kept the bloody recent history of the region close in his thoughts. "In the Soudan, Mahdism during the ten years of its unchecked

## A Quasi Battleground

control was responsible for the death of over half the population and meant physical and moral ruin ..."[17] As to Persia, and Arabia at large, Roosevelt had only the crudest consideration of the Mahdis or the Egyptians as individual peoples, yet he had a clear appreciation of their homelands as part of the international system of politics. He understood that it is necessary "to consider each of the several centres of interest as not separate, but having relations to the whole; as contributory to a general balance ..."[18] Africa was a tinderbox, and so was Europe, which was connected in an underlying way to all global contacts, no matter how distant: if the Algeciras treaty went unsigned and the whole matter caught fire again, there was no telling what Wilhelm might do.

Waiting for the Moroccan Sultan to decide to sign the Treaty of Algeciras, Roosevelt worked hard to keep his temper in check. "*Allah ma elsaberin, izza sabaru* – God is with the patient, if they know how to wait," was a favorite Arab motto of his.

"Each one of us has in him certain passions and instincts," Roosevelt warned a YMCA audience in 1900, "which if they gained the upper hand in his soul would mean that the wild beast had come uppermost in him." To control his passions, to prevent the wild beast from gaining the upper hand in his soul, Roosevelt was prone to taking what his friend Leonard Wood called "tramps." These were long and arduous walks to which he often subjected unsuspecting visitors, and which were part tests of character and endurance and part pleasure, rough climbs through Rock Creek Park and the rugged cliff and banks of the Potomac above Washington. "He especially delighted in taking out officers of the Army and Navy and giving them what he called a tryout. The crossing and recrossing and scrambling about the banks of Rock Creek when the waters were high and the walking difficult gave him particular pleasure. A tramp with the President usually meant that the invited ones would appear rather smartly turned out. They usually departed ... more or less complete wrecks."

That summer, Mulai Abd-al-Aziz IV at last ratified the Algeciras treaty. The Germans were appeased. The world took "a step back on the ramp to war."[19]

Haroun Al-Roosevelt was satisfied.

For now.

On July 12, in Paris, Captain Alfred Dreyfus was officially exonerated by a military commission. The day after his exoneration, he was readmitted into the army with the rank of Squadron Chief. A week later, he was made a Knight in the Legion of Honour, and subsequently named to the artillery command at Vincennes.

Honor had been restored to a military man who had been unfairly accused by his superiors.

Eight years earlier, Captain Dreyfus had been accused and convicted of treason, selling secrets to France's new field artillery piece, the French Modèle 1890 120mm Baquet howitzer, to Germany. Alfred Dreyfus was Jewish, and the charges against him were hopelessly far-fetched: yet he was convicted by a military tribunal. All France had watched his disgrace. In the main courtyard of *L'Ecole Militaire* on Paris' Place Fontenoy, Sergeant-Major Bouxin, "a helmeted giant with flowing mane" had

## A Quasi Battleground

systematically torn the decorations from his superior's uniform. "Long live France!" and "I am innocent!" Captain Dreyfus had exclaimed, trembling with emotion. Dreyfus was shipped to Devil's Island, a brutally primitive penal colony off the coast of French Guyana.

All of France had been caught up the Dreyfus Affair. Dreyfus' brother, Mathieu, had fiercely believed in Alfred's innocence, and Mathieu was not without resources. He was determined not to repeat the passivity with which past attacks on Jews had been met, "of receiving blows and not protesting, of bending the spine, waiting for the storm to pass…"[20] Mathieu persuaded the writer Emile Zola to help the cause, and on May 16, 1896, Zola's editorial *"Pour les Juifs"* set fire to the affair. "Let us return to the depth of the forest, let us begin again the savage war of species against species; let us devour one another …" Zola wrote. *"La verite est en marche et rien ne l'arreta."* Truth is on the march and nothing can stop it. Three weeks later, Emile Zola was put on trial. The charge was criminal libel. It was what Zola had hoped for: a forum to place the entire affair under public scrutiny. Hundreds of journalists descended on Paris to report the trial. The *London Times* decreed: "Zola's true crime has been in daring to rise to defend the truth and civil liberty … [and] for that courageous defense of the primordial rights of the citizen, he will be honored wherever men have souls that are free …"

The French government realized its mistake. At length, the injustice was undone. Dreyfus was pardoned in 1899. Now, in July of 1906, a military tribunal officially exonerated Captain Alfred Dreyfus, returning him to honor, and to the French armed forces.

## CHAPTER 5

# Forward Observer

Did you know that if a publisher owes you one thousand dollars in March they can put it on the April statement and pay you in December? They can.

> -- *John Cheever to his friend John D. Weaver, commiserating on their chronic money woes*

**DECEMBER, 1943**

Just before Christmas, 1943, on the grounds of the Astoria movie studios in Queens, Lenny Spigelgass introduced one young writer to another.

One writer was John Downing Weaver. The other was John Cheever.

The old Paramount movie studios in the Astoria section of the Queens borough of New York City was bustling with Army personnel as well as with actors, cameramen, and sound and lighting technicians. The cinema people were there to help the Army Signal Corps Motion Picture Center produce technical films

# Teddy's Tantrum

for the war effort. The two young writers were there to help as well. Lenny, who knew both, figured they should get along all right.

John Cheever was a New England writer who had been kicked out of Thayer Academy for smoking. He wrote a story about the experience, "Expelled," which was published in *The New Republic* magazine in 1930. Since then he had lived in Europe and in the artists' colony at Yaddo and published a steady stream of stories in *The New Yorker*. In 1941, he had married Mary Winternitz, a "brainy" Sarah Lawrence graduate who was a trainee-typist in the office of Cheever's literary agent, Maxim Lieber. John Cheever was one his generation's most promising young writers.

The resourceful Major Lenny Spigelgass had sought out Sergeant Cheever in the Spring of that year and eventually managed to roust him from Fort Dix in southern New Jersey, telling the young writer that he "considered it unpatriotic for him to be in the infantry."[1]

In a letter written that year, Cheever reflected that his life in the Signal Corps had "never been so well regulated, moderate, and quiet. Mary meets me at the door with a floury apron in the evenings. We eat dinner, play with Susan, read the paper, and go to bed. It's very pleasant, of course, but I sometimes wish it were more exciting, and that I could see more of the war. But the army is very big, moves very slowly, and the war may be very long."[2]

The two young writers did indeed become fast friends. "I met another writer, John Cheever," wrote Weaver to Harriett, that night. "I can see that we will get along very well."

# Forward Observer

### December, 1944

"Please repeat those coordinates," said the raspy voice on the walkie-talkie. The Germans were coming in fast.

The forward observer did so.

There was a pause.

"That will be right on you!" the artillery officer at headquarters yelled into the phone. "I can't do that!"

"Fire it!" Lieutenant John Fox, the forward observer, yelled back inot the phone.

He had already asked for a smoke screen to cover a withdrawal by the handful of American soldiers and partisans who could still walk. Now he was ordering a heavy concentration of mortar and 105mm shells on the surrounded observation post.

His own post.

On the day after Christmas, 1944, Lieutenant John Fox of the all-black 92nd Division, one of the rare black American soldiers to see combat in the European theatre, was in a hopeless position. He and "a scant two platoons" -- seventy fellow soldiers -- were trying to slow "a massive German assault"[3] in a small town on a mountainside in northern Italy. The town was named Sommocolonia, and while Lieutenant Fox may not have been able to pronounce its name, he was surely prepared to defend it against the advancing enemy.

The rift between Germany and England which Theodore Roosevelt had always feared had blasted open once again. World war engulfed Europe and the Pacific. Poland, Austria, and France had fallen. The Teutonic peoples whom Roosevelt warned "had reduced savagery to a science" had rounded up the weaker tribes, imprisoned them in concentration camps, and were now systematically exterminating them by the hundreds of thousands.

The United States' 92d Infantry Division had arrived on the shores of Europe to help save the free world from Nazism.

In the years after Brownsville, the 24th Infantry had tended to resist harassment. In Houston in August, 1917, "insults and abuse" heaped upon the young black men of the 24th resulted in 19 deaths (17 white, two black). The Inspector General of the Army flew into Houston and told the troops, "If you know anything about the matter, you'd better start talking now, because there is going to be a big hanging." No members of a General Court-Martial had yet been assigned to try the case. Thirteen soldiers were hanged for the incident.[4]

Few black American soldiers drew combat assignments during World War I. The black 92nd Division, 369th, 371st and 372nd Infantry regiments were among those that served with the French Army at such battles as Metz and Monthois. In an attempt to accommodate their American brethren, the French command sent the following directive to its officers in August, 1918:

> *To The French Military Mission Stationed with the American Army*
>
> *Secret Information Concerning Black American Troops*
>
> *We must prevent the rise of any pronounced degree of intimacy between French officers and black officers. We may be courteous and*

> *amiable with the last but we cannot deal with them on the same plane as white American officers without deeply wounding the latter. We must not eat with them, must not shake hands with them, seek to talk to them or to meet with them outside the requirements of military service. We must not commend too highly these troops particularly in front of white Americans. Make a point of keeping the native cantonment from spoiling the Negro. White Americans become incensed at any particular expression of intimacy between white women and black men.*[5]

When World War II broke out, a federal judge named Hastie delivered a report to Theodore's younger cousin, Franklin, now President, calling for full integration of the armed forces. Franklin Roosevelt rejected the Hastie recommendation, as did Dwight Eisenhower, Supreme Commander of the Allied Forces in Europe. "Please give thousands of young American Negroes the chance to serve in the *actual* combat units of the U.S. Army. Let *our* country live up to the Democratic Concepts that it is now fighting for," wrote William C. Wyatt of Rolla Missouri to Franklin Roosevelt on December 15, 1941. Four young black men from New York City wrote to Eleanor Roosevelt, hoping she would be more sympathetic than her husband. "Wanting to be part of the Colored Tenth Cavalry, whose proud history they knew well, these men showed up at the Tenth's New York City enlistment office, only to be turned away. 'The very fact that there should be separate divisions for white and colored in such a democratic nation as this is bad enough,' they implored. 'But to deprive those who really wish to serve their country of the opportunity to do so because of their race is intolerable and something drastic should be done to eliminate the situation.'"[6]

Black soldiers remained segregated, drawing assignments confined to service and support.

The all-black 92nd Division was an exception. When they arrived in Italy, they were greeted by their commanding officer, Gen. Edmund Almond, with "I did not send for you." The white commandant of the 92nd Division was not happy to see them. "Your Negro newspapers, Negro politicians and white friends have insisted on your seeing combat, and I shall see that you get combat and your share of casualties."

Lieutenant John Fox was a forward observer for Cannon Company, 366th Infantry Regiment, 92d Infantry Division.

On Christmas night, 1944, Fox had watched as Nazi soldiers had infiltrated the town in civilian clothes, and by early morning the town was largely in hostile hands. Commencing with a heavy barrage of enemy artillery at 0400 hours on 26 December 1944, an organized attack on Sommocolonia by uniformed German units began.

"Being greatly outnumbered," most of the Americans withdrew from the town. "Lieutenant Fox and some other members of his observer party voluntarily remained on the second floor of a house to direct defensive artillery fire. At 0800 hours, Lieutenant Fox reported that the Germans were in the streets and attacking in strength.

"He then called for defensive artillery fire to slow the enemy advance.

"As the Germans continued to press the attack towards the area that Lieutenant Fox occupied, he adjusted the artillery fire closer to his position.

"Finally he was warned that the next adjustment would bring the deadly artillery right on top of his position. After acknowledging the danger, Lieutenant Fox insisted that the last adjustment be fired as this was the only way to defeat the attacking soldiers.

"Later, when a counterattack retook the position from the Germans, Lieutenant Fox's body was found with the bodies of approximately 100 German soldiers."[7]

Few lived to tell of Lieutenant Fox's gallant actions. His supreme sacrifice, and those of his fellows, went forgotten. A small marker on the side of the hill was the only reminder.

CHAPTER 6

# Justice or Death

We, the soldiers of the United States, do hereby warn cowboys, etc., of San Angelo and vicinity, to recognize our rights of way as just and peaceable men.

If we do not receive justice and fair play, which we must have, someone will suffer; if not the guilty, the innocent. It has gone too far; justice or death.

-- U.S. Soldiers, one and all

*Handbill written by U.S. Army soldiers, black and white, in San Angelo Texas, February 3, 1881, the day a black private was killed by a professional gambler and a white soldier by another civilian.*

AUGUST, **1906**

"A delightful summer," wrote Theodore Roosevelt to his friend Henry Cabot Lodge on August 6.

He also mentioned Pennsylvania Republicans and the new Hamilton book, which he was now reading and recommended highly.[1]

# Teddy's Tantrum

The first week of August found Theodore Roosevelt in Oyster Bay, a hamlet founded by the Dutch on the north shore of Long Island. He went fishing and rowing in the bay, read books, camped out with his children on the beach, and took long walks with his wife, Edith.

Theodore's first love but his second wife, Edith was erudite and calm, frank and loyal. She made a good partner for her rambunctious husband. Like his closest advisors, she served the role of sentinel, reining him in often without a word. She and Theodore had been childhood sweethearts until a teenaged fight in the gazebo at the Roosevelt family compound: no one else had heard the exchange, but it had precipitated a complete falling-out, which lasted five years. Roosevelt went to Harvard, where he met, fell in love, and married Alice Hathaway Lee, a very different kind of woman – pretty, rich, sweet-tempered and frail. Alice had died on the blackest day of Roosevelt's life, February 14, 1884, the same day Theodore's mother had died. The day had sent him into a two-year downward (or at least westward) hejira. Alice Hathaway Lee's name was never spoken in Edith Roosevelt's house.

On August 9, the President wrote Frederick Scott Olivier, the author of the Hamilton book, to compliment him. "Jefferson ... was infinitely below Hamilton. I think the worship of Jefferson a discredit to my country," he wrote, in typical full-throttle enthusiasm for his subject. "Jefferson led the people wrong, and followed them when they went wrong." Lincoln, on the other hand, "carried out the Hamiltonian tradition ... a true democrat."

# Justice or Death

Theodore Roosevelt did not care for Thomas Jefferson, although he should have.

Jefferson appeared to be an ardent supporter of the Constitution, a man with a passionate belief in strict limitations on the President's actions. Unless the Constitution expressly gave a power to the chief executive, he argued, the president did not have that power, the states did. Yet, once Jefferson himself rose to the office, he set a clear precedent for the President breaking the articles of the Constitution whenever he deemed it necessary, especially Article 1, Section 8.

Jefferson twice broke Article 1, Section 8, both times in spectacular fashion. First, in 1801, he discharged the U.S. Navy to fight off the Barbary pirates in North Africa, notifying the Congress of his actions only when the ships were too far to be called back. That same year, he sent envoys to Paris to buy the port of New Orleans for $2 million from Napoleon. Instead, they returned with an agreement to buy the entire Louisiana Territory. So, in 1803, without constitutional justification, Jefferson borrowed $15 million from Great Britain and made one of the most massive land purchases in history. Now that he was president, it seemed, the ideas he had formerly held about states rights and executive power seemed… different. "What is practicable must often control what is pure theory," as he explained it to Congress.

If Thomas Jefferson broke Article 1, Section 8, then Theodore Roosevelt shredded it. Violating the Constitution, for which he had an open disregard, was for Roosevelt a weekly event. Like Jefferson, he considered this document to be a collection of guidelines to action in the real world. "I do as I see fit, and let the rules catch up," was one of the many ways he expressed this. Another way was this: "The country needs and, unless I mistake its temper, the country demands bold, persistent, experimentation." Theodore Roosevelt rarely mistook the nation's temper, and "bold, persistent experimentation" is as clear a description as we need for his presidential philosophy.

Theodore Roosevelt understood history. He was an avid history reader. He wrote history – not just the Oliver Cromwell biography, but a popular history of the West called *Winning the West* as well as half a dozen histories -- before entering politics, and clearly realized that he was creating history once he did so. "The vision of the great historian must be both wide and lofty," he wrote. "… In any great work of literature the first element is great imaginative power. The imaginative power demanded for a great historian is different from that demanded for a great poet; but it is no less marked. Such imaginative power is in no sense incompatible with minute accuracy. On the contrary, very accurate, very real and vivid, presentation of the past can come only from one in whom the imaginative gift is strong. The industrious collector of dead facts bears to such a man precisely the relation that a photographer bears to Rembrandt. There are innumerable books, that is, innumerable volumes of printed matter between covers, which are excellent for their own purposes, but in which imagination would be as wholly out of place as in the blue prints of a sewer system or in the photographs taken to illustrate a work on comparative osteology. But the vitally necessary sewer system does not take the place of the cathedral of Rheims or of the Parthenon; no quantity of photographs will ever be equivalent

## Justice or Death

to one Rembrandt; and the greatest mass of data, although indispensable to the work of a great historian, is in no shape or way a substitute for that work."

Roosevelt deserved a delightful summer. It had been a busy eighteen months.

He had recently ended the Russo-Japanese War, the largest and deadliest war in the history of mankind. Most of his countrymen were unaware of that particular fact. Roosevelt often preferred that his countrymen be unaware of particular facts, since that allowed him freedom to do as he saw fit. In this case, he had seen fit to correct an imbalance in the world order. Much as he had done in Morocco, and also in Venezuela in 1902, Roosevelt set out single-handedly to stop an apparently trivial incident from mushrooming into a worldwide conflict, and succeeded. After the Russian fleet was decimated that night in the straits of Tsushima, Roosevelt had invited the Russians, whom he loathed, and the Japanese, whom he mistrusted, to a secluded compound in Portsmouth, Maine. Roosevelt and his intermediaries browbeat them into a truce which, while it favored the Russians, ended the great Russo-Japanese War.

In June, Roosevelt had taken aim at Standard Oil. On June 22, his Attorney General had announced an investigation into Standard Oil, headed by Frank B. Kellogg and owned by the dour John D. Rockefeller. As in the matter of the Russo Japanese negotiations, Roosevelt made an effective use of duplicity. In the court of law, he pressed for a breakup of Standard Oil with the full force of the Sherman Act. In the court of public opinion, he fanned the flames of resentment against Rockefeller, who was slow to respond. Yet, when entertaining his enemies, Roosevelt showed no sign of the rabid passion with which he pursued them in all other arenas. In early March of 1906, Roosevelt showed to the Standard Oil executives the friendliest possible face. "He exhibited no personal animosity or unkindly feeling," wrote Rockefeller Junior of the meeting. "Nor could they judge from anything said that he himself was at the bottom of this investigation."[2]

It was a delicate game. Roosevelt had learned to hold his anger in check, for his goal was not an open fight with the trusts but a curbing of their power. It was a disciplined process, showing the carrot and then the stick, pretending to unaware of the savage game even as he pursued it. Roosevelt sought a balance of the warring forces. What Roosevelt wanted was integration: compromise. All Americans working together.

In Oyster Bay that summer, the President took his children camping out overnight on the beach, catching the fish they would eat for dinner. He spent hours gardening. He shaped world events in his mind.

He wrote a letter to the Honorable W.W. Rockhill, of Peking, China, urging him to stay in close communication with the representative of the Associated Press stationed in the Middle Kingdom. Failing that, might the American Minister confide in Mr. Melville Stone? The President hoped Mr. Rockhill would stop giving his information to the London Times. "The three centers of special world interest for the immediate future bid fair to be Russia, the Balkan Provinces, and China," he reminded the loose-lipped Mr. Rockhill.

## Justice or Death

Roosevelt also found time in Oyster Bay to write Andrew Carnegie in Scotland regarding the Hague Conference, during which letter he found cause to mention Robespierre, the Kaiser, and the European armaments race, ending "with warm regards to Mrs. Carnegie, believe me."

Another letter commended the President of Yale on his recent article regarding football in the American college.

To his friend, the illustrator and fellow frontiersman Frederic Remington in nearby Chippewa Bay, he wrote:

> *My Dear Remington,*
>
> *We hail the coming of the original native oyster.*

He wrote a telegram to the President of Chile offering a "tribute of sorrow and sympathy" regarding the awful disaster that had befallen Valparaiso.

It was a delightful August.

On the morning of Monday, August 13, 1906, Sergeant Mingo Sanders of the 25th Infantry had reason for concern.

The 25th Infantry's new home -- Fort Brown, Texas -- was not at all like Nebraska.

Fort Brown sat at the foot of the Rio Grande, where it met the Gulf, deep in the borderlands on the south Texas Plains, as south as you could go and still remain in the United States. During the boom years of the Civil War, the Rio Grande valley had seen a huge influx of cotton workers, railroad men, and Mexican agricultural workers. The mix of Yankee, southern, Mexican and

Indian border cultures made for a lively, often explosive mix. "During Brownsville's heyday as a major Gulf port in the 1860's, Hispanics got along well with black Union soldiers ... but within four decades, this amiability had disappeared, along with the town's hopes for ... prosperity."[3] By the turn of the century, in towns all along the Rio Grande corridor, Hispanics tended to clash with black Union troops. "Bring out your nigger soldiers," an angry mob had yelled at nearby Fort McIntosh in Laredo in March of 1899, when members of the 10th had assisted Texas Rangers in enforcing a quarantine. Fewer than a dozen black families existed in Brownsville to welcome the men of the 25th.[4]

Texas towns had a checkered history with their uniformed protectors. The men of the 9th had heard the stories of powerful rancher-rustlers like King Fisher of Maverick County[5] who controlled local law enforcement and intimidated jurors. They did not wholly trust the Texas Rangers, many of whom considered themselves to be sole arbiters of the law. They were also aware of the gangs of Mexican smugglers whom Mexican President Porfirio Diaz made little effort to quell.

Mingo Sanders and his soldiers had no way of knowing that in the days before the 25th arrived, "all were loud in their denunciations of colored soldiers."[6] The white soldiers of the departing 26th heard repeated threats against their replacements. One of the town's police officers, Victoriano Fernandez, bragged, "I want to kill a couple of them."

So far, sentiments among the townsfolk did not seem positive.

# Justice or Death

One of the townsfolk recounts the following exchange between "an adolescent girl, the daughter of a local Jewish family named Cowen," who struck up a conversation with a black guard:

> [The guard asked ]if she was a "half-blood nigger" or a "half-blood Mexican." When she answered that her mother was Mexican, the guard responded, "You look like it," whereupon the girl shot back, "You look like an ape."[7]

Sanders' company had only been in Texas ten days, but there had been small incidents already. Private August Williams was walking along a Brownsville street with another soldier when they passed a white man, customs inspector Fred Tate, who turned on them and said, "You black son of a bitch, don't you know this is a white man's town?" On the previous Sunday night, Newton and Lipscomb of Company C were passing through a small group of townsfolk on the Elizabeth Street sidewalk when a man struck Newton on the side of the head with a Colt .45, dropping the soldier to the sidewalk. A second customs officer confiscated a pen from Private Adair, and another (A.Y. Baker) knocked Private Reed into the Rio Grande. The company commander, Captain Edgar Macklin, made light of the incidents.

Hollomon, the company moneylender, did not take proper care when it came to maintaining a low profile in town. He had somehow managed to set up a saloon across from the Twixell Brothers' place. That could not be a good thing. Private Burt Conyers was spending too much time with the baseball team. Private Reed had been shoved into the river by a customs officer. These young men needed supervision, especially here in their new home.

Saturday, payday, went smoothly, but tension simmered in the hot air.

Then, on Monday afternoon, August 13, the *Daily Herald* newspaper hit the streets with an inflammatory headline: *"INFAMOUS OUTRAGE Negro Soldier Invaded Private Premises Last Night and Attempted to Seize A White Lady."*

In four years and two months in Fort Niobrara, no member of the 25$^{th}$ had invaded a home to seize a white lady. Sanders could not imagine that there was any truth to this report. Even so, the mayor, Fred Combe, met with Major Penrose to defuse the mounting tension. All passes were cancelled as of 8:00 p.m. Three patrols were sent out to round up stray soldiers.

Sanders went to bed that night thinking that this was not a situation that was going to go away.

Shots rang out around midnight on Monday night. They came from the vicinity of the garrison wall which separated the town from the garrison.

Raiders moved up Elizabeth Street, firing indiscriminately into lighted areas. A bullet grazed bookbinder and editor Paulino Preciado.

In the Cowen house on Fourteenth Street, a block away from the fort, a birthday party was just ending. Mrs. Anna Cowen couldn't sleep; the night was too hot. Her husband Louis was at Weller's Bar, buying a bottle of Schlitz beer when the shooting

## Justice or Death

started. When the shooting lulled, he walked fifty feet to the Ruby Bar, where young Frank Natus was tending bar. He asked Natus if he had a gun.

"Just the one," said Natus, and he showed Cowen a small nickel-plated Smith & Wesson. The pistol was in Natus' hand when a bullet struck and killed him. Private Joseph Howard, the sentinel guarding the area closest to the wall, believed the fort to be under attack from outside the reservation and fired three shots to sound the alarm.

Anna Cowen had convinced her eldest daughter, Gertrude, to stay up with her. The loud sounds of shooting scared her children, who ran into the living room saying "Fire, Mamma, fire."

"Children, it is the soldiers," she replied. She assumed the police and the soldiers had got into a shooting scrape, as used to happen frequently in the old days.

When the shooting sounds came closer, she ordered her children under the beds. "Pray God to save your lives," she told them. "If we are alive tomorrow, we will all go and thank God in church."

Shots burst the lights and splintered a mirror.

"Madam," said the servant girl, Amada, as she crawled along the floor. "I believe it is the day of judgment. The soldiers are going to kill us."

Two policemen moving along Elizabeth Street called up to Widow Katie Leahy in the second-story window of the Miller Hotel. "Where's the fire?" Like many others, they assumed the shots were an alarm.

# Teddy's Tantrum

Mrs. Leahy ran downstairs, bundled them into the hotel, and told them to stay there, which they did.

Major Penrose heard the shots and assumed the fort was under attack, perhaps in retaliation for the alleged molestation.

Mingo Sanders was asleep with his wife in the quarters reserved for married noncommissioned officers when he was awakened by a hammering on the door. "What's the matter?"

"There is a fire out here or something!" a man shouted.

Sanders could hear the trumpeter of the guard sounding the call to arms. *That's not a fire,* thought Sanders as he scrambled into his uniform. He raced the five hundred yards to his barracks. He was certain that he heard bullets passing ten or twelve feet over his head. After the Cuba and the Philippines campaigns, Sanders had no trouble identifying the sound of Winchester rifles. He also thought he heard Mausers and perhaps a Remington, and pistol shots, which he took to be .45s. Neither the Army's new Krag-Jorgenson nor its new Model 1903 Springfield rifle was involved in the mixed fire.

Police lieutenant Joe Dominguez was sitting on the markethouse steps waiting for the schoolhouse bell to ring at midnight when he heard the first shot. He mounted his large gray horse and set off at a fast trot down Washington Street.

"What does all the shooting mean?" he called to Genaro Padron, whom he saw standing in the middle of the street.

"The soldiers are shooting up Cowen's," came the reply.

Dominguez spurred his horse across Thirteenth Street and called out to the Miller Hotel residents to "escape themselves" and put out the lights.

## Justice or Death

He continued down Thirteenth Street toward Elizabeth and made it as far as Twelfth, but coming around the corner, his horse stumbled and fell down, dead. The firing continued as Dominguez struggled to get out from under the horse and stumbled up Elizabeth Street. His arm was shattered by a bullet. Two Mexicans helped the policeman to the drugstore, where he lost consciousness.

When Mingo Sanders reached the B Company barracks, he darted into his office, grabbed his rifle, then rushed out to the parade ground with a half-dozen of his men. He snatched a lantern from Sergeant George Jackson and ordered the company to fall in. Shots could still be heard on the town side of the garrison wall.

Meanwhile, a mob was forming in the lobby of the Miller Hotel; men with guns were gathering to march on the garrison. Mayor Combe stood on a barrel and argued against such a move, since the troops would be "splendidly armed," and besides, it was better to remain within the law. Anna Cowen was crying, much to the annoyance of Widow Leahy, who had no sympathy with a woman in hysterics.

At dawn, the men of the three companies of the 25th Infantry stood reveille. After rigorous inspection, not one of their rifles showed any sign of having been fired. All ammunition was verified: not a single bullet was missing.

Captain Macklin walked to the town side of the garrison wall and returned with a handful of spent cartridges – cartridges for the Army's new Springfield rifle, Model 1903.

"Well Macklin," said Major Penrose, "I am afraid our men have done this shooting."

The white lieutenant, Lawrason, ordered seven men of B Company to step aside.

# CHAPTER 7

# Studio 55

Patriotism means to stand by the country. It does not mean to stand by the president or any other public official...

-- *Theodore Roosevelt*

**April, 1950**

"There is the happiest guy in New York," says Robert Mitchum to Janet Leigh.

He nods his head in the direction of a seal in the Central Park Zoo. The seal claps as Mitchum tosses the remainder of his hot dog into the seal's enclosure.

"He'll never be Vice President of the First National Bank."

Janet is intrigued by Mitchum's remark, and by his casual cynicism. It is December. Pretty snow is falling in Central Park. She delves deeper, asking what he means. What's his story?

"I made the mistake of listening to people," he tells her. "'Do something sensible,' they said. 'Sell something – cut a few throats, get yourself an executive suit.'"

Mitchum is buying Janet Leigh lunch in Central Park. This is noteworthy because she has just gotten him fired. A charming, financially strapped widow with a young son, Janet has a job as a comparison shopper. She had bought a toy train from Mitchum without asking how much it cost: Mitchum recognized her as a corporate spy, but decided not to turn her in to management because he liked her. He was fired within the hour.

Janet asks Robert about himself, about how he came to be a clerk in a toy store. It turns out that Robert is a boat builder, bound for San Diego, where he has a small yet promising shipyard waiting for him. Caught in the commercial gears, Janet must soon choose between Mitchum and her sincere, patient ("We've had almost two years!") lawyer suitor, Wendell Corey. Janet, playing Harriett Weaver, chooses Mitchum.

The a view of values and priorities expressed by Robert Mitchum in the 1949 film adaptation of John D. Weaver's short story "Holiday Affair" closely reflects the Weavers' own values: happiness before commerce.[1]

Such a choice came with consequences.

In the spring of 1950, John D. Weaver was not a wealthy man. He was never a wealthy man.

Except for a brief period in 1943, when MGM bought the film rights to the holiday short, John and Harriett had never known financial stability. John's letters are filled with surprisingly even-handed references to their often-dire financial straits. "By the end of June," he wrote once to his friend John Cheever, "Harriett just about exhausted our savings account, our total earnings for the first six months of the year having come down to exactly nine dollars (from the Danish rights to a short story). An income of five cents a day struck me as cutting things a bit thin, but in no way discouraged Harriett from prowling the Hollywood hills in search of a house. 'Not enough closet space,' she [will] say airily."[2]

Harriett Weaver did not believe in debt. Harriett believed in real estate, which would prove to be a good rule in post-war Southern California.

She did her own repairs. For their little cement-block house in the Hollywood Hills, she had woven a wall-to-wall carpeting for the living room, built a desk for John's workroom, and laid the bricks for three patios. John benefited from Harriet's pragmatism, and enjoyed contrasting his own family's extreme casual attitude towards home repair to Harriett's. Here is a passage from his 1959 memoir, *As I Live and Breathe* that describes Harriett's first visit to his family retreat in the Shenandoah Valley. In it he introduces his bride to his family, a collection of eccentrics living in genteel poverty in the Shenandoah Valley town of Gooney:

> *"You remember that old roof leak?" Mother said as we started towards the kitchen. "It hasn't come back this year. I always knew it would go away if we just left it alone. I think leaves or something got in it."*
>
> *"One winter, I told Harriett, "Mother and Dad spent the Christmas holidays here and when I got home, I found they had ice on the dining room floor."*
>
> *"We didn't mind," Mother said, lighting the coal-oil stove. Harriett glanced curiously at the electric stove, which seemed brand new, and Mother explained that it didn't work. "It*

works, but every time I turn it on, it blows out a fuse." Last time it was six weeks before we could get a new fuse put in."

"Can't you put them in yourself?" Harriett asked in her innocence.

"Oh no. We wait till somebody comes along. That's the nice thing about Gooney. Somebody always comes along." She turned to me. "Remember the summer Ed Baxter fixed the downstairs bathroom? I often wonder what ever became of Ed. He was a good old soul. Only summer we could ever use that bathroom."

Harriett, while Mother was breaking eggs into her black iron skillet, went to the sink for a drink of water. She had the glass to her lips when Mother snatched it away. "I forgot to tell you. We can't drink the water here. We had a state test run and they said it wasn't safe. I don't know why. We've been drinking it for twenty-five years. We get our drinking water down the road at Greenberry Manuel's. He's got a real nice well."

I knew Harriett was too shy to ask the question, so I asked it. "Has the state tested his water?"

"Oh no, but we've been neighbors for twenty years and never a cross word between us."[3]

# Studio 55

Harriett was somewhat alarmed by the Weavers, who were "sublimely indifferent to long-distance [telephone] rates," and called one another just to talk. The first time the phone rang in their apartment, she handed it to John, assuming it was a family emergency. While John's family members were all mechanically challenged, leaving broken appliances to fix themselves, Harriett could fix anything. On Harriett's first visit to the Weaver family home, they watched in admiration as she took down a crooked closet door, shaved the bottom, and re-mounted it. John Cheever marveled that she could cook chicken dinner on a clothes iron.

"Always put a little something aside for a rainy day," Harriett's mother had told her. Ever Saturday morning, Harriett had carried the savings book to the bank.

Harriett had a dozen recipes for leftovers.

"You save money on trivial luxuries so you can do the things you really enjoy,"

Harriet had declared on the couple's first trip to New York.

John had never seen a budget before. By the end of their first year of marriage, Harriett had taken charge of the family finances. By the end of the second year, Harriet gave John a "carrying dollar," in case he encountered an emergency requiring funds. Yet there were strict limits to the alluring power of money: a defining moment for the young couple came early in their marriage.
In 1942, Harriett had quit her job, and they were living on a strict budget of $25 per week. John's agent called with a golden opportunity: David O. Selznick, producer of *Gone With the Wind*, was looking for an assistant, "a bright young man to bounce ideas off." The job paid $250 a week, and both John and Harriett were

tempted to say yes until the agent mentioned that Selznick was a hard driver, and might well be calling him at two o'clock in the morning. "No one ever calls you at two o'clock in the morning to go anywhere," said Harriett. John declined the offer.[4]

John took any writing assignment he could find – short fiction, magazine pieces, travel articles. John wrote a novel about the Bonus Marchers who had so deeply affected him. *Another Such Victory*, published by Viking in 1948, was subtitled *The Story of One Small Family Whose Love Was Tested and Proven During a Fateful Summer Not Too Long Ago*. The book was not a success.

John Weaver and his friend John Cheever commiserated over their money troubles. "I am tired of borrowing and hedging, of living like a bum," wrote Cheever. "Towards the end of the night I felt like killing myself, I have so little to pass on to my children."[5] In another letter, he shares advice on royalties: "Did you know that if a publisher owes you one thousand dollars in March they can put it on the April statement and pay you in December? They can."[6] In a third letter, later in his career, he relates a rare victory: "I seem to have scored a victory with the *New Yorker*. I went there with a manuscript and said the price would be five thousand dollars. Everybody turned white and went to the men's room but then they read the story and said five thousand was what they were going to pay anyway."[7]

Here is Weaver's note to his agent, discussing his reluctance to undertake books: "As you know, I have no outside income. I depend entirely on my earnings from writing and, for the last three years, I have not been able to make a living from the magazines. And when I think of doing a book I remember the year

I spent on *Another Such Victory* and the $1,000 advance I received, and never another red cent."

One hundred twenty kilometers south of the straits of Tsushima, where Captain Vladimir Semenov had witnessed the destruction of the Russian fleet in 1905, another small Asian nation lined up against a world power.

This time the Asian nation was South Korea, and Russia was again the aggressor. North Korea was controlled by Soviet Russia and backed by Russian advisors and weaponry.

Theodore Roosevelt had found that the Russians "responsible for managing her foreign policy betrayed a brutality and ignorance, and arrogance and short-sightedness, which are not often combined." Not much had changed.

The correspondence among nations was weak. The working-class President, Harry Truman and his Ivy-League Secretary of State, the pragmatic Dean Acheson, had little meaningful contact with either opposing or third-party nations that could head off war with the hard-headed Communists, Mao Tse-Tsung and Joseph Stalin.[8] So war broke out once again in Asia, a war that would bring about three million deaths.[9]

North Korea decided to invade and take over the Republic of South Korea on June 25, 1950.

On June 27, President Harry Truman ordered the U. S. Air Force and Navy into Korea.

By June 30, American ground forces were sent in from military bases in Japan to stop to help the free people of South Korea fight off tyranny. Among them were the all-black 24th Infantry.

Walter White, the boy who had gripped his rifle so tightly as the lynch mob approached his father's porch the day of the deadly Atlanta riots in September, 1906, had grown into an accomplished scholar.

Walter White was now Chairman of the NAACP.

After graduating from Atlanta University in 1916, he had joined the national staff of the National Assocaition for the Advancement of Colored People in New York. In 1931, he had taken over as Executive Director. He waged a long and campaign for federal anti-lynching legislation in Congress.

In his plain way, Harry Truman told his fellow Americans to knock it off. With Walter White standing at his side, Truman called for state and federal action against lynching, and an end to inequality in education and employment.

> *When I say all Americans, I mean all Americans.*
>
> *Many of our people still suffer the indignity of insult, the narrowing fear of intimidation, and, I regret to say, the threat of physical violence. Prejudice and intolerance in which these evils are rooted still exist. The conscience of our nation, and the legal machinery which enforces it, have not yet secured to each citizen full freedom of fear.*

# Studio 55

> *We cannot wait another decade or another generation to remedy these evils. We must work, as never before, to cure them now.*

White was sure it meant political suicide for Truman.[10] White also lobbied hard for a complete integration of the armed forces, and on July 26, 1948, President Harry Truman issued Executive Order 9981, calling for "equality of treatment and opportunity for all persons in the armed services without regard to race, color, religion, or national origin." President Truman also established a Presidential committee to help establish the best way to implement a plan of integration. The committee advised that military efficiency would be improved with full utilization of black soldiers, and that segregated units were inefficient. The implementation of these military policies took place slowly, so that by the outbreak of the Korean conflict in 1951, all-black units still fought.

The North Koreans' main thrust was along the Seoul/Pusan axis. The U.S. 25th Infantry Division (Tropical Lightning) was positioned to back South Korean troops in the central sector and prevent an enemy drive on Taegu. When the town of Yechon fell into enemy hands, it was retaken by the all-black 24th Infantry Regiment of the 25th Division.

Here is how the protagonist of the battle, Lt. Charles Bussey of the 77th Engineer Combat Company, describes the combat at Yechon once he had climbed a hill and spotted a large (250 soldiers) body of white-clad Koreans coming toward the American position:

*"I watched the group of farmer-soldiers coming ever closer and reckoned that farmers scatter and turn if you send a long burst of machine-gun fire over their heads, but soldiers flatten out like quail and await orders from their leader ... I sent a burst from the .50 caliber machine gun dangerously close above the heads of the approaching group ... True to the form of soldiers, they flattened into the paddy as the bullets flew past them ... Bullets raked and them up mercilessly ... The advancing column was under tight observation from somewhere on the mountain because large mortar rounds started ... overhead. I was nicked by a fragment. The gunner on the .30 caliber machine gunner was hit badly, and his assistant was killed. The enemy mortar was accurate. The shells were bursting about twenty to forty feet overhead, showering us with shell fragments. And we were now drawing small-arms fire from the rice paddies below ... I chopped the North Korean troops to pieces ... I was ashamed of the slaughter before me, but this was my job, my duty, and my responsibility. I stayed with it until not one white rag was left intact."*[11]

Associated Press war correspondent Tom Lambert reported it as the "...first sizeable American ground victory of the Korean War." Bussey, who had served as a black fighter pilot during World

War II, won a Silver Star as a combat engineer. "Back in the U.S., blacks began appearing at the recruiting offices, asking to get in that 24th Regiment."[12]

The U.S. Army, however, did not acknowledge the victory at Yechon, or even that there was an engagement with the enemy.

After Yechon, things seemed to go haywire for the 24th Infantry. North Korean forces engaged and overwhlemed three battalions from the 1st Cavalry. At Sangju, the North's "relentless attacks" cause the South Koreans soldiers guarding the right flank to collapse. Military historian Roy Edgar Appleman wrote that "The tendency to panic continued in nearly all the 24th Infantry operations west of Sangju. Men left their positions and straggled to the rear. They abandoned weapons on positions."[13] Lieutenant Roger Waldon of Company F gave a very different account, describing an enemy roadblock and a redeployment, not a retreat.

The retreat from Sangju seemed to cast a pall over the battalion's reputation.

The performance of the black American troops in Korea was so controversial that no agreement could be reached.[14]

In late September, 1950, Major General William B. Kean requested that the all-black 24th Infantry regiment be disbanded. The regiment, he declared, had proven in combat that it was "untrustworthy and incapable of carrying out missions expected of an infantry unit."

## Teddy's Tantrum

**October, 1952**

"Well then, you're an *astrologist*, of course," said Louis Untermeyer sarcastically.

The audience in Studio 55 roared with laughter.

The contestant blinked, afraid to answer or to give anything away by a careless non-answer. He looked to the host for guidance.

"No! I'm afraid not, Louis," replied the urbane host, John Charles Daley, smiling as he did so. He knew the audience enjoyed Untermeyer.

"Our guest is *not* in fact a student of the stars."

Clever, warm, avuncular, Untermeyer was a favorite on the television quiz show *What's My Line*, the most popular show on the CBS network.

In a Mahattan television studio, the poet Louis Untermeyer leaned back from the micriphone and smiled. John and Harriett Weaver's affable, literate friend was a leading player on the widely viewed game show, in which the celebrity panel tried to guess the occupation of each show's "mystery guest." The occupations were usually obscure and unexpected: hat check girl, diaper executive, baseball player (mystery guest Phil Rizzuto). Untermeyer and the other panelists -- columnist Dorothy Kilgallen, former New Jersey governor Harold G. Hoffman, comedy writer Hal Block, sometimes actress Arlene Francis – did their best to uncover the guests' odd job choices by asking the fewest number of questions they could. If they failed it was all the more amusing.

# Studio 55

On October 12, Louis Untermeyer came to work and was told that he was no longer on the show. As his friend, the playwright Arthur Miller, recounted it:

> *Louis Untermeyer, then in his sixties, was a poet and anthologist, a distinguished-looking old New York type with a large aristocratic nose and a passion for conversation, especially about writers. He married four times, had taught and written and published, and with the swift rise of television had become nationally known as one of the original regulars on What's My Line?, a popular early show in which he, along with columnist Dorothy Kilgallen, publisher Bennett Cerf, and Arlene Francis, would try to guess the occupation of a studio guest by asking the fewest possible questions in the brief time allowed. All this [was done] with wisecracking and banter, at which Louis was a lovable master, what with his instant recall of every joke and pun he had ever heard.*
>
> *One day he arrived as usual at the television studio an hour before the program began and was told by the producer that he was no longer on the show. It appeared that as a result of having been listed in Life magazine as a sponsor of the Waldorf Conference (a meeting to discuss cultural and scientific links with the Soviet Union), an organized letter campaign protesting his appearance on*

> *What's My Line?* *had scared the advertisers into getting rid of him.*
>
> *Louis went back to his apartment. Normally we ran into each other in the street once or twice a week or kept in touch every month or so, but I no longer saw him in the neighborhood or heard from him. Louis didn't leave his apartment for almost a year and a half. An overwhelming and paralyzing fear had risen him. More than a political fear, it was really that he had witnessed the tenuousness of human connection and it had left him in terror. He had always loved a lot and been loved, especially on the TV program where his quips were vastly appreciated, and suddenly, he had been thrown into the street, abolished.*[15]

A year after the accusations surfaced, Untermeyer bowed out of *What's My Line* and was replaced by the urbane book editor Bennett Cerf.

The fall of their friend Untermeyer affected the Weavers deeply. Genuine affection and mutual support runs through the forty-year correspondence between the Weavers and Untermeyers. Untermeyer tells Weaver in one letter that he hopes for a good advance from Holt on an anthology of stories, and promises to include one of Weaver's stories ("… although," Untermeyer admits with some chagrin, "since our budget is stricter than last year's, you probably won't get more than $40.00 for the reprint rights!").

# Studio 55

He gives updates on his three sons ("John ... is getting a raise in pay and a promotion at Raytheon ...").

After the *What's My Line* shock, a shadow falls across Untermeyer's chatty letters to Weaver. Inevitably, no matter where the letter begins, the narrative turns to his troubles. "I received one timid letter of commendation," from his legions of fans, he notes. "CBS had me on the carpet," he writes in another, "and were (finally) very gracious to me when I convinced them (or am I deceiving myself) that I am not, never was, and never will be ..." And again: "'Lie low,' they say. The time may come when you can speak up – and prove you're innocent."[16]

The time never came. Untermeyer never returned to the quiz show. In the months and years that followed his dismissal, he was unable to remove the stigma that had stained his reputation.

The typewriting in his letters to the Weavers begins to falter, and handwritten notes explaining the subtleties of his dilemma begin to appear along the bottom of his letters. "I'm sick about the rapidity with which this has happened," he writes in one marginal note. "You are almost the only people to whom I can say all this – a frightening thought in itself." The vague nature of his supposed offense torments him. "I challenge my traducers to find a single line [ in all my writings ] ... which might even remotely be considered disloyal."

Screenwriter Carl Foreman, actress Marsha Hunt and screenwriter Isabel Lennart were other Weaver colleagues whose careers were damaged by the blacklist. An immensely talented writer and producer who created such films as *High Noon, Champion, Bridge Over the River Kwai, Guns of Navarone*, and

A *Hatful of Rain*, among many others, Foreman was forced to leave America to live and work in London. Lennert, who also wrote *Anchors Aweigh* and *Funny Girl* as well as the screenplay for Weaver's *Holiday Affair*, was told by her employer, MGM, that she had to testify if she wanted to remain a scriptwriter in Hollywood. In May, 1952, she gave the names of twenty-one people who she knew had been members of the Communist Party. She never got over her regret for doing so. "I believe with all my heart that it was wrong to cooperate with this terrible Committee in any way," she told an interviewer in 1970. "I believe that I was wrong. I believe I did a minimum of damage, but I still believe it was wrong. I had a much bigger reaction to it than I thought I would. I've never gotten over it. I've always felt an inferior citizen because of this."

Decades later, friends like Jim Perry say that in reflective moments, no matter the circumstance, John Weaver would turn to the "blacklisting" and the havoc it brought to its innocent victims. It was an injustice he could never forget: he was powerless to stop it, or correct it, or help repair the shredded reputations of its victims, his talented friends.

## CHAPTER 8

# Einen Wilden Baren

> [Roosevelt was] always playing a game ... forcing optimism, forcing enjoyment with the desperate instinctive appreciation that if he let the pretense drop for a moment, the whole scheme of things would vanish away.
>
> -- Gamaliel Bradford

### SEPTEMBER, 1906

"In the past year the work of the Negro hater has flourished in the land," declared William DuBois on August 13, speaking to a small crowd in a pretty green space in West Virginia.

He was speaking of racially intolerant white Americans, who represented one front of his ongoing struggle.

"Our weaker brethren are actually afraid to thunder against color discrimination as such," he said, "and are simply whispering for ordinary decencies. Our weaker brethren are actually afraid to thunder against color discrimination as such and are simply whispering for ordinary decencies."

Here he was addressing the second front of his war, namely his weaker brethren Booker T. Washington, whom he often regarded as a truer enemy than white racists. "Our enemies," that is, the accommodating blacks like Booker T. Washington, "triumphant for the present, are fighting the stars in their courses. Justice and humanity must prevail. We live to tell these dark brothers of ours -- scattered in counsel, wavering and weak -- that no bribe of money or notoriety, no promise of wealth or fame, is worth the surrender of a people's manhood or the loss of a man's self-respect. We refuse to surrender the leadership of this race to cowards and trucklers."

DuBois, a deeply suspicious man, thought Richard Greener, a member of the small group to whom he addressed his remarks, was a spy in their midst, sent by to Harper's Ferry by his nemesis, Washington, to monitor their plans.

He was correct.[1]

The pretty green space was the campus of Storer College, and the occasion was "one the greatest meetings that American Negroes ever held." DuBois and Greener and William Trotter and two dozen colleagues in a loose association they called the Niagara Movement (after the site of their first meeting) assembled in Harpers Ferry, West Virginia to discuss how black men and women could attain full civil rights. Attendees walked from the college grounds to the nearby farm of the Murphy family, then the site of the historic fort where John Brown's quest to free four million enslaved African Americans had reached its bloody climax.

## Einen Wilden Baren

Booker T. Washington had not been invited. He had asked Greener, the first black graduate of Harvard and a diplomat under McKinley and Roosevelt, to report back to him.

Dubois harbored an exquisite contempt for Washington, whom he called "The Great Accommodator." At Washington's death, DuBois had this to say: "In stern justice, we must lay on the soul of this man a heavy responsibility for the consummation of Negro disfranchisement, the decline of the Negro college and public school, and the firmer establishment of color caste in this land."

Like Roosevelt, he held out modernity, the "increased complexity of life," as a villain in human events; specifically, DuBois felt it was responsible for the rise in the crime rate among blacks. Like Roosevelt, he saw classifications of people as a natural, even desireable fact of evolution; like Roosevelt, he felt that it was the upper caste, the exceptional men, this top "Talented Tenth" section of the citizenry which can and must save the day. Another part of DuBois' philosophy was identity: America was the white man's nation, part of a world that denied the black man his own identity, "a world in which yields him no true self-consciousness, but only lets him see himself through the revelation of the other world..." Black society needed its own, separate identity, if not its own separate economy.

Washington, for his part, made repeated gestures of peace and collaboration towards DuBois and his allies. Washington tried three times to hire DuBois at the Tuskegee Institute, and each time DuBois declined. Washington supported members of the DuBois faction any way he could, advertising in their newspaper (*The Voice*), writing introductions for their books, offering praise on their behalf to President Roosevelt. Washington stood for vocational education and accommodation with white America. Confrontation would never work, he felt: white America outnumbered black America. Booker Washington was hopeful about the possibilities of progress. "We went into slavery pagans; we came out Christians. We went into slavery pieces of property; we came out American citizens. We went into slavery with chains clanking about our wrists; we came out with the American ballot in our hands." To DuBois and the elite, Washington's message was, "It is at the bottom of life we must begin, not at the top," by which he meant beginning with practical job training for working-class blacks. "There is another class of colored people who make a business of keeping the troubles, the wrongs, and the hardships of the Negro race before the public. Having learned that they are able to make a living out of their troubles, they have grown into the settled habit of advertising their wrongs."

While it was not a significant topic at the Harpers Ferry conference, the Brownsville raid would supply the Niagara movement with a powerful opportunity to test its mettle. DuBois, the man who mocked the Negro accommodators and who commanded his brethren to "Stand up for the right, prove yourselves worthy of your heritage" would soon have his chance to do the same.

On the day after the shooting, confusion reigned in Brownsville, Texas – confusion, but not armed conflict.

## Einen Wilden Baren

Families had scattered, some across the river to Matamoros, some to outlying ranches and farms. "While armed and angry men converged on the center of town, their women and children huddled behind locked doors and bolted doors."[2] Damage to the town was inspected – Tillman's saloon, the Cowen house, bullets in the Starck home on Washington Street, which sat next to the home of Fred Tate, the customs inspector who had mistreated Private Newton. The soldiers were aiming for Tate's house and mistook it, the townsmen theorized.

On Elizabeth Street there was a growing sentiment to march on Fort Brown. Captain Kelly, a veteran of First New York Mounted Rifles, heard some bold talk. "One man told me he could take fifty men and go and clean out the whole Negro unit. That man had never been a soldier."[3] The realization that the armed men of the 25th would be putting up considerable resistance to any lynching eventually prevailed, and there was no rush on the Fort.

"I do not want any of this talking," Brownsville's Mayor Ray Combes announced. "I will arrest anybody who keeps it up."

He called a meeting. At 11:00, up to 500 citizens of the town met in the courtroom of the Federal courthouse.

"I took the chair and addressed the people," Mayor Combe later explained. "I told them what had occurred last night, as they knew it by this time, and went on to say that I agreed with them that unquestionably it had been by some ruffians of the battalion now stationed at Brownsville, but that we should not condemn all the men and all the officers; that so far they had deported themselves as good citizens, and I appealed to them and requested them to continue to do so; that we would appeal to the highest authority in the land, if necessary, but under no circumstances to take the law in their own hands, because it would lead to trouble and maybe the ruination of Brownsville."

Captain Kelly was assigned to investigate the raid. Kelly assembled a committee, selecting "mostly northern men, who had no special animus against Negroes as such."

The members of the committee went directly to see Major Penrose. Penrose had on his desk the statements of two sentries swearing that no soldiers had left the barracks area, and three noncommissioned officers insisting that the rifle racks had remained locked. It seems that Private Newton had been on guard duty all night. He could not have participated in the shooting. It was not Newton, seeking revenge on Tate, who had shot at the Starck house.

Captain Kelly and his committee then set up shop in a law office. They invited townspeople to come in and tell what they had seen the night before. A newspaperman had heard the raiders' voices and knew them to be Negro voices. "I was raised among them and know their voices pretty well," he said. As Kelly questioned him, he revealed that "he had made his identification on the basis of three mono-syllables, 'We got him.'"[4]

Others concurred that the voices had been Negro voices. None had actually seen Negro men. One citizen, Jose Martinez, reported that he had heard a noise "like somebody – big crowd – jump the fence."

"Were they Negroes or white men?" he was asked.

"Negroes."

"Did you see their uniforms?"

"No; I saw their – what you call it? – bulk."⁵

The testimony went on for two days.

The next day's Brownsville *Daily Herald* warned that if the soldiers tried to repeat "the dastard outrage," they would find no easy victims but "people fully prepared to defend themselves."

Captain Kelly's committee concluded that between twenty and thirty soldiers "carrying their rifles and an abundant supply of ammunition" had emerged from Fort Brown a few minutes before midnight August 13, and, after firing about two hundred shots, had returned to their quarter, having killed one citizen and wounded "the lieutenant of police, who rode toward the firing."

The report went on to warn that the soldiers had threatened to attack again. "We do not believe their officers can restrain them, there being but five commissioned officers. Our condition ... is this: Our women and children are terrorized and our men are practically under constant alarm and watchfulness. No community can stand this strain for more than a few days." It concluded with plea to transfer the black soldiers out of Fort Brown at once.

The Secretary of War, Taft, was vacationing in Canada, so the Military Secretary, Major General F.C. Ainsworth, responded on his behalf. He wired Penrose, asking if he could indeed restrain his troops from further violence. Penrose responded that he had no doubt that he could.

On Saturday, Major Augustus Blocksom of the Inspector General's Department arrived to make his own assessment of the situation. "Troops under proper control," he reported, "although town people are still very excited, and men all carrying arms." He downgraded the logistics of initial reports, estimating that between nine and fifteen soldiers carried out the raid, firing seventy-five to a hundred rounds. As to the source of the problem: "Causes of disturbance are racial."

The men of the 25th Infantry troops did as they were trained to do: they stuck together. They weathered the long weeks following the midnight raid in worry, waiting for hearings to clear them. As discouraged as they were when it seemed the entire state of Texas was ready to lynch them, as they knew had happened elsewhere, the men of the 25th Infantry felt some comfort in the fact that it was their comrade-in-arms who now occupied the White House. Teddy Roosevelt, the foolhardy Rough Rider who had shared their grub and climbed the deadly slopes of Kettle Hill beside them, that bloody day in Cuba eight years earlier, would stand for justice.

Beneath the crystal chandeliers, the alluring Belle da Costa Greene and John Pierpont Morgan, age 68, did an impromptu war dance on the carpet of the Morgan library in midtown Manhattan.[6]

Belle da Costa Greene, Morgan's young curator and confidante, had just returned from a trip to Europe. She had managed to smuggle a painting, three bronzes, and a special watch past the customs officers in her suitcase. These treasures would serve to enrich the Morgan collection, an already impressive private collection which they hoped would one day rival those in the British Museum and France's *Bibliotheque Nationale*.

J. P. Morgan was not a particularly good dancer, but it nonetheless delighted his companion, whom Morgan biographer Jean Strouse describes as "small and slender, with dark hair and

## Einen Wilden Baren

olive skin dramatically set off by light green eyes, exotic looks which she attributed to her Portuguese grandmother."[7] Belle and her boss, whose code name in their veiled correspondences was "Flitch," were close confederates in the great game of acquiring artifacts from long-dead civilizations. "His love for beautiful things and pretty clothes was as intense as a woman's," said his friend Annette Markoe. And Belle had the same ambitions for Morgan's collection as he did (she sometimes called it "our collection"). The two shared details of their unorthodox private lives as well.

Belle fiercely protected Flitch from middlemen and dealers who imagined the Morgan money being thrown about carelessly. Once, Belle had heard from a London book dealer that Lord Amherst intended to sell his library of perfect editions of early printer William Caxton. The British Chancellor of the Exchequer would sponsor the British Museum to buy it for thirty thousand pounds. Belle made an offer of twenty-five thousand, in cash, to the book dealer the night before the auction. The Caxton books now resided in the Morgan collection.

Since the French first emerged from the Egyptian sands with alluring, exotic antique treasures in the 1790's, Americans had admired Egyptian decorative splendors, mute objects that "speak with golden eloquence and whose message is now being revealed to the world,"[8] and marveled at the mysterious civilization's longevity. By the Civil War, "every self-respecting bookcase … contained at least one book on Egypt."[9] American fascination with ancient civilizations was spurred by von Schliemann's discovery of Troy in 1872. The Egyptians' art was a "sincere expression of the national temper … Nothing was made simply to be set up and looked at for the sake of its beauty; everything was made to be of use," Mrs. Schuyler Van Rensselaer wrote in the *North American Review*.[10] From Egyptian art, Americans could learn to make their art in service to a community, to craftsmanship, and to a higher aesthetic. "Both of these lessons we need to learn, we *must* learn, if in America good taste is to grow and great art is to develop."[11]

J. P. Morgan, a friend of Theodore Roosevelt's father, a complex man with interests beyond earning money, fostered the study of ancient civilizations in America. He hired Harvard professor Albert Lythgoe to run the Metropolitan Museum's Egyptian department and underwrote the initial expeditions, as well as collecting for his own museum. Morgan had rented a houseboat to travel 35 miles on the Nile to visit the excavation at Lisht, where Senwosret and his predecessor, Amenemhat I, who founded Egypt's Twelfth Dynasty 12th Dynasty had built temples. Morgan and his party had walked the Great Oasis at Khargeh and the *Deir el-Bahri*, the magnificent temple complex within the ancient city of Thebes.

The great pharaohs like Senwosret and Amenemhat I held their power through a strong and loyal imperial army. In the early periods of the Egyptian empires, the Pharaohs' armies were purely Egyptian. Seti I speaks of "the good son of Amun, who smites multitudes of persons … He loves the infantry and chariotry, the great noble, who protects the youth and brings up the militia of Egypt."[12] Then, as the empire expanded, the Egyptian army absorbed conscripts and foreign prisoners of war. The army often destroyed captured villages in order to frighten other foes into submission. Bodies were displayed to the public or hung from the prow of a ship. Conquered territories were annexed.[13] By the 19th and 20th Dynasties, Egypt struggled to guard her borders. The army relied on mercenaries hired from the east and the north.[14] In the Late Period, Ionians and Carians, Jews and Aramaeans, Phoenicians and others fought for Egypt. "Jewish contingents were stationed at Elephantine and Aramaeans at Syene after Egyptian troops were considered to be unreliable," some deserting and fleeing into Nubia.[15] "These mercenary troops were often officered by foreign commanders, at times of a different ethnic group, and their obedience was not always assured."[16] By the middle of the 12th century, sixty per cent of the soldiers were non-Egyptians.

J. P. Morgan, Egyptologist, also served as a one-man United States Federal Reserve.

Before America had a government body to act as a steadying influence on the volatile economic markets, J.P. Morgan made it his personal mission to do so. In the tumultuous decades of meteoric growth and wildcat oil, railroads and speculation and on at least three occasions brought the nation back from ruin.

One of these occasions was in 1877, when the government ran into gold problems as a result of Civil War debt. Together with August Belmont and the Rothschilds, Morgan floated $260 million in US government bonds. He then bought $200 million worth of government bonds with gold, thereby preserving the credit of the United States.

A second instance came in 1895, at the depths of the Panic of 1893: the Federal Treasury was nearly out of gold. President Grover Cleveland arranged for Morgan to create a private syndicate on Wall Street to supply the U.S. Treasury with $65 million in gold, half of it from Europe, to float a bond issue that restored the treasury surplus of $100 million

As Morgan and Belle Green celebrated their Egyptian cuneiforms, a third crisis was brewing. Monetary markets had shrunk from the pressure of the Russo-Japanese War. Roosevelt's suit against the railroads caused uncertainty, as did his blithe threats to place all of the railroads under government control. But thoughts of Wall Street panics did not distract J.P. Morgan from dancing with his alluring young associate.

As for Belle Greene, she was in fact Belle Marion Greener, the mulatto daughter of Richard T. Greener, Harvard graduate, diplomat under McKinley and Roosevelt, and nemesis to William DuBois. There was no Portuguese grandmother. "The matrilineal Portuguese/Dutch descent was pure fiction."[17] In one of the more successful identity transformations of the day, Belle Greener had become Belle da Costa Greene.

Theodore Roosevelt lived with a powerful sense that all hell was about to break loose.

"We stand at Armageddon," he would say, or "We are fighting in the quarrel of civilization against barbarism, of liberty against tyranny," or "I believe that the next half century will determine if we will advance the cause of Christian civilization or revert to the horrors of brutal paganism." He warned repeatedly of "the general smash-up of our civilization" and the "endless crusade against wrong … the never-ending warfare for the good of humankind." None of this was mere rhetoric, but rather reflected a passionate

## Einen Wilden Baren

conviction. His apocalyptic foreshadowing cropped up in all facets and at all junctures of his life. When he said, "If I must choose between righteousness and peace, I choose righteousness," it was yet another of his reminders to himself and his countrymen that the stakes could not possibly be any higher.

One of the many agents of the coming apocalypse was Germany. He admired the Teutonic races, but feared them as well. Roosevelt "enjoyed a lifelong sense of racial kinship with the German people."[18] Here is the song Roosevelt used to celebrate the hunting trophies of the American frontiersman in his book *The Winning of the West*:

> *Danach schlag er weider einen Buffel*
> *und einen Elk*
> *Vier starkes Auer neider und einen*
> *grimmen Schelk,*
> *So schnell trug ihn die Mahre, dasz ihm*
> *nichts entsprang;*
> *Hinden und Hirsche wurden viele sein Fang.*
> *… ein Waldthier furchterlich,*
> *Einen wilden Baren.*

Thereafter he knocked down again a buffalo
and an elk
Four strong mighty oxen and a
furious schelk,
His mare bore him so swiftly that nothing
escaped him;
Many hart and hind became his prey
… a terrible animal is the forest
A wild bear.

Germany was a nation whom Roosevelt believed had "reduced savagery to a science." He had gone to school in Dresden. He corresponded regularly with Wilhelm II (Wilhelm once sent a birthday telegram to Roosevelt *You and I, there are no others*") and considered him to be a dangerously unbalanced man. Germany's seething relations with England and France caused a perpetual balancing act for Roosevelt, in Morocco, in the Russo-Japanese negotiations.

Another corrupting force was the "trans-Atlantic elite," a class which plagued Roosevelt. Not only did they "pursue money upon money," and seek soft virtues over hard, but it was they who had brought the black man to America to do work they themselves should have been doing.

There were villainous threats creeping among common Americans. Low birth rates among the dominant races, for one; "depleted craftsmanship" for another. Overcivilization and lax morals threatened the best among us. He had seen his own brother Eliot fall into the abyss. Eliot, "a dangerous maniac" who was "absolutely lacking in any moral sense," fell into a spiral of alcoholism, as would Roosevelt's son, Kermit. He also pointed to national extravagance -- that is, expenditure of money which is not warranted -- and "industrial chaos," a catch-all phrase by which he meant a spectrum of evils personified by Standard Oil, running rampant. These and other shadowy counter-forces were many, and he constantly alerted his comrades, and called out their remedies so all Americans might aid him in the ongoing war against the forces of darkness: fructification, a term he used to suggest not only productive farmland but also a high birth rates among well-educated whites; an army "kept at a high pitch of perfection;" a naval fleet built up to such strength "as to render it unsafe for any foreign power to attack us" the Panama Canal, fortified; self-control; the capacity to conduct savage warfare; and vigorous physical exercise.

Roosevelt had little patience for those who, knowingly or not, stood in the way of progress, and on occasion he allowed this impatience to flash. The British writer H.G. Wells records a conversation with Roosevelt in the White House garden. The subject came up of Wells' most pessimistic book, *The Time Machine*, in which all the devices and constructions of modernity have failed, leaving mankind living like feral dogs at the mercy of a harpy-like race of bestial morlocks:

> *"He became gesticulatory," Wells recalled, "and his straining voice a note higher in denying the pessimism of that book ..." Gripping at the back of a garden chair with his left hand, Roosevelt had stabbed the air with his right, the familiar platform gesture.*
>
> *"Suppose after all that should prove to be right, and it all ends in your butterflies and morlocks. That doesn't matter now. The effort's real. It's worth going on with. It's worth it – even then."*
>
> *"I can see him now," Wells recalled, "... and the gesture of the clenched hand and the – how can I describe it? The friendly peering snarl in his face, like a man with the sun in his eyes ..."*[19]

## Teddy's Tantrum

So that the President could monitor the national temper, and mix with his fellow citizens, White House luncheons were open to the public, and as Roosevelt's biographer William Roscoe Thayer recorded, "he always reserved time when any American, rich or poor, young or old, could speak to him freely. He liked to see them all and many were the odd experiences which he had." Such luncheons, according to Thayer, were varied meals. "Sometimes there were only two or three guests at it; at other times there might be a dozen. It afforded the President an opportunity for talking informally with visitors whom he wished to see, and not infrequently it brought together round the table a strange, not to say a motley, company."

Thayer offers the following exchange as typical.

Theodore Roosevelt had spent the morning attending to his many correspondences and dictating letters. He entered the White House dining room and, surveying the gathering, took a seat beside an elderly woman.

He asked the old lady what he could do for her.

"Nothing," she said. "I came all the way from Jacksonville, Florida, just to see what a live President looked like. I never saw one before."

"That's very kind of you," the President replied; "persons from up here go all the way to Florida just to see a live alligator."

On the morning of September 22, 13-year old Walter White was worried.

## Einen Wilden Baren

His father, Walter Sr., was quiet. He looked seriously concerned. And with good reason.

Walter, a light-skinned boy with traces of Afro-American heritage, lived with his family in a trim house on Houston Street in Atlanta. The day before, the boy had convinced his parents to let him accompany his father, a mail carrier, on his rounds. They had started out at the main post office on Marietta Street. Walter saw signs of tension in the streets of the city, as "little bands of sullen, evil-looking men talked excitedly on street corners." The city's newspapers, battling for readers, had helped fan the flames of racial tension. A series of disturbing incidents broke out, unwarranted attacks on Atlanta's black citizens. Editorials warned of impending danger, a vision drawn on much the same lines as Theodore Roosevelt's nightmare visions of racial war. The *Atlanta Journal* warned of the negro's growing malice:

> "He grows more bumptious on the street, more impudent in his dealings with white men, and then, when he cannot achieve social equality as he wishes, with the instinct of the barbarian to destroy what he cannot attain to, he lies in wait ... and assaults the fair young girlhood of the south ..."

This recurring image of armed black males assaulting white girls helped incite savage gang murders on Atlanta's streets. Young Walter had heard the reports. He was curious, a little excited, but not frightened.

Not yet.

## Teddy's Tantrum

Turning onto Peachtree Street, Walter and his father heard a sound, "a roar the like of which I had never heard before," White wrote later.

Suddenly, "we saw a lame Negro bootblack from Herndon's barber shop pathetically trying to outrun a mob of whites. Less than a hundred yards from us the chase ended. We saw clubs and fists descending to the accompaniment of savage shouting and cursing. Suddenly a voice cried, 'There goes another nigger!' Its work done, the mob went after new prey. The body with the withered foot lay dead in a pool of blood on the street."

This chilling sight of the cold-blooded murder haunted the boy. The police were doing nothing to stop these white mobs and their random lynchings. As far as Walter could see, the police strategy was to confiscate firearms from the city's black citizens.

In the morning, friends came by the house on Houston Street to warn them that more trouble was coming. They told them that the hats and caps of the previous night's victims had been hung on the iron hooks of telegraph poles all along Peachtree Street. "Plans had been perfected," they said, "for a mob to form on Peachtree Street just after nightfall to march down Houston Street to what the white people called 'Darktown,' three blocks or so below our house, to 'clean out the niggers.'"

Walter and his father peered up Houston Street from the front porch of their small house. Night fell. Walter's father ordered his wife to take their daughter and move inside, to the back of the house, where bullets and bottles and rocks might not reach.

"There had never been a firearm in our house before that day," recalled Walter. There was now. Both he and his father held rifles.

# Einen Wilden Baren

Around midnight, they heard it: that same sound, that horrible roar, turning onto Houston Street. It was coming towards their house. Here is Walter's description what happened next:

> *My brother George was away, so Father and I, the only males in the house, took our places at the front windows of the parlor. The windows opened on a porch along the front side of the house, which in turn gave onto a narrow lawn that sloped down to the street and a picket fence. There was a crash as Negroes smashed the street lamp at the corner of Houston and Piedmont Avenue down the street. In a very few minutes the vanguard of the mob, some of them bearing torches, appeared. A voice which we recognized as that of the son of the grocer with whom we had traded for many years yelled, "That's where that nigger mail carrier lives! Let's burn it down! It's too nice for a nigger to live in!" In the eerie light Father turned his drawn face toward me.*
>
> *In a voice as quiet as though he were asking me to pass him the sugar at the breakfast table, he said, "Son, don't shoot until the first man puts his foot on the lawn and then—don't you miss!"*
>
> *The mob moved toward the lawn. I tried to aim my gun, wondering what it would feel like to kill a man. Suddenly there was a volley of shots. The mob hesitated, stopped.*

*Some friends of my father's had barricaded themselves in a two-story brick building just below our house. It was they who had fired. Some of the mobsmen, still bloodthirsty, shouted, "Let's go get the nigger." Others, afraid now for their safety, held back. Our friends, noting the hesitation, fired another volley. The mob broke and retreated up Houston Street.*[20]

# CHAPTER 9

# Fire in the Hills

> "Someday," she said, before lapsing again into an embarrassed silence, "I would like to live on the highest hill I can find."
>
> -- *Harriett Weaver to her future husband, John, on their first date*

### Los Angeles, 1967

"All right, thank you ma'am," said Deputy Fire Chief Anthony Giordano brusquely from the dais, cutting the red-headed lady off in mid-sentence. "Now, let's move on to other business -- "[1]

Now a little man shot up beside the red-headed lady.

"You will NOT dismiss this woman's opinions!"

He was dapper, trim, and seemed to be hellishly protective of his wife.

"She practically WROTE the existing fire code regulations," the man continued, clearly angry. "In fact, she knows more about the fire code than anyone in this entire room! She deserves the respect of this entire city. And, what's more ..." The Chief placed his hand over the microphone and looked at the agitated little man stoically, as though he might be sucking a particularly sour lemon drop.

The man went on to say that the Chief damn well better listen to her, otherwise we'll have the entire city council down here tomorrow asking why he didn't. The little man shook his finger in the direction of the dais, where Chief Giordano and other officials of the Los Angeles Fire Department were conducting a public hearing. The new command at the LAFD had little patience for citizens designing brush ordinances and discussing flame retardant, much less swimming in the murkier waters of the politics within the LAFD and the still deeper waters of California's high-risk insurance carriers.

"All right," said Giordano at the end of the dressing-down. "Thank you, Mister and Missus ... Weaver." He mumbled a few words acknowledging Mrs. Weaver's contributions.

In fact, the remarkable Harriett Weaver had initiated a widespread campaign to prevent fires in the thousands of canyons and hillsides throughout all of Los Angeles County. Now that she lived in the high hills, she worked hard to protect them. Richard Reeves describes her this way in his *New Yorker* profile of California personalities: "Harriett Weaver is considered one of Los Angeles' experts on brushfires. She has many titles, among them chairperson of the Mayor's Brush Clearance Committee." He quotes her "A third of the city is in brush. In Los Angeles County, they joke that they don't fire maps. Because the whole thing would be red – 'extremely hazardous.' ...The deadwood underneath the green you see out there is soaked with resin and oils. It literally explodes."[2] As Harriett pointed out to Reeves where the hidden dangers of the landscape lie, she dropped a disturbing fact: "a hundred acres of brush fire five feet high can produce the same amount of heat as the atomic bomb that was dropped on Hiroshima." She had worked for years to assemble, write, and distribute new code regulations in the city government bylaws which governed clearing flammable brush from the canyons. She had worked almost single-handedly to distribute the regulations to homeowner and hillside associations across the city. According to Fire Captain Jim Perry, who was present at the confrontation with the LAFD officials, "I'd say that every brush fire after the Bel Air fire in 1961 and the Topanga fire was better managed because of Harriett's brush fire ordinance and her spearheading political pressure on the elected officials to get things done." John was her constant partner in this, as she was his partner in all his writing: their friend John Cheever called John and Harriett Weaver "the two most civic-minded people I know."

At the time, John Weaver was working on his most important project to date, a biography of Earl Warren, a controversial figure on whom Weaver was eager to set the record straight. Warren had 1953, Warren was appointed by President Eisenhower "He represents the kind of political, economic, and social thinking that I believe we need on the Supreme Court," said President Eisenhower when he appointed Warren as Chief Justice of the United States in 1953. "[H]e has a national name for integrity, uprightness, and courage ..." But Warren turned out to be a maverick, and more liberal than most had thought. The Warren court issued a number of significant decisions, including *Brown v. Board of Education*, (1954), which overthrew the segregation of public schools; *Hernandez v. Texas*, which gave Mexican-Americans the right to serve on juries; and *Miranda v. Arizona*, which required that certain rights of a person being interrogated while in police custody be clearly explained, including the right to an attorney (often called the "Miranda warning"). President Eisenhower would regret the appointment: nominating Warren for the Chief Justice seat "was the biggest damned fool mistake I've ever made in my life."

Weaver had worked long and hard on the book, getting to know members of the Warren family in the process. He was also writing articles for magazines, and was considering compiling a history of Los Angeles. He wrote novelizations of popular films under exotic pseudonyms (several of them "weaver" in a different language). But the couple would have been financially strapped if not for Harriett's real estate savvy. "Harriett knew the market backwards and forwards, better than many realtors," according to her niece, whom she helped scout for homes in the early 1970's. It was a good time to know the housing market: Southern California real estate was on a steep growth curve. The Weavers took advantage of the appreciating prices, buying and selling homes with Harriett serving as both broker and contractor. "She wove wall-to-wall carpeting for the living room, built a desk for my workroom, and laid the bricks for three patios," John wrote of Harriett Weaver in *Glad Tidings* of her expertise in renovating the Hollywood Hills house they bought in 1948.

Harriett, in marrying John, "turned her shapely back on the mink-and-chrome fetishes of Status and Society and goes her own quiet way."[3] In a photo on one of his books' back covers, both John and Harriett look genuinely happy, content with the bargains they had made. Their friend Carl Reiner calls the Weaver marriage one of the most romantic he has known: the couple owned over 200 pieces of sheet music, and one would often sift through the stack and leave a love song on top, one that contained a particular message for the spouse to see. "Harriett was very pretty – she reminded you of Harriet Nelson," recalls Pamela Fiore, John's friend and editor at *Travel and Leisure*. "She sounded like Harriet Nelson." Harriett served to "keep him aloft" amid the realities of life. 'John was 'brainy.' He was happiest at the UCLA library."4

In 1967, Lyndon Baines Johnson violated the third rule of combat, which is this: *Apply sufficient force to overwhelm the enemy.*

It was the same mistake that his predecessor, John Kennedy had made, only Johnson made it much worse. In December, 1961, President Diem of South Vietnam had made a forceful appeal to America's leader. "In the course of the last few months, the Communist assault on my people has achieved high ferocity. Mr. President, my people and I are mindful of the great assistance which the United States has given us ... But Vietnam is not a great power and the forces of international Communism now arrayed against us are more than we can meet with the resources at hand. We must have further assistance from the United States if we are to win the war now being waged against us."

President John Kennedy had replied: "We shall promptly increase our assistance to your defense effort ... I have already given the orders to get these programs underway."

By increments, but never enough to win, this assistance had grown. The number of American troops was mounting close to 400,000, and still it was not enough. No one knew the point at which sufficient force would overwhelm the enemy.

Lyndon Johnson had always feared the American action in Vietnam. He described it as "the damnedest worst mess that I ever saw," in a conversation with his political mentor, Senator Richard Russell of Georgia. "I do not see how we are ever going to get out of it without getting in a major war with the Chinese and all of them down there in those rice paddies and jungles."[5]

Johnson felt that his destiny was to bring civil rights and prosperity to America. He knew also that failure in Vietnam would ruin everything. "LBJ was great in domestic affairs," the American diplomat Averell Harriman put it. "If it hadn't been for ...Vietnam he'd have been the greatest President ever."[6] Johnson himself phrased it more graphically. "If I left the woman I really loved – the Great Society – in order to get involved with that bitch of a war on the other side of the world, then I would lose everything at home. All my programs. All my hopes to feed the hungry and shelter the homeless. All my dreams to provide education and medical care to the browns and blacks and the lame and the poor. But if I left that war and let the Communists take over South Vietnam, then I would be seen as a coward and my nation would be seen as an appeaser and we would both find it impossible to accomplish anything for anybody anywhere on the entire globe."[7]

Everything depended on victory in Vietnam. And the combat in Vietnam was going poorly.

JANUARY, 1968

Dak To, in Kontun Province, was a small town with an airstrip in the central highland, the tri-border region where Vietnam meets Laos and Cambodia.

The Peoples' Army of Vietnam (PAVN) wanted to flush out camps of U.S. Special Forces which dotted the isolated villages of the province. In late 1967, the PAVN launched a series of attacks on the border provinces. Six thousand North Vietnamese troops were diverted from Pleiku and other regions to Kontun. In response, the U.S. moved two battalions of the 173rd Airborne Brigade into Dak To, then three companies of the 503rd Airborne Infantry. Over 200 bombing strikes and two thousand air sorties were called in to support the ground efforts.

On January 14, Dwight Johnson of Detroit, Michigan was assigned a new tank.

A black twenty-year old Specialist in Company B, 1st Battalion, 69th Armor, 4th Infantry Division, Dwight "Skip" Johnson had grown up in Detroit, "a good boy," Explorer Scout, altar boy, a good student who had done all that was expected of him. His mother warned him to stay out of fights. "The only time he fought was on one occasion when older boys set upon his younger brother, and the anger came out. The neighbors had to pull a kicking and screaming Skip away from the fight."[8] He had been drafted in July, 1966, months after his high school graduation, and did his basic training at Fort Knox, Kentucky.

The following day, January 15, Skip Johnson and his newly-assigned tank were moving through the thick jungle near Dak To in order to aid elements of his platoon under fire.

A sudden barrage of enemy rocket fire exploded on the column. Two tanks took direct hits. Johnson's tank was struck and disabled. Then "a battalion-sized enemy force appeared from nowhere."[9] Seeing his old tank on fire, Johnson "leaped from his own vehicle and ran through sixty feet of crossfire" armed with only a .45 pistol to try and rescue his crew members. "He pulled a barely recognizable but still breathing crew member from the turret and carried him to the ground."[10] At that moment, the tank's ammunition ignited, exploding the tank into shards of metal and burnt and blackened bodies.

Then Dwight Johnson lost his temper.

He ran towards the enemy, "despite intense hostile fire," firing his pistol. His ammunition ran out. As his Medal of Honor citation tells it, Johnson continued fighting. "Returning to his tank through a heavy volume of antitank rocket, small arms and automatic weapons fire, he obtained a sub-machine gun with which to continue his fight against the advancing enemy. Armed with this weapon, Specialist Johnson again braved deadly enemy fire to return to the center of the ambush site where he courageously eliminated more of the determined foe. Engaged in extremely close combat when the last of his ammunition was expended, he killed an enemy soldier with the stock end of his submachine gun.

## Fire in the Hills

"Now weaponless, Specialist Johnson ignored the enemy fire around him, climbed into his platoon sergeant's tank, extricated a wounded crewmember and carried him to an armored personnel carrier.

"He then returned to the same tank and assisted in firing the main gun until it jammed. In a magnificent display of courage, Specialist Johnson exited the tank and again armed only with a .45 caliber pistol, he engaged several North Vietnamese troops in close proximity to the vehicle. Fighting his way through devastating fire and remounting his own immobilized tank, he remained fully exposed to the enemy as he bravely and skillfully engaged them with the tank's externally-mounted .50 caliber machine gun; where he remained until the situation was brought under control.

"When his clip was spent, he returned to his own tank and retrieved a submachine gun and again took the fight directly into the enemy's ranks. When the submachine gun ran out of bullets, he used his rifle as a club and killed an enemy soldier with the stock."[11]

By Spring, the North Vietnamese had withdrawn from Dak To and the Kontun Province, retreating to sanctuaries across the border. American commanders debated the cost of victory. "We had soundly defeated the enemy without unduly sacrificing operations in other areas," declared General William Westmoreland. "The enemy's return was nil."[12] But Marine Corps General John Chaisson questioned the numbers. "Is it a victory when you lose 362 friendlies in three weeks and by your own spurious body count you only get 1,200?"[13]

# Teddy's Tantrum

Plagued by the memory of Dak To and unanswerable questions – *Why was he ordered to switch tanks the night before the attack?* -- Johnson could not find steady work. He resented making public appearances to help recruit young black men to the armed forces, and went AWOL on more than one occasion. He was treated for psychiatric disorders at the Valley Forge Army Hospital in Pennsylvania. His psychiatrist noted that "'There is evidence the subject learned to live up to the expectations of others while there was a buildup of anger he continually suppressed.' He may have suppressed that anger, but he was aware of it. That's why he was afraid."[14] Dwight Johnson's epic temper tantrum at Dak To, his magnificent display of courage, served somehow to release darker forces which soon destroyed him. On April 29, 1971, he walked into the Open Pantry Market in Detroit and asked for a pack of cigarettes. "When the storeowner opened the register, Johnson pulled a .22 caliber pistol and told him to step aside.

"The owner reached under the counter for his own gun.

"'I hit him with two bullets,' said the store owner afterwards, 'but he just stood there, with the gun in his hand, and said "I'm going to kill you." I kept pulling the trigger until the gun was empty.'"[15]

# CHAPTER 10

# Special Order 266

I remember Mr. Roosevelt. I let him in myself. He went from room to room. He found just the right place. He sat down. People came in a ring. He talked to everybody at once. Mr. Theodore Roosevelt was a great man – a very great man; but he was kind o' heedless like.

-- *A black cook remembering Roosevelt's visit*

### OCTOBER, 1906

William Howard Taft returned from Canada ten days after the raid to find his desk cluttered with communications regarding the midnight raid in Brownsville, Texas. Telegrams were constantly coming in from one Texas military post or another, complaining in dire and elaborate terms of apocalyptic events that more often than not turned out to be ugly but short-lived racial incidents.

William Howard Taft, an Ohio judge whom McKinley had persuaded to take on the organization of the Philippines, did not enjoy being Secretary of War. He did not enjoy being the close confidant and heir apparent to Theodore Roosevelt. He had enjoyed governing the Philippines, and was reluctant when Roosevelt asked him in 1904 to return to Washington and serve as Secretary of War.

Taft took naps – often during midsentence, either his own or a visitor's – because he was unhappy. He would nod off when the mood took him, whether standing up or sitting down, at church or the dinner table or a meeting, often picking up in mid-sentence when he awoke. "He has no nerves and sleeps while the rest stay awake," wrote Captain Butt of Taft's narcolepsy. "If sleep overpowers him while he is talking to the Chief Justice or anyone else, he promptly closes his eyes and takes cat naps between sentences." Those close to him felt that Taft also gained weight because he was unhappy. Since Roosevelt had asked him to come home from Curzon and installed him in a Washington office, he had been getting larger and larger, and he now weighed over 300 pounds. His Nellie had called in an English physician who promised to help Taft lose seventy pounds.

Taft, a genial man, would have preferred to be on the Supreme Court to being in his friend Teddy Roosevelt's cabinet. His affableness and intelligence made him a good companion for Roosevelt. In the matter of the Texas raid, he would prove to be genial to a fault.

One of the Texas telegrams, from one Major Penrose of Fort Brown, read:

> "I am convinced that the killing of the citizen and wounding of the chief of police at Brownsville last night was done by seven

# Special Order 266

> *to ten men of this command, abetted by others in post."*

Police chief wounded? Such news would have been disturbing, except for the fact that every week brought similarly dire cables from Laredo, and Fort McIntosh, and Waco, and Houston, and San Antonio. The two Texas senators, Culberson and Bailey, were particularly fond of sending such warnings. It seemed the Texans could not get their fill of florid descriptions of barbarous acts by the lesser races.

From Laredo: *"The cause of these negro-Mexican disturbances were that the negroes were given too many liberties,"* and *"These Mexicans are an inflammatory people and are liable to catch fire at any times and no telling what …"*

To their most recent urgent cable regarding the apocalyptic consequences of black troops along the Rio Grande, Taft had sent a reasonable answer:

*"The fact is,"* he had written back to Culberson, *"that a certain amount of race prejudice between white and black seems to have become almost universal throughout the country, and no matter where colored troops are sent there are always some who make objections to their coming. It is a fact, however, as shown by our records, that our colored troops are quite as well disciplined and behaved as the average of our other troops, and it does not seem logical to anticipate any greater trouble from them than from the rest."*

It was a lawyerly answer; Taft had recited the facts but begged the question, as he usually did. However, if indeed a man lay dead in the streets of Brownsville, then such an answer would not suffice.

William Howard Taft liked to get along. As Secretary of War, he sought to avoid crisis. It was a smallish Department, and Taft managed to keep things on course - signing the billets, overseeing promotions, receiving complaints. Elihu Root had organized it splendidly before he left.

Taft was getting caught up in a whirlwind. Roosevelt, whom Taft had met over a decade earlier in New York when the two young politicians lunched together, was a most unpredictable man. The presidency had the courage of his convictions, which were many, and passionately held. With all his talk of the forces of evil, he was sometimes as much a zealot as a politician, and that worried Taft. He has tried to balance Theodore, to moderate his erratic tendencies, but it was getting harder and harder, particularly with the success of the Canal effort.

He was increasingly aware of Roosevelt's temper. He had seen Roosevelt almost rip the head off a Buffalo journalist who had criticized the President's private dinner with Booker T. Washington. Hand shaking with rage, Roosevelt had vowed to take away the unfortunate man's press access for the rest of his life: it was a savage thing to witness, as though some titanic inner struggle had suddenly spilled out into the open. *"Men must trust to emotion for that safety which reason ... can never give,"* Roosevelt was fond of saying. At some point, Taft might have to distance himself from Roosevelt. That, he knew, would be unpleasant.

# Special Order 266

Roosevelt's reaction to this Texas business, he was sure, would be a measured one. Roosevelt had served with those very same black troops in Cuba. He had mentioned it on several occasions.

Theodore Roosevelt felt, or wanted to feel, that William Taft was his ideological twin. "I believe with all my soul that Taft ... represents the principles for which I stand. His policies ... purposes, and ideals are the same as mine." It was not true. Taft was a conservative man whose true opinions were far less progressive than Roosevelt knew. Either Taft's extreme desire to go along or Roosevelt's tendency to see things in his own image, or a combination of the two factors, produced a bubble in the relationship, a false intimacy that one day had to end.

Taft's wife Nellie saw it coming. "I do hope," she wrote her husband, "that you are not going to make any more speeches on the 'Roosevelt policies' as I think they need to be let alone for the present." The charade of close kinship with all things Roosevelt took its toll on Taft. "I hope that somebody, sometime, will recognize the agony of spirit that I have undergone."

"Incredible folly," the New York Times called the Army's decision to post black soldiers in south Texas. "If there must be negro troops, which is far from evident, it would seem to be the part of wisdom to station them elsewhere than in Texas, or anywhere in the South."

In the national black community, grave concern over the Brownsville shooting was tempered by a deep admiration for Theodore Roosevelt. This was the man who had fought alongside the 25th that day in Cuba, the man who had invited Booker T. Washington to dine with him in the White House, the man who said, honestly if somewhat bluntly, "I have not been able to think out any solution of the terrible problem offered by the presence of the Negro on this continent, but of one thing I am sure, and that is that in as much as he is here and can neither be killed nor driven away, the only wise and honorable and Christian thing to do is to treat each black man and each white man strictly on his merits as a man."[1] "[Roosevelt] had appointed black officeholders in the face of white opposition ... and had given the impression that he meant to give a 'square deal' to each American. Photographs of Washington and Roosevelt together had become extremely popular wall decorations for black homes and were referred to as 'Social Equality' pictures."[2]

Sergeant Mingo Sanders and all the men of the 25th swore that no soldier among them had gone into the streets of the town and shot at houses, families, the bartender Natus, or Dominguez. All the men of the regiment were innocent, they insisted.

Twelve of the soldiers were arrested, including Privates Howard and Allison. Eight of them had confirmed alibis. "If you men had told what you knew about the shooting, Major Penrose told them when he visited them in jail, "you would not [be] in confinement."

A Grand Jury was convened. The judge, in his directions to the jurors, made his own feelings clear: the raid, he told them, was an "unprovoked, murderous midnight assault committed by the Negro soldiers," who had acted with "fiendish malice and hate, showing hearts blacker than their skins." For three weeks

# Special Order 266

the grand jury "made a very thorough investigation, but failed to find an indictment against any of the parties under arrest."[3] As the U.S. Commissioner explained, "the evidence did not point with sufficient certainty to any individual or individuals to justify or warrant them in bringing an indictment."

The twelve men were released from arrest.

The battalion was transferred to Fort Reno, Oklahoma.

There, the Inspector General of the Army, General E.A. Garlington, took their testimony "in affadavit form before a summary court in accordance with the provisions of the articles of war applicable." Again, no testimony or evidence of guilty parties could be produced. Garlington issued an extraordinary threat in an effort to make the soldiers talk: unless the enlisted men with knowledge of the true facts of the incident came forward, every soldier serving at Fort Brown on the night of the incident would be not only discharged from the Army but also debarred from federal employment in either a military or a civilian employment. This was a substantial evil, since many ex-soldiers took government jobs after military service: postal carrier or policeman was a far step above the other employment opportunities available to black males, shoeshine or bootblack or farm worker.

A second report was prepared in Brownsville by Major Blocksom, and a third by Lieutenant Colonel Leonard A. Lovering. All concluded that there was insufficient evidence to indict any man of the 25th.

Despite the conviction of much of the town that the black troops were responsible for the shooting, hard evidence was difficult to find. Eyewitnesses provided vague descriptions of men moving in the darkness. Blocksom was sure that the soldiers were hiding the truth, particularly the sergeant of the guard, the sentry, and the non-commissioned officer in charge of the barracks. All three had the same story: no members of the regiment participated in the raid. "There is little prospect of conviction on evidence thus far obtained," he concluded. The stalemate would last through multiple hearings. The Corpus Christ newspaper suggested that the raid may have been perpetrated by "persons disguised in uniforms, which are easily purchasable, and using government ammunition, which is no less easy to be secured." The soldiers waited for their day in court. The first Texas investigation came to no conclusion regarding the identity of the guilty parties.

"The Brownsville "Affray," as it came to be known, began to attract a cast of varied characters.

Bill MacDonald, a headline-chasing Captain of the Texas Rangers, decided he could "go down and settle that Brownsville business." He arrived without any authority and began investigating, interviewing a soda-water salesman. He marched on Fort Brown and told the twenty black soldiers, "I'll show you niggers something you've never been use' to." The local authorities shunned him, and within a week Bill McDonald had barged in and barged out.

Henry Weaver, a soft-spoken, literate man, did not belong in Texas. As a court reporter for the hearing, this literate man, "a lawyer, a parliamentarian, and one of the fastest shorthand writers in the world"[4] was a member of the six-man corps of Official Reporters who recorded every word spoken on the floor of the House of Representatives for the *Congressional Record*. Much of the

# Special Order 266

testimony heard by Captain Kelly's citizens' committee had been hurriedly transcribed, and was useless: with the Official Reporters, that would not happen again. Henry Weaver was somewhat absent-minded: his wife, the practical one, would give him a single dollar bill, "for emergencies," for his daily commute to and from work. The father of five children, Henry stayed in Texas only a short time, perhaps a week, to record the hearing proceedings, then he returned to his Shenandoah Valley.

William G. Baldwin was the head of a Roanoke, Virginia detective agency. Herbert J. Browne was the former editor of the Roanoke *Times*. Sensing that they could find a role to play in the coming Brownsville drama, Baldwin and Browne the two Virginians teamed up to approach Senator Foraker, head of the Senate Military Affairs Committee, the body which would eventually review the hearings. Foraker quickly realized the pair were charlatans, producing inflated, if not invented "reports" with little basis in truth. Foraker would sever his relations with Browne and Baldwin, the pair from Roanoke.

As the Congressional elections loomed, pressure was mounting for a resolution in Brownsville. "The Congressional elections of 1906 were important to the Republicans and especially to Roosevelt. At stake was the control of Congress and Roosevelt's actions against the trusts. If the GOP could retain control of Congress, the party could claim a mandate for the presidential policies."[5] Concern over Roosevelt's anti-trust legislation was high. The South was critical, and Roosevelt was concerned that his centralized-government message would be interpreted correctly in a region that treasured states' rights. Government control of railroads, government control of corporations – these were progressive ideas that needed a proper explanation. "It is my very good fortune," he told an audience in Georgia, "to have the right to claim that my blood is half southern and half northern." His dinner with Booker T. Washington was fresh in the memory of many southern voters, politicians, and journalists. Wherever he spoke, he was pleased to see that he was forgiven for his "Negrophilist" views and accepted for his other perceived virtues. The Atlanta riots had inflamed passions across the country.

The mob that had turned away from Walter White's picket fence on Houston Street in Atlanta the previous month had not dispersed.

Thousands of angry white men roamed the streets for five hours that day, looking for blacks to murder on sight. They found fifteen more, in addition to the man whom Walter saw murdered on Peachtree Street, as well as scores they merely pummeled. Victims were pulled from moving street cars and wrestled away from police protection to be put to death.

The Mayor had practically lit the fuse with his response to early signs of trouble: "The best way to prevent a race riot," he had declared, "depends entirely on the cause. As to the present trouble in Atlanta, I would say the only remedy is to remove the cause. So long as black brutes attempt to assault our white women, just so long as will they be unceremoniously dealt with."[6] Even worse, if possible, than the Atlanta Mayor were the two candidates for Georgia Governor, Smith and Howell. Both Hoke Smith and Clark Howell ran campaigns based on open hostility to negroes. Gregory Mixon adds commerce as a factor in his book

# Special Order 266

*The Atlanta Riot: Race, Class and Violence in a New South.* His thesis is that the recent success of black-owned businesses fanned the resentment of whites.

The rest of the nation saw clearly what was happening in Atlanta, and in Brownsville. A San Francisco Chronicle headline put it plainly: *"All South Ready for War Upon Negro."*

Garlington had concluded two things: first, that the men were guilty, although he could not procure any evidence to prove it; and secondly, that there was a conspiracy of silence. He was convinced that the men "so uniformly and persistently denied guilt" that they must be colluding in order to suppress the truth.

Garlington had recommended that the entire battalion should be found guilty of the shooting and of a conspiracy to conceal the facts. Surely at least one of the troops knew something, yet the entire battalion colluded to say nothing. This, he wrote, would set an example for the entire army. He requested that the President approve a discharge without honor.

Roosevelt wholly agreed with Garlington. A quiet fury which had simmered from the moment he heard about the Brownsville Raid finally found its expression.

On November 5, 1906, the day after the Congressional elections, while his Secretary of Army was absent, and without any advice and consent from any other government body, President Roosevelt directed the War Department to issue Special Order 266, an order dismissing the three black Texas companies "and forever debarring the men from serving their government either as soldiers or civilians."

# CHAPTER 11

# A Stray Remark

> The greatest historian should also be a great moralist. It is no proof of impartiality to treat wickedness and goodness as on the same level.
>
> -- *Theodore Roosevelt, History as Literature*

O<small>N A</small> V<small>IRGINIA</small> S<small>ATURDAY EVENING</small> in the spring of 1967, John D. Weaver was pouring cocktails for his mother and a friend.

They were looking through the family scrapbook. They came across a photograph of John's three older siblings playing in a cow field.

"Where was that taken?" Weaver asked his mother.

"Texas, dear," answered John's mother.

John looked up. The family had never spent time in Texas, at least not that he had known.

"And what were we doing in Texas, Mother?"

The elderly Martha Weaver explained that John's father had served as the court reporter in a civil hearing there one summer before John was born.

"Some Negro soldiers shot up the town," she explained, "and Teddy Roosevelt kicked them out of the Army."

"Did Dad report their trial?" John asked.

"They didn't have any trial. He just kicked them out."

"But, Mother, not even the President can go around kicking people out of the army without a trial."

"Well, he did."[1]

The incident stayed with Weaver. He had no memory of any connection between the state of Texas and his own family, and the idea of Teddy Roosevelt perpetrating a blatant injustice on black soldiers ... well, it made no sense.

*Texas? Teddy Roosevelt?*

Roosevelt had fought with black troops on San Juan Hill, everyone knew that. Roosevelt was a progressive: he had dined with Booker T. Washington in the White House. John Weaver knew history, and he had never heard of such an event.

Determined to prove that his mother's memory was faulty, John Weaver decided to look into it.

PART TWO

# THE DETECTIVE

The Brownsville episode arose when Roosevelt had, in a fit of rage, ordered the dishonorable discharge of several units of Negro troops ...

--- *Taft biographer Judith Icke Anderson*

# CHAPTER 12

# Aftermath

*Yes, I think Mr. Roosevelt began to be sadly badgered by the 'Brownsville nightmare'; his phrase.*

*-- Julia Foraker*

NEWSPAPER HEADLINES SCREAMED AT THE dismissal of the men of the 25th Infantry before any trial was held.

"*Negroes are not fools, at least not all of them, and this after-election order is well understood by them,*" the Washington Bee declared.

"The picture of a President whose chief merit is supposed to lie in his fearless bravery dodging an issue like this one, until after the votes are counted, is not pleasant to look upon, even though it stamps him as a clever politician," the Waterville, Maine *Sentinel* observed. "No media coverage, black or white, doubted that the affray originated with former Confederates' disdain for armed blacks."[1]

"The impact of the Brownsville incident on the black population was tremendous."[2] "Reaction to Roosevelt's order came swiftly and bitterly in the Negro press."[3] The timing of Special Order 266 was not lost on anyone. Benjamin J. Davis, editor of the

## Teddy's Tantrum

*Atlanta Independent,* put it plainly: "No self-respecting Negro man would have voted the republican ticket last Tuesday in the face of this flagrant violation of our constitutional rights." In the next day's newspaper, Davis went further, comparing Roosevelt to two notorious racists: "The hand of Ben Tillman nor Vardaman never struck humanity as savagely as did the iron hand of Theodore Roosevelt. His new dictum is lynch-law, bold and heartless."[4] The silence of the men of the 25th was seen as heroic, not villainous ("That noble bands stood mum"). "The fact that he withheld his decision until after the election emphasizes the fact that he is about as much of a politician as he is a statesman," wrote John Mitchell of the *Richmond Planet*. He called for his readers to remember it during "many elections to come."

Black churches, too, condemned the decision. The Reverend William Decker Johnson of Thomasville, Georgia "reminded the nation, Roosevelt, and the black community of that day at Kettle Hill:

> *Let us not fume, and fret and grieve because Theodore Roosevelt, the President of our Country, has dismissed in disgrace eon hundred and seventy Negro soldiers, we remember, too well, that he would never have reached the Presidential chair, had it not been for the bravery of these disgraced soldiers.*

Johnson went on to make a prediction that was indicative of the feelings of the black community:

# Aftermath

*The Spanish American was not the last was this country is going to be involved in, there will yet dawn a day when this country will be glad, yea, will court and beg the services of the Negro in time of warfare.*

"Bitter denunciation of Roosevelt's actions came from all quarters of the black community." The Colored American Magazine, part-owned by Booker T. Washington, turned on Roosevelt quickly. Booker T Washington himself, however, did not. "The most notable silence was that of Booker T. Washington who, as Roosevelt's political referee, was unwilling to make any statement denouncing the President."[5]

Reverend Charles Morriss of the Abyssinian Church of New York went right to the point, urging his congregation to elect a Democratic President in 1908. "Thus shall we answer Theodore Roosevelt, once enshrined in our love as our Moses, now enshrouded in our scorn as our Judas."

Taft received his share of blame. "Secretary Taft might make a good judge of the Supreme Court, where no politics are necessary," wrote B.J. Davis, "but he does not measure up to presidential timber."[6] Taft's inaction in the Brownsville episode was unfavorably contrasted to his successful intervention in a similar case in Athens, Ohio – on behalf of white troops.

In the hallways of the rambling home on Sixteenth Street, Julia Foraker heard muttering. It was coming from her husband's study.

# Teddy's Tantrum

*"No, no, no ... this can't be ..."*

Julia, the smart, loyal wife of Ohio Senator Joseph Foraker, heard her husband reading over the transcripts of the Texas investigation.

Foraker was a lawyer, and a good one at that. He had fought in the Civil War with Company A of the 89th Regiment, Ohio Volunteer Infantry and rising to Captain. He had attended Cornell Law School after the war and ran for office, eventually winning the governorship in 1885 and the Senate seat in 1896. His political career only slightly impeded by his infrequent disagreements with Ohio Republican bosses like Mark Hanna and McKinley. The Forakers were a popular couple with a wide set of acquaintances, and they entertained frequently in the close-knit Washington community; they had recently given a party for their friends Will and Nellie Taft.

Foraker could not believe the shoddy proceedings he was reading.

He was Chairman of the Military Affairs Committee. It was his responsibility to see that these soldiers received fair treatment.

His lawyerly eye was finding gaping holes in the case against the soldiers.

In the unsworn testimonies of the eyewitnesses he found "loose, conflicting, disjointed, and contradictory." The investigators he found to be less than competent, and less than unbiased. He referred to Blocksom as "... beyond any other, unfitted for this special work" due to his family's history of opposing black civil rights. And the soldiers themselves seemed to have been shut out of the inquiries: where were their statements? A midnight

## Aftermath

raid firing at houses and random targets seemed an unlikely undertaking for trained military men intent on doing harm. As to the investigation, it seemed stacked against the supposed culprits.

*The New York Times* agreed. "No evidence had been gathered prove a conspiracy on the part of the … battalion. The whole proceeding in fact was based on the assumption of the officers who made the inquiry that those who did not take part in the riot at Brownsville 'must know' who did."

The deeper Foraker delved into the documents of the Brownsville raid, the less he liked it. In the days that followed, his wife writes of Foraker "writing, wiring, sending men out to Texas to take sworn testimony, to secure exact details; spending hours and hours in a thickening jungle of newspapers, clippings, letters, and calf-bound books."[7] Foraker would go on to clarify the legal conundrum which had trapped the soldiers.

"Did you or the others ask [Major Penrose] to tell you how you could prove that you did not know anything about it except by saying you did not know anything about it?" Foraker asked Private Howard.

"No, sir," Howard replied.

"Has anyone else ever told you how you could prove that you were innocent, except by denying it?"

"No, sir."

The soldiers were stripped of their arms and confined to their post. "I never experienced such sadness in my life," Private Boyd Conyers told the court inquiry. The men were summoned to the adjutant general's office in groups of eight or ten, given their pay, their separation papers, and their travel fare. "Quietly they went their separate ways."⁸

The Roosevelt family was enjoying the view aboard the *U.S.S. Lousiana.*

The *Louisiana* had embarked at Piney Point, Maryland, on November to carry the President and his family to the Panama Canal.

The *Connecticut*-class battleships were the finest in the world, equipped with heavy broadside batteries, superior seakeeping capabilities and a top speed of 19 knots. Twelve months later, the *Louisiana* would be among the "Great White Fleet" which Roosevelt sent around the world to impress America's might upon all the nations.

"It is a beautiful sight, these three great war-ships standing southward in close column, and almost as beautiful at night when we see not only the lights but the loom through the darkness of the ships astern," the President wrote his son Kermit. "We are now in the tropics and I have thought a good deal of the time over eight years ago when I was sailing to Santiago in the fleet of warships and transports."

"I think Mother has really enjoyed it," he added.⁹ "Mother and I walk briskly up and down the deck together, or else sit aft under the awning, or in the after cabin, with the gun ports open, and read; and I also spend a good deal of time on the forward bridge, and sometimes on the aft bridge, and of course have gone over the ship to inspect it with the Captain. It is a splendid thing to

## Aftermath

see one of these men-of-war, and it does really make one proud of one's country ..."[10] "As for me, I of course feel a little bored, as I always do on shipboard, but I have brought on a great variety of books ..."

One of the works he cherished most was Edward Gibbons' multi-volume history of Rome, *History of the Decline and Fall of the Roman Empire* was one of the President's favorite works.

Roosevelt read Gibbon constantly, taking volumes with him on a long train trip or on a hunting expedition.[11] He understood very well one of Gibbon's primary themes, that Rome fell from internal decline.[12] "The enemies of Rome were in her bosom," wrote Gibbon. He portrayed with a fine point how her rulers lost their barbaric edge. Septumius Severus and his contemporaries, wrote Gibbon, "...in the enjoyment of the peace and glory of his reign, forgave the cruelties by which it had been introduced."[13] Roosevelt had read Gibbon's account of the Illyrian emperors of the late third century, doomed by their inability to see and understand the moral rot of the state. Edward Gibbon saw history in moral terms, and so did Theodore Roosevelt. Nor did Theodore Roosevelt ever forget the cruelties by which the nation had been introduced.[14]

Gibbon also blamed Rome's soldiers for Rome's fall.[15] "The rougher trade of arms was abandoned to the peasants and barbarians of the frontiers ... With bloody hands, savage manners, and desperate resolutions, they sometimes guarded, but much oftener subverted, the throne of emperors."[16] Roosevelt had no intention of letting the military slip into disarray, moral or physical or otherwise: such a mistake had cost Rome and empire.

# Teddy's Tantrum

Gibbon is visible in many of Roosevelt's habits, and values, and rhetoric. Here is how Gibbon describes the virtue of Marcus Aurelius Antoninus. "At the age of twelve years, he embraced the rigid system of the Stoics, which taught him to submit his body to his mind, his passions to his reason; to consider virtue as the only good, vice as the only evil, all things external as things indifferent."[17] Here is Gibbon's version of Roosevelt's famous remark on critics who cling to the sidelines, and rulers who may make mistakes, but leave something great in their passing. "Whatever evils either reason or declamation have imputed to extensive empire, the power of Rome was attended with some beneficial consequences to mankind …"[18] "The correspondence of nations was in that age so imperfect and precarious, that the revolutions of the North might escape the knowledge of the court of Ravenna, till the dark cloud, which was collected along the coast of the Baltic, burst in thunder upon the banks of the Upper Danube. The emperor of the West, if his ministers disturbed his amusements by the news of the impending danger, was satisfied with being the occasion and the spectator of the war." [19]

Under Theodore Roosevelt, the correspondence of nations was never so vigorous.

Mary Terrell's phone rang.

This was a first, since the device was newly installed in her Washington home, and Mrs. Terrell was not aware that it actually working. She answered.

# Aftermath

It was a long-distance call. "John Milholland, the wealthy white sponsor of the Constitution League, wanted her to go over to the War Department"[20] and ask Taft to reverse Special Order 266.

So the next day, when Will Taft returned to his office, he found Mary Church Terrell, president of the National Association of Colored Women, waiting in the lobby of his office.

Mrs. Terrell told the Secretary of War that she had come on behalf of the colored soldiers.

"What do you want me to do about it?" Taft replied. "President Roosevelt has already dismissed them and he has gone to Panama. There is nothing I can do."

"All I want you to do, Mr. Secretary, is to suspend the order dismissing the soldiers until an investigation can be made."

"Is that *all* you want me to do?" he responded.

Perhaps moved by Mrs. Terrell's plea, perhaps following his own lawyerly instincts towards caution and moderation, Taft cabled Roosevelt and point out that the process of discharging the soldiers had barely begun. Special Order 266 could still be suspended, pending further study. "Much agitation on the subject," he advised Roosevelt, "it may be well to convince people of fairness of hearing by granting rehearing."[21] Taft confided to his Nellie, "I do not think [Roosevelt] realizes quite the great feeling he has aroused on the subject."

In response to Taft's plea for moderation, Roosevelt shot back, "Discharge is not to be suspended unless there are new facts of such importance as to warrant your cabling me."

## Teddy's Tantrum

Taft had no stomach for confrontation. Whatever his true feelings about it, that would be the last time he would question Roosevelt's decision in the Brownsville matter.

On November 18, the U.S. Attorney General filed suit in Missouri to dissolve Standard Oil and sixty-five companies under its control. Named in the suit were a "pantheon of chieftains," executives and directors who were charged with charged with monopolizing the oil industry and conspiring to restrain trade. Standard Oil then controlled 87 per cent of all the heating oil in the nation and was twenty times larger than its nearest rival, Pure Oil.

Roosevelt and his Bureau of Corporations had been marshalling seven different lawsuits against Standard Oil and its subsidiaries, in conjunction with multiple suits from states like Texas, Minnesota, and Missouri. The most explosive of these would come to fruition in Indiana, where the flamboyant judge "Kenesaw Mountain" Landis would levy the staggering fine of $29 million against the trust.

"*It is a greater work than you yourselves at the moment realize,*" Roosevelt told his comrades in the Grand Army regarding their work on the Panama Canal, which was but one small panel in the grand tableau of progress which he was imagining.

Control of an intersea canal was a dream that predated Roosevelt by 300 years, and several were the nations who

## Aftermath

foundered on that vision. Scotland was first. France was
the second.

Pretty as poison, the Isthmus had proven fatal to men with plans for hundreds of thousands of years. Fooled by the seductive beauty of its coves and plants, fertile soils and friendly natives, Europeans had reaped nothing but horrific death and defeat from the land bridge. Among the earliest Europeans to grasp the enormous value of capturing the Isthmus trade were the Scots. At the end of the seventeenth century, seeing its own economic fortunes failing while rivals like England and Holland and Spain gobbled up New World territories for their empires, Scotland made a bold gamble: they sent an expedition to capture the Isthmus. The unfortunate thousand who sailed from Glasgow in July, 1698 suffered terribly on the isthmus: those who did not die of excruciating fever perished on the voyage home, and barely three hundred survived. They had learned nothing, and the second voyage was cut down by disease in less than a year. A single boat returned.

William Paterson, a Scot who was one of the founding directors of the Bank of England, proposed to build a permanent trading colony in the port of Darien, on the western shore of the Isthmus. If a colony could be established there, all merchant ships would pay a commission for a reliable transport across the land bridge, saving weeks of dangerous journey around Cape Horn, the remote tip of South America.

A rush of subscribers financed an initial voyage in July, 1698. The Dutch and English regarded this as and embargoed the Scots. Five ships set out of Leith harbor, laden with combs, mirrors and wigs to trade to the long-haired natives. They arrived in the thick mud of Darien in November, and by March the band of colonists was all but ravaged from disease and starvation. Dutch and English settlements refused to help. Paterson's wife died, and only a single ship made it back to Scotland. A second expedition left Scotland in August of 1699, and met the same fate. A neighboring settlement, Toubacanti, besieged the ruined Darien colony and a handful of Scots returned to tell the grim story.

The Isthmus venture wrecked Scotland. Her finances and morale were broken at a time when crucial advances in global empire were being made by the other nations of Europe. Empty of money and will to adventure, Scotland remained on the sidelines while men like Drake and Pisarro and Cortez conquered new lands for their monarchs. Scotland had no choice but to sign the Act of Union, joining England as the junior partner in the united kingdom of Great Britain. England paid the debts left from the Isthmus adventure.

France was next.

The ambitious entrepreneur Ferdinand de Lessops, who built the Suez Canal, raised seven million dollars and attempted, between the years1881 and 1889, to dig a sea-level canal through the Isthmus of Panama. His attempts failed. He had a grand vision of a canal across the Isthmus, one that would bring fortune to France and her investors. He presented the plans for a sea-level canal to investors at a sumptuous dinner in Paris. Enthusiasm ran high. He discounted the yellow fever that seemed to shadow previous efforts. He had, after all, faced and defeated cholera in his effort to build the Suez: Panama would be no different.

# Aftermath

So convincing was de Lessops that he had raised $17 million by the sumner of 1880. His team began digging the Culebra Cut even before his engineers had provided a system of removing the dirt. The French excavating machines were too light, and could not remove the large boulders which ancient glaciers had left for them. De Lessops' contract with Colombia, which owned the Isthmus, was conditional, which frightened off investors.

Yellow fever murdered 10,000 of his workers. A brilliant young man named Henri Bionne died of "brain fever." Then his colleague, Etienne, a graduate of the Polytechnic, was taken. The fever raged through the Isthmus cities, with their open sewers. De Lessops fought back against the epidemic, pouring money into a hospital at Ancon and a sanitarium at Taboga. But his doctors did not understand the disease, and could not stop it. De Lessops was forced to fold his company, bankrupting a good portion of the French aristocracy in the process.

Theodore Roosevelt, understanding history as he did, committed the full might of the American empire to build the isthmus canal. Having wrested the rights to the land from the Colombians, whom he identified as "homicidal corruptionists" and "monkeys," Roosevelt spared no expense to get the job done. The great naval fleet he was building to needed to pass through the Isthmus at will, and thereby patrol the world: anything less would hinder American destiny. "This nation demands that results be achieved," he reminded his army of workers and engineers. The United States agreed to pay the new nation of Panama $40,000,000 – forty *million* dollars -- for the unconditional rights to this strip of land. It was an unimaginable sum of money.

## Teddy's Tantrum

Wallace, the first Chief Engineer, was paid an annual salary of $25,000, more than any other government employee except the President. The lock system was debated in Congress. Roosevelt assembled an army of men and machines for the task: great berm cranes on gantries; concrete mixers weighing 470 tons; shunting towers 62 feet tall, with cantilevered arms to move sand and gravel to the hoppers; fifty 95-ton Bucyrus steam shovels; drill towers to prepare the dynamite charges; 220,000 feet of pipe laid in the Culebra Cut to power the drills; air compressors located at Rio Grande, Empire and Las Cascadas.114 rising steam valves, with 120 cylindrical valves; a train of waiting dump cars to carry off the dirt; pyramid-like scaffolding to hold mold boards in place while concrete is poured; 92 leaves of iron plates each 65 feet wide, 7 feet thick, and from 47 to 82 feet high, used to form the lock gates; elevators to the operating-tunnels; twenty No.12 McCully gyratory crushers, to reduce boulders to chunks of five inches or less); an oceangoing ladder dredge, *The Corozal;* almost 2000 tons of Scottish-built bucket chains; navigational range markers.

Passages from David McCullough's description of the Roosevelt visit in his detailed, epic 1977 book, *The Path Between the Seas* give a flavor of both the man and the great enterprise:

> *As the official welcoming committee stood at the end of the pier, all eyes searching for signs of life on the big ship, an amazing figure called "Good morning" from shore. He advanced into their midst. He was wearing a white suit and a seaman's sou'wester, the*

# Aftermath

*brim of which reached his shoulders. The pince-nez glistened with fine raindrops. He had been rowed ashore two hours earlier, he explained, and had been having a grand time "exploring" the waterfront.*

*By noon he had toured the bay in a seagoing tug and had walked unannounced into one of the employees' mess halls at La Boca, where, with several hundred "gold roll" men, he and Mrs. Roosevelt sat down to a 30-cent lunch of soup, beef, mashed potatoes, peas, chili con carne, plum pudding and coffee. According to the official schedule, he was supposed to have attended a large luncheon in his honor at the Tivoli Hotel.*

*"He seemed obsessed with the idea that someone was trying to hide something from him," Frank Maltby would recall. "...He was continually pointing to some feature and asking, 'What's that? ... Well, I want to see it'... he was continually stopping some black man and asking if he had any complaint or grievance."*

*He walked railroad ties in Culebra Cut, leaped ditches, splashed through work camps, made impromptu speeches in the driving rain. "You are doing the biggest thing of the kind that has ever been done," he said, "and I wanted to see how you were doing it."*[22]

# Teddy's Tantrum

Roosevelt was obsessed with the idea that someone was trying to hide something from him because of the Eerie Canal.[23] When he was Governor of New York, scandalous corruption had been discovered in a vast improvement project for the Eerie Canal. A special investigation committee reported that "improper expenditures" on the canal improvements totaling at least one million dollars. The entire budget had been spent, yet the channel was only two-thirds deepened.

In the eighteen months since John Findley Wallace had resigned, Roosevelt had consolidated the overseeing committee which had so tortured Wallace and hampered his progress. The divided authority was united. Wallace's successor, Colonel George Goethals, was the right man for the job. Dr. William Gorgas had roving brigades draining swamps, hauling garbage, burning brush and digging drainage ditches in a relentless campaign to stop the *Anopheles* mosquito, who needed shady, wet breeding grounds. Roosevelt noted with pleasure the absence of mosquitoes.

He rode the railroad. He scrambled up a hill to get a better view of the dam at Gatun. At the Pedro Miguel locks, he climbed into a steam-shovel carriage "and was soon sitting at the driver's seat," according to a delighted newspaper reporter.

He and his entourage crossed a rickety plank bridge and came upon a breathtaking panorama: giant cranes were lowering the gates into place, abetted by what seemed like thousands of swarming black men. Explosions in the high rock sent shards skittering down the cliffs as if to punctuate the process. River dredges were pumping mud from the Culebra Lake as quarry barges from Porto Bello crossed in front of the Gatun gates,

# Aftermath

carrying massive rocks to shore up the breakwaters. A gleaming locomotive pulled away, carrying tons of dirt and gravel dug out of the canal channel. The Gatun Gates, the centerpiece of the Isthmian Canal, waited to be installed. Gigantic iron doors twenty stories tall, so massive they had to be transported from the Scottish shipyards on the *Titanic's* sister ship, the *Olympia*, the 92 leaves of lock miter gates loomed 65 feet wide and 7 feet thick.

It was all as he had hoped.

On his return from Panama, Roosevelt declared the incident closed. It did not stay closed.

Roosevelt admitted there was a "conflict of evidence" regarding the exact chain of events, but he dismissed the contradictions as a "wholly unimportant matter."[24] Blame lay squarely upon the shoulders of the men of the 25th Infantry, if for nothing else, then for their stubborn silence. "If the colored men elect to stand by criminals of their own race because they are of their own race, they assuredly lay up for themselves the most dreadful day of reckoning," he proclaimed. "Every farsighted friend of the colored race in its efforts to strive onward and upward should teach first, as the most important lesson, alike to the white man and the black, the duty of treating the individual man strictly on his worth as he shows it."

On Monday, December 3, the Fifty-Ninth Congress convened. Senator Foraker was about to demand an investigation of the Brownsville matter when Senator Boeis Penrose of Pennsylvania, a close ally of Roosevelt's, leapt to his feet. He proposed his own investigation of the Texas shooting in order to shut Foraker out of the investigation; his bill "requested" all material from the President "if not compatible with the public interests." Such a bill, if passed, would allow Roosevelt to control what documents were shown to the Senate. Foraker jumped to his feet to propose a sweeping investigation, one that demanded *all* of the records. Foraker's bill was the one which eventually passed.

Support rallied around him in his defense of the soldiers. Gilchrist Stewart, a member of the Constitution League, a civil rights organization, wired Taft directly: "Soldiers in no conspiracy. Not allowed to present their side and investigation farce." Reverend Francis Grimke Washington churchman called it an "exercise of arbitrary and despotic power on the part of the President."

Roosevelt had let Booker T. Washington know in advance what his actions would be. To Washington's written plea to reconsider, Roosevelt was firm: "I could not possibly refrain from acting as regards those colored soldiers. You cannot have any information to give me privately, to which I could pay heed, my dear Mr. Washington, because the information on which I act is that which came out of the investigation itself."

Washington next turned to Taft. "I have never in all my experience with race," he wrote the Secretary of War, "experienced a time when the entire people have the feeling that they have now in regard to the administration." Once Taft had tried to intervene and failed, Washington relented. He circulated his correspondence with Roosevelt to his supporters, so they would know he tried. "I did my utmost to prevent his taking the action he did. I feel that I

# Aftermath

did my full duty in the matter which the enclosed copy of a letter from him will show."[25]

Roosevelt defended himself vigorously. "The action was precisely such as I should have taken had the soldiers guilty of the misconduct been white instead of colored men." Perhaps the situation was not being clearly understood, he suggested: the soldiers' course of action, gone unpunished, "would mean not only that the usefulness of the Army was at an end but it had better be disbanded in its entirety at once." And he, for one, would not stand for it. "Under no conceivable circumstances would I submit to such a condition of things."

It was to Roosevelt the familiar clatter of cynics amassed along the sidelines. Roosevelt gave it no thought. "I care nothing whatever for the yelling of either the politicians or the sentimentalists."

Besides, he had just won the Nobel Prize for Peace.

On December 10, he was awarded the Nobel Peace Prize for his role in negotiating peace in the Russo-Japanese War. Roosevelt directed his envoy Herbert Pierce to accept the Nobel Prize in Oslo and read a statement from him. "I am profoundly moved and touched by the ... Nobel Peace Prize. There is no gift I could appreciate more and I wish it were in my power fully to express my gratitude. I thank you for it." He then reminded all that he was able to accomplish the peace "only as the representative of the nation of which, for the time being, I am president." He directed that the prize money be given to a permanent industrial peace committee that would seek equitable relations between capitalists and wage workers, and between industrialists and farmers.

# Teddy's Tantrum

Taft eventually took Roosevelt's side in the Brownsville matter, and regretted whatever sympathy he might have shown to Mrs. Mary Church Terrell. "I think [Roosevelt's] order is fully sustained by the facts and the evidence which I have read," he wrote to a friend, "and it is quite embarrassing to me to have it thought that I differ with him on the subject."

Roosevelt dug in, ever more deeply, casting himself as a lone voice for justice. "There has been great pressure not only by sentimentalists but by the Northern politicians who wish to keep the Negro vote," he wrote to a newspaper editor. "In a case like this, where the issue is not merely one of naked right and wrong but one of vital concern to the whole country, I will not for one moment consider the political effect."

On the evening of January 26, the mood was light and expectant just before the Gridiron Club dinner at the New Willard Hotel. The gentlemen's establishment was buzzing with good humor as cigar smoke wafted towards the arched ceilings. This was an annual event (still very much in practice) where journalists and the politicians they write about are able to assemble and review the year's event. Clinks of silverware mixed with conversation under the high chandeliers which spilled light on giant oriental rugs and heavy wooden tables.

Senator Jim Watson of Indiana, the evening's master of ceremonies, concluded his introductory remarks and asked President Roosevelt to say a few words. Lines of tuxedoed waiters

# Aftermath

emerged for the swinging kitchen doors carrying steaming silver platters with soup tureens.

Roosevelt opened with a stern lecture against big business.

"It has been a year of excesses," he began.[26] "Wall Street, with its infinite greed, should be thankful that this administration is engineering the reforms over its behavior and not the mob, whose measures would be far more distasteful, I assure you."

The President glared down the table at J.P. Morgan. The eminent financier flushed at the unexpected challenge and began to stand and leave before he was pulled back.

Roosevelt continued to attack big business. Journalists in attendance would later say that Roosevelt seemed like a mad dog. Other men at the head table commented that the President was in one his "preachment" moods. The wolf within Roosevelt had risen: this would not be a lighthearted evening.

"It has also been a year of protracted academic discussions," said the President, turning to a new target. "I refer to the Senate's discussion of the Brownsville matter."

Joseph Foraker raised his head at the mention of Brownsville. The President looked directly at him.

"The legislative branch has no constitutional authority to review or reverse an action taken by the executive branch," he told the assemblage. "Has he gone mad?" came the murmurs. The Congress has every right under the Constitution to review actions taken by the executive branch; this is the very heart of the system of checks and balances the founders designed to prevent any one arm of the government from gaining too much power. The second and third courses were waved away; lines of confused waiters bumped into one another under the high chandeliers of the dining hall.

The President "had done what he took to be his duty, and he would brook no interference from anyone in discharging the obligations of his office.

This was a direct threat to Foraker. A chill fell over the great chamber. Unlike J.P. Morgan, Foraker would not be backing down from the challenge. He rose and made his way to the podium ("I did not know where to commence," he later wrote to his son). His face was white as a sheet, recalled an audience member.

He had, Foraker told the President, voted "according to my judgment and the obligations of my office, as befits any patriot. A Senator's duty is no less sacred and inviolate as a President's oath." He went on to say that no man stood so high or so low that, if guilty, he would not be punished and, if innocent, would not be granted the law's full protection. The President's action in the Brownsville matter, Foraker said, had betrayed that principle: many men with splendid records as soldiers who were innocent had been branded as criminals, and dismissed without honor.

Roosevelt seethed and nearly jumped up to give a rebuttal, but was restrained. "*That is not so*," he muttered. "*I will not stand for it.*"

Foraker reminded Roosevelt of a happier time, when "I loved him as though one of my own family." Their differences had always been in the open, he added, and pointed out that he "had fired no shots from ambush."

"When legal and human rights are involved, all persons look alike to me," Foraker concluded declared. "I did not come to the

# Aftermath

Senate to take orders from anybody, either at this end of the line or the other. Whenever I fall so low that I cannot express my opinion on a great question freely, and without reservation or mental evasion, I will resign and leave my place to some man who has the courage to discharge his duties."

He sat down to loud applause. "Newspapermen and their guests leaped up, cheering, crowding around the Senator and offering their congratulations."[27] Roosevelt's reply was savage. "Some of those men were bloody butchers. They ought to be hung. The only reason that I didn't have them hung was because I couldn't find out which ones of them did the shooting."

As time and multiple hearings dragged on, accounts became murkier and more and more conflicting. In the thirty months after Roosevelt's Special Order 266 in November, 1906, no definitive conclusions were ever reached. The soldiers were not exonerated, nor was any credible proof brought against them. The white officers, Macklin and Lyons and Penrose, heard the charges and counter-charges and determined that the black troops could not have participated in the midnight raid. Taft, who appears to have known exactly the difference between right and wrong in the matter, kept his silence after the dismissal. He had little use for this Brownsville business, and Nellie liked it even less. "The papers are still full of the Foraker row and I am glad you are not here to be wounded by it," wrote Nellie. "I fear it will be injurious to your chances."[28]

Julia Foraker reports that her husband "appears white and fagged" as the process wore on. Foraker himself wrote to his son that "there is no happiness in politics."

The same month of the Gridiron dinner, Theodore Roosevelt wrote a foreword for Seattle photographer Edward Curtis' privately published multi-volume project on the American Indian, *Vanishing American.* The twenty large-format books collected photographs text and drawings of the remaining tribes. "You have begun just in time," Roosevelt told Curtis, "for these people are at this very moment rapidly losing the distinctive traits and customs which they have slowly developed through the ages. The Indian, as an Indian, is on the point of perishing, and when he has become a U.S. citizen, though it will be a much better thing for him and for the rest of the country, he will lose completely his value as a living historical document."

A pretty sentiment from the man who had once declared "I don't go so far as to think that the only good Indians are the dead Indians, but I believe nine out of every ten are, and I shouldn't like to inquire too closely into the case of the tenth."[29]

The publisher of *Vanishing American* was J.P. Morgan.

In December, 1908, Foraker would propose the establishment of a commission of five retired general who could impartially review the evidence. The tribunal would give the soldiers a chance to confront their accusers. "If there be a guilty man in that battalion, no man should throw a straw in the way of having that guilt established ... Five investigations had failed to produce

# Aftermath

evidence on which charges could be brought a single member of the three infantry companies."

Foraker attacked the "eyewitnesses" savagely.

"I have shown that the testimony first submitted by Major Blocksom, although only loose-jointed, unsworn, inconsistent and contradictory statements, was regarded by the President as 'conclusive'..."[30]

"The testimony taken originally was *ex parte* and not sworn to ... the men had no notice of the proceeding, and ... had no one present to cross-examine the witnesses, or to represent them in any way whatever ...The evidence before this court fails entirely to prove the guilt of a single soldier..."

Foraker did more than bat aside the flimsy evidence: eventually, he was ready to put forth a far different scenario for who committed the crime and for what reasons.

"I have ... striven to ferret out the persons engaged in this crime ...I have had close personal contact with almost all the soldiers discharged...My investigations have tended to the conclusion that the shooting up of Brownsville was not an affray, but a crime committed by person not in the military service of the United States Government."

This was a most inflammatory charge, and one he was prepared to back up. "...I offered to produce testimony of an affirmative and positive character," wrote Foraker in his autobiography, "giving the names of the participators in and the details of an alleged conspiracy to commit this crime.

Foraker felt betrayed by Taft. He makes reference in his memoirs to Taft's "peculiar ability to disappoint and make enemies where it would be easier and more natural to meet expectations and make friends."

On March 14, Wall Street crashed.

The stock market lost 8.3% of its value when a speculator named Augustus Heinze bought the Knickerbocker Trust bank and began speculating aggressively, trying to corner on United Copper.[31] Other banks shunned him, and refused to honor Knickerbocker checks and soon both Knickerbocker and The National Bank of North America failed and the run was on.

The Secretary of the Treasury, George Cortleyou, shored up the panic with a gigantic investment ($35 million) of federal money. It was not enough. The markets were still unsettled.

Once again, J.P. Morgan saved the nation.

Morgan assembled a team of bank and trust executives to redirect funds between banks and secure international lines of credit. They bought plummeting stocks of companies like United Copper, with the President's blessing, and succeeded in restoring order.

As Theodore Roosevelt would later recall those events, "In the fall of ... 1907 there were severe business disturbances and financial stringency, culminating in a panic which arose in New York and spread over the country. The damage actually done was great, and the damage threatened was incalculable. Thanks largely to the actions of the Government, the panic was stopped before ... it became a frightful and Nation-wide calamity, a disaster fraught with untold misery and woe to all our people."

# Aftermath

This was not quite accurate: it was thanks largely to the actions of J. P. Morgan, although he did not particularly want the credit

"The entire agitation over Brownsville was in large part not a genuine agitation on behalf of the colored men at all, but ... the effort by the representatives of certain law-defying corporations to bring discredit upon the administration," proclaimed Roosevelt.

To Brooks Adams. "I believe you are right in saying that Foraker has been representing Wall Street in attacking me on this issue." Again and again he blamed the "capitalist reactionaries."

Taft would hire the two Roanoke, Virginia "investigators," Harold Browne and William Baldwin, to conduct yet another round of investigation. The pair interviewed various members of the scattered battalion and returned with dramatic results, giving for the first time "the true secret history of the Brownsville raid."[32] The President promptly submitted it to Congress. "This report enables us to fix with tolerable definiteness ... the criminals who took the lead in the murderous shooting of private citizens at Brownsville." Once again, Roosevelt declared the matter settled beyond all possibility of doubt. "It establishes clearly the fact that the colored soldiers did the shooting."

The President was typically resolute, and spoke of the incident in typically absolute terms. "The soldiers were the aggressors from start to finish ... The act was one of horrible atrocity, and, so far as I am aware, unparalleled for infamy in the annals of the United States Army."

## Teddy's Tantrum

In a lengthy session in Congress, Foraker broke down the President's case against the soldiers, line by line.

First, he attacked the contradictory and often unlikely nature of the testimony colelcted by Captain Kelly's citizens committee as well as the Blocksom and Garlington hearings. "Does any man believe that fifteen or twenty men, who had been off engaged in an excitement of that character, shooting up the town, trying to murder people, rushing back under such circumstances, could get into camp, could join their commands ... and avoid being detected in doing so?" Second, he attacked the logic of the "conspiracy of silence." There was nothing to indicate that the regiment members could actually identify the raiders; punishing them for not doing so was absurd. What if the men did not confess because they were innocent? The President had acted not on the basis of conclusive evidence, Foraker said, but on the basis of no evidence.

Roosevelt said that the soldiers were lucky not to be hung. "People have spoken as if this discharge from the service was a punishment," Roosevelt claimed at one point in the battle of rhetoric. "I deny that emphatically ... because as punishment it is utterly inadequate. The punishment for mutineers and murderers such as those guilty of the Brownsville assault is death."

After Foraker's public attack, Roosevelt looked to bolster his case against the men of the 25th. Resources were gathered from three departments – War, Justice, and Treasury – to question the townspeople yet again.

Foraker found evidence suggesting other parties did the shooting. Both Mingo Sanders and combat veteran Sergeant Samuel Harley testified that the guns they heard that night were

# Aftermath

not Springfields. "It was more like the reports of six-shooters and Winchesters." Two of the townsfolk had reported they saw revolvers in the hands of the raiders – guns which were common in town but absent at the fort.

The results of Roosevelt's three-department foray to Texas were delivered to the Senate on January 14. The additional evidence, Roosevelt declared, made it "likely that there were very few, if any, of the soldiers dismissed who could have been ignorant of what occurred." It was now "impossible to question the conclusion on which my order was based."

Foraker disagreed, and in equally hyperbolic terms.

"In all the history of crime and its detection nothing more atrocious, disreputable, and disgraceful has ever been recorded." These confessions obtained by the two Virginia men were fraudulent, he claimed, citing an Associated Press account from a reporter who had been present during several of the interviews. Such "wicked fabrications" violated "the elementary principles of common-law justice." He supplied affadavits refuting the Roosevelt report for his fellow legislators to examine.

Foraker's committee, The Senate Military Affairs Committee, investigated the raid in 1908. The testimony would take up three thousand pages. Foraker was outraged at the treatment of the battalion. "The vilest horse thief, the most dangerous burglar, or the bloodiest murderer would not be required either to prove his innocence or to submit to a trial before a judge who had ... expressed the opinion that the defendant was guilty."

These men "are at once both citizens and soldiers of the republic ... In every war in which we have permitted them to participate they have distinguished themselves for efficiency and valor. They have shed their blood and laid down their lives in the fierce shock of battle, side by side with their white comrades ..."

In March 1908 the Committee voted nine to four that the soldiers were guilty.

Foraker filed a minority report.

Roosevelt turned the full fury of "his dangerous enmity" against Joseph Foraker. Support from his fellow Congressmen gradually vanished.

Perhaps coincidentally, the newspaperman William Randolph Hearst charged Senator Foraker with accepting an illicit $15,000 payment from Standard Oil. "Like a flash, the whole situation was changed." Hearst made a speech in which he accused Foraker of collusion with Standard Oil. Hearst possessed letters between Foraker and John Archibald of Standard Oil that seemed to show a series of payments, presumably bribes. When Foraker was a practicing lawyer in Ohio, Standard Oil had been a client.

Foraker replied immediately. "I rendered the company such service as I could, charged for it and was paid ... That employment ended before my first term in the Senate expired. I have not represented the Company in any way since." He was portrayed as a symbol of corporate greed and corruption, representing the very companies which had been sued by the federal government for monopoly practices

Foraker saw the attacks as groundless. As for the $50,000 check, it had been promptly returned. Back and forth, the issue played out, with accusations, counter-charges, and editorials published in newspapers.

# Aftermath

Then, Roosevelt and Taft weighed in on Hearst's side. From Foraker's viewpoint, this sealed his fate. "President Roosevelt gave an interview of such hostile character, and President Taft assumed such an attitude of opposition, if not of hostility ... the tide turned against me."[33]

Foraker answered the charges immediately, identifying the payments as fair compensation from a client for legal work, not a surreptitious bribe. "That employment ended before my first term in the Senate expired. I have not represented the company since." Hearst then read at a speech from a letter regarding another deposit, this time for $50,000. Foraker produced documentation proving it was a loan, returned a month later. His protests were not heard as widely as Hearst's accusations.

Taft kept silent. The absence of a vigorous defense from his "intimate old-time friend" (as described by Julia) was seen as giving credence to Hearst's charges. Taft declined to appear on the same platform as Foraker, making his censure unmistakable. Foraker, either naïve or unskilled at such maneuvering, was left to turn on the wind.

The wave engulfed Foraker, as his wife would later describe it. His political career was over. He and Julia would return to Ohio. Before he left, he tried one last time to protect the men of the 25th, now scattered across the country. He pushed for a bill which would specifically state that any soldier not found guilty would be able to re-enlist. He did not get it: he was forced to compromise and accept a bill which authorizing the Secretary of War to appoint a court of inquiry. If the tribunal found any soldier "qualified for reenlistment," they could reinstate him. This arrangement, Foraker knew, left too much up to the tribunal. Mingo Sanders repeatedly applied for reinstatement times and was denied.

In the end, outrage in the black press amounted to little, at least in political terms. The black vote remained in the Republican column. "Most historians ... concede that Negroes remained true to the Republicans for a number of reasons. Democrats failed to take advantage of the Booker T. Washington placed the survival of his cause above the episode, and worked "to minimize the effect of Brownsville on Negro voting habits,"[34] DuBois squandered whatever political impact he might have had, spending his energies on writing essays and squabbling with Washington. "Black leaders ... consistently failed to take major issues to the grass roots level."[35] Where, in the Dreyfus incident, for example, intellectuals joined with other social sectors to create a powerful opposition to the government's unjust action. Here, men like DuBois and Trotter remained aloof from events, as Roosevelt surely counted on them doing. "Black leaders have too often been guilty of dealing with issues on an intellectual plane and have tended to ignore the practical aspects ... It is this failure ... that has consistently hurt Negroes."[36] Ironically, the Atlanta riot got in the way of a unified black response to Brownsville. Coming so close on the heels of the raid, this "cataclysmic event ... made Brownsville seem pale in comparison."[37] Booker Washington and Richard Greener had not needed to spy on the Niagara Movement. Trotter and DuBois could not agree over whether or not white people should be included in the organization and in the struggle for Civil Rights (Du Bois felt that they should) and the movement

# Aftermath

soon fell apart. DuBois' followers accused Washington of using his influence to stifle press coverage of the movement.

A black vote to punish Roosevelt and Taft never materialized. "The Brownsville episode did not lead to a marked defection of Negroes from the Republican party, nor did Taft appear to have suffered personally because of his part in the affair." In the election of 1908, Taft's margin of victory was smaller than Roosevelt's in some states with significant black populations (Ohio, Pennsylvania, Illinois) but larger in other such states (New York, New Jersey).

Foraker eventually lost his bid for re-election. He and Julia left Washington to return to Ohio, where he resumed his law practice.

"The President and his friends have not the courage to confess their original error," *The New York Times* wrote. "The endeavor to escape its consequences leaves them distinctly ridiculous."

*The New York World* agreed:

> *"To be successful a farce should lead up to a grotesque climax. The court of inquiry has done all that could possibly be asked of it to make this Brownsville burlesque upon justice a triumph of absurdity."*

Multiple Brownsville hearings droned on.

Mingo Sanders would apply for reinstatement and would be denied. The hearings were inconclusive. Roosevelt continued to guard Special Order 266 like a dog with its teeth bared: "If they pass a resolution to reinstate these men," he warned, speaking of the Congress, "I will veto it. If they pass it over my veto, I will pay no attention to it."

The nation's pressing business moved on.

# CHAPTER 13

# Weaver Investigates

> Weaver's book attacked the accepted version at all points ... As a piece of historical investigation, the book offered the first judicious and balanced appraisal of the case that had been mounted against the accused men.
>
> -- *Historian Lewis Gould*

SEVERAL DAYS AFTER THE VISIT with his mother, back in Los Angeles, John Weaver's seven-year-old Buick chugged up Hilgard on the UCLA campus, cutting left on Melnitz by the Art Center, emerging at the Charles E. Young Research Library, a pleasing three-story stone and glass structure under shady trees. He trolled along Young Drive, hoping for a parking space, but finally parked in the P5 lot across from the Fowler Museum.

Curiosity about the long-ago Texas hearings was nagging at him. The whole episode seemed incongruous. It would be so out-of-character for this particular president, Teddy Roosevelt, to strike out against soldiers, for one, but in particular black soldiers.

# Teddy's Tantrum

Wouldn't he have heard of it, if it had truly happened? Weaver descended to the 800s, the stacks holding texts on American history. He began tracking down references to Teddy Roosevelt's dismissal of a regiment of black soldiers in a Texas town.

He could find none.

He found no record of a scandal in Texas involving the dismissal of black soldiers.

Weaver found admiring profiles of Roosevelt everywhere, and, at first, he found no references to Brownsville.

Almost 500 books had been written about Theodore Roosevelt. Most followed the general line of Roosevelt's own version. "The fame of other men may fear the onslaught of time; but the fame of Roosevelt need not fear it," Calvin Coolidge had written in a preface to a Roosevelt biography, and he was right. History's decision was overwhelming that Roosevelt had been both an effective president and an irreplaceable icon of the American spirit at the birth of the modern nation. "Roosevelt, like Lincoln, was in a true sense a preserver of our National unity. Lincoln saved us from section cleavage, Roosevelt saved us from class cleavage. He pointed out the road of straight Americanism where all could walk in amity towards the same goal."[1]

Many accounts of "TR" and his administration failed to mention the Brownsville Raid. As Weaver began to find mentions of the episode, they presented it as a minor incident, a typical border scuffle perpetrated by black Union soldiers stuck in a hostile southern post. None seemed to detail Roosevelt's part in what sounded to Weaver like the conviction of men presumed innocent before a fair trial.

## Weaver Investigates

John Weaver, however, knew his way around a library.

No books reflected that such an event had taken place. He found Brownsville on a map, at the very tip of Texas, across from Matamoros. It seemed so far away from everything familiar. Had the family really spent a summer there? He searched for military trials in 1910.

He found references to Roosevelt's invitation to Booker T. Washington to dine at the White House. Perhaps these black soldiers had mutinied. Why wouldn't a military journal publish articles on it, then? He descended to the Special Collections, where he rooted through stacks and microfiche viewers holding old journals and newspapers. All the references to Roosevelt he could find were unabashedly positive, often bordering on worshipful. After all, he was one of only four presidents with their faces on Mount Rushmore. It was hard to imagine the Rough Rider, the people's president, firing three companies of black troops without just cause.

He scrolled through the various histories of Texas. Surely his mother had been mistaken. He could find no record of a scandalous Texas shoot-out or military incident involving Teddy Roosevelt. *Nothing.* Surely such an incident, involving one of our most renowned presidents, would have been much scrutinized by historians.

Then he found it.

He uncovered four sand-colored volumes of *The Report of the Brownsville Court of Inquiry* in the Senate Documents, Sixty-first

# Teddy's Tantrum

Congress, Third Session, 1910-11. On the opening page, he saw that the court's five generals were present at its first meeting in Washington, May 4, 1909, and that "Henry B. Weaver was duly sworn in as reporter."

*A military dismissal and racial incident involving Teddy Roosevelt, yet it's virtually unknown.*

*How can that be?*

He found a 1943 article by one James Tinsley, apparently a graduate student. Yes, Roosevelt had indeed discharged 167 members of the 25th Infantry. Historians seemed to agree that Roosevelt had acted "hastily"– not completely out of character for him – but they did not challenge the finding that some kind of violence had occurred "as a result of the deeds of the black troops" caused the violence that night in Brownsville.[2] The broad outlines of the story were bad enough: reading the details was damning to Roosevelt.

Weaver found accounts of Roosevelt's high emotions during the Brownsville fray. White House visitors found the President "in an astonishing frame of mind," according to a *New York Times* account which Weaver found, his anger "raised to the white hot pitch" against the black "butchers" who had assaulted the townspeople. He found a protagonist: Senator Joseph Foraker of Ohio, stood in Congress and demanded justice for the troops, not because they were black, but because they were men. Foraker demanded a fair trial for the 25th: Roosevelt resisted, and gradually Foraker's allies seemed to distance themselves. John Weaver, a child of Washington, understood very, very clearly what he was seeing happen to the men of the 25th Infantry.

## Weaver Investigates

Weaver began digging seriously into the Brownsville Affray. It was a sprawling, complex affair: there were eight separate hearings over the span of five years, and two administrations. The Affray had involved a large cast of characters on the national stage, and each subsequent round of hearings had been covered extensively in newspapers. Roosevelt hunted down the scattered battalion members to hasten their descent into lives of poverty, in his desperate hope to regain face from his ill-conceived dismissal.

Weaver found his bombshell in a thin green, half-sized document binder entitled *Letter from the Secretary of War, by Direction of the President*. Neat, rounded hand-lettering along the label at the top announced the subject of this letter as "Employment of Browne and Baldwin at Brownsville."

The same two "investigators" who had approached and been rejected by Foraker had gone straight to the President. Roosevelt found them to be just the men he needed to prove his case. And what efforts they had made! Over the space of eight months, Harold Brown and William Baldwin had been paid the considerable sum of $15,000 for their efforts to frame the men of the 25th. The report ended with a letter from William Howard Taft, Secretary of War, verifying the contents.

He found Report #355 of the Sixtieth Congress Committee on Military Affairs, Foraker's Committee, "On the Brownsville Affray." Here were 107 pages of detailed testimonies from "eyewitnesses" to the raid.

# Teddy's Tantrum

"Oh, I think if only I could taste a little success!" John Cheever wrote to his friends.[3]

He tasted a little success in 1958, when his family memoir, *The Wapshot Chronicles*, won the National Book Award, and even more when his novel The Swimmer was made into a successful movie. His collection of short stories, The Way Some People Live, had sold well, and Knopf had advanced him money on the contract for the next collection. The paperback rights were auctioned off for over $200,000.

John Weaver never attained the success of his good friend. Among their extended network of genteel friends and associates, Weaver's achievements were modest: he and his wife made do with a steady if unspectacular succession of writing assignments.

So, at the time, John was in no position to divert his efforts from the *Travel and Leisure* articles and freelance assignments upon which they depended to pay the monthly bills in order to write a new account of a very old episode. An entire book on this "American Dreyfus" affair would take a year, or more. Besides, he had almost completed his contract with Simon & Schuster to write a book on Supreme Court Chief Justice Earl Warren. The manuscript was on its way to the copy editor, and John had a number of last-minute alterations. They were in a rush to beat another Warren biography, by McGraw Hill, to market, so the clock was ticking, but John wanted desperately to get it right. Timely and substantial, the Warren book was one of the meatiest projects of his career. The breadth and depth of the subject suited John's restless intelligence, and it could be an important career step, a book that showed he could write bestselling nonfiction.

# Weaver Investigates

There was still so much to review on the manuscript: research always seemed to stretch further than the contract time.

Weaver became fascinated by the detective work into the Brownsville Raid. "I filled shoe boxes with cross-indexes of the location at every moment of every person known to have been connected with the disturbance." If other scholars had fellowships to underwrite their research, he had Harriett: her habit of buying homes and fixing them up and selling them for a profit allowed him to slice of more and more time to devote to what appeared to be a clear case of injustice buried beneath slanted histories. She supported him because she shared his outrage: Cheever called them "the most civic-minded couple I know."

He quickly came to understand the outlines of the incident: the shoddy case brought against the soldiers in the eight hearings; the repeated denial of the soldiers that they knew anything about the raid; the rifle shells which did not match the soldiers' rifles; the multiple inconclusive hearings; Foraker's championing of the troops; Taft's complicity; the vendetta against of Foraker. Weaver saw that they were "discharged without honor" rather than given "dishonorable discharges" because the latter would have required court-martial proceedings … presumably to be avoided, since the Army had no evidence.

These soldiers had walked into an ugly situation. Racial prejudice had been rampant in Texas, and similar tensions had boiled up all along the Rio Grande. Whether they had actually shot up the town or not was unclear. What was quite clear is that

Roosevelt had jumped the gun in dismissing them: there was too little hard evidence against them, the press reaction was quite clear about that. The whole thing seemed never to have gone to trial. *Was that possible? Why had this story never been told?*

The documentation on the Brownsville Raid and it subsequence hearings

was sprawling, including as it did scores of records, testimony from nine local and federal hearings, countless newspaper articles as well as personal correspondence from the scores of participants, all over a time period of at least four years. Weaver set out to examine everything. He was convinced that he had to be exhaustive in his research. In the end, his focus was the 1909-1910 federal court of inquiry, the court which upheld the president's decision and closed the case against the soldiers.

He found that Roosevelt's November, 1906 temper tantrum against the men of the black regiment had turned into a sustained vendetta that outlasted his own presidency and carried into Taft's, a deliberate and purposeful campaign against all of the men and their chief defender which was personally directed by Roosevelt. True to his big-stick philosophy, he struck his antagonists hard, with all his might, with no warning, and did not relent until his enemies were destroyed. Roosevelt himself remained little-scathed.

He found the weather report for August 13, 1906. There had been no moon and an overcast, utterly dark sky. Visibility on such a night was next to nothing. Standing at the head of the alley on Elizabeth Street, the citizens of Brownsville could not possibly have seen the color of the raiders' skin.

## Weaver Investigates

He found the 1932 memoirs of Julia Foraker. He had found the transcripts of two of the four rounds of Texas hearings. He had tracked down an out-of-print biography of Texas Ranger Bill McDonald, whose actions he had always found suspicious. Perhaps most remarkably, he had found the reports of two henchmen, Herbert Brown and William Baldwin, whom Roosevelt and Will Taft (his Secretary of War) had hired to bribe and bully the men of the 25th into false confessions. He had their own accounts of browbeating Dorsie Willis and John Hollomon and a dozen others. No attempt had been made to hide the fairly embarrassing fact of a sitting President paying "investigators" five thousand dollars with funds from a dubious government account: yet it had never been questioned.

He kept looking for credible evidence against the soldiers – a confession, a reliable eyewitness, and could find none. He concluded that the soldiers had been framed.

John Weaver developed a theory as to who might have done it, and why.

Not trusting secondary sources, Weaver traveled to Texas, Ohio, and the Washington D.C. to do his own research in primary sources. He cites the Texas History Center in Austin, the University of Texas Archives, the Texas State Library, the National Archives in Washington D.C., the Library of Congress, the Cincinnati Historical Society, and the Brownsville *Herald* archives among his many sources.

Weaver uncovered a shocking figure buried in the documentation: "Two months before the Republican Convention, the president and his secretary of war had quietly tapped a military contingency fund for the first of their unauthorized ... payments" to Baldwin and Browne. The payments totaled to $55,000, a very substantial figure for the United States government to spend on framing innocent soldiers. Weaver found their report to be completely phony, "based on deceit, coercion, and manufactured evidence." Yet Baldwin and Browne knew their employers well. They assured Roosevelt and Taft that "the guilty men would be unmasked before the voters went to the polls in November."[4]

Weaver found a letter from a Cleveland correspondent to Foraker regarding Roosevelt's misuse of federal resources:

> I suppose you noted the fact that the President has sent Secret Service men down to Brownsville to work up the case against the colored soldiers. Doubtless he has overlooked the fact that the appropriation bill passed last winter Congress specified explicitly that the Secret Service men were to be used for the detection of counterfeiters and for protecting the life and person of the President, and for no other purpose. Perhaps he will contend that ... he is using them protect himself against you.[5]

Weaver focused his attention on four aspects in particular which form the core of his rediscovery of the extended Brownsville episode: the rifle shells; the shoddy testimony of eyewitnesses; Roosevelt's personal direction of the campaign against the soldiers; and the sinking of Foraker.

## Weaver Investigates

Weaver walked the alleys and streets of Browsnville, so he could judge the testimonies for himself. He was struck by the statement of Herbert Elkins,n the teenaged candy-store employee who was certain he had seen eight to fifteen Negro soldiers in the alley between Elizabeth and Washington Streets, just east of the Cowen house.

"And you state positively that they were colored soldiers?" he was asked.

"Yes. I could see them plainly."

"What light was there in the vicinity of the Cowen house?"

"None," answered Elkins, "unless there was one at the corner; but it was not very dark."

Weaver viewed this as far from credible. The night was in fact extremely dark. "...Not only had young Elkins recognized these ... raiders as Negro soldiers at a distance from thirty to forty paces, he had even been able to idenify the color of their trousers (yellow khaki) and, in one instance, a summer Army shirt (blue)."[6]

In "The Brownsville Affray Hearings" from 1907 (Volumes 1,2,3) he found extensive details of the episode. Eight pages of photographs of Brownsville's streets and buildings were included, along with a fold-out map of the town. In two slimmer volumes *Report and Message* Dec. 10, 1906, he found that Roosevelt himself had written a damning four-page introduction in a vain attempt to close the door once and for all on the incident. The President's direction of the case against the soldiers had been close and constant.

## Teddy's Tantrum

The men of the 25th had disappeared into the fabric of American society, never to be heard from -- singly or as a unit -- again.

As Foraker became Weaver's hero, Taft became his secondary villain. Foraker was furious that Taft, whose career he had supported, would not back him in the Brownsville matter. "Taft was even more apathetic about black rights than was Roosevelt, and he consistently and openly declared that the dismissals were justified."[7] "Roosevelt told Taft not to let people think Foraker was getting the best of the argument or that he was afraid of standing up to the senator." "If possible," Roosevelt urged Taft, "you should give Foraker a mauling."[8]

He also came across two charges which Roosevelt had found particularly galling. First, Senator Nathan Scott of West Virginia made the following remark: "...If it had not been for the gallant and courageous action of the Tenth Regiment of Cavalry at the battle of San Juan we might not now have the privilege of having in the White House that brave soldier and 'square deal' and patriotic President of ours." Second, a front page story in *The New York Times* profiling Mingo Sanders quoted two unnamed Republicans who felt that the black man had "a better record as a soldier" than the President. If it had not been personal for Roosevelt before this point, it certainly became so afterwards.

Roosevelt personally blocked Mingo Sanders' reinstatement. As he was leaving office, Roosevelt took the time to write the Secretary of War the following note: "First Sergeant Mingo Sanders in spite of his reputation for personal courage, was as [thoroughly] dangerous, unprincipled and unworthy a soldier as ever wore the United States uniform, and that under no conceivable circumstances should he ever be allowed again in the army."

John got up early to write. He often swam the first thing in the morning. Harriett rebuilt the house on Deervale Drive so John could have a pool. The Mitchum movie had paid for the Hollywood Hills home, then they had moved (serving as their own movers) to the Sherman Oaks home, which was traded up for the Beverly Hills home.

The Brownsville matter frustrated him at many turns. Records were partial, and tracking the former soldiers was next to impossible. Weaver called it "a good day" when he finished a page. In the afternoon he did lighter work, such as articles for *Travel and Leisure*. Harriett reviewed and edited his typed pages.

"Although even black historians and many others have consistently taken the soldiers' guilt for granted," he told Gladwin Hill of *The New York Times*, "I found there wasn't a shred of evidence implicating them in the riot at all. It apparently was some local vigilante types who were sore at the black troops being stationed there and the effect on local businesses like saloons. They just roared through town shooting wildly, mostly at lighted rooms in houses. A couple of people just accidentally got in the way of bullets."9

Hill's profile describes Weaver's trek through the voluminous evidence. He "studied the Army's 12-volume report in the University of California library, records in Brownsville and Austin, Texas, Senator Foraker's papers in Cincinnati, and the National Archives in Washington, where he even examined the bullets recovered from the incident."[10] The Coffee-colored bound volumes of the Congressional Record and National Archives revealed ongoing treasures. They reproduced a string of Browne and Baldwin reports: "Conyers has confessed," reports Browne; the President "will be glad to hear" that "sufficient evidence to convict and hang" has been gathered; or "evidence is conclusive," or that they "would like to continue work" and references to their own "careful and persistent questioning." They identified John Hollomon as "the chief conspirator." The reports, Weaver was sure, were complete fabrications.

As Weaver widened his search, he traveled across the country to find the records he needed to tell the complete story of this long-running drama. He drove to Cincinnati to find Foraker's papers, many of which were crumbling. He sought out private letters from the various combatants until he had assembled a clear picture of the proceedings against the men of the 9th Infantry. It was an ugly picture.

Weaver found that Roosevelt's vendetta against Foraker was long and unrelenting. "He is a very powerful and very vindictive man," he wrote to Lodge, "and he is one of the most unblushing servers and beneficiaries of corporate wealth that I have ever met." Foraker, Roosevelt speculated, was so angry over Roosevelt's rescue of the Republican Party and the nation from ruin that he, Foraker, intended to fight the President on every point, good or bad.

# Weaver Investigates

*The Brownsville Raid* by John D. Weaver was published in 1970 by William Morrow.

In it, Weaver retells the story of the entire Affray. Its ambitious parameters stretch from 1906 to 1911. The book includes the perspective of all the major participants of the Affray and weighs the results of all the hearings.

His exposition begins with a narrowly focused, minute-by-minute, almost documentary-style recreation of the night of the raid. Then he broadens his lens to take in the scandal as controversy and hearings spread to all of Texas, to the White House, to the halls of Congress, to the great Victorian house at Sixteenth Street, and to Burt Conyers' small farmer's cottage in rural Georgia.

It is the accumulation of detail that makes Weaver's account so compelling.

Weaver found the original billet advertising the evening at the Gridiron Club when Roosevelt and Foraker clashed. He found the bullet shells picked up on Twelfth Street on the night of the raid. He located a photograph of the Company B baseball team. He found an unpublished manuscript by Mary Terrell, a minor but vivid character in the sprawling drama. He details the nighttime visit of Roosevelt's henchman, Boies Penrose, who visits the Foraker home in Sixteenth Street after dark to offer a bribe: drop the Negro business and the President will make him ambassador to any nation he pleased (Foraker declined). Set against the Rough Rider's bold statements of purpose, Weaver's painstaking account such bullying tactics forms a stark contrast to the friendly TR we have come to know from the other five hundred histories.

# Teddy's Tantrum

In the 300-page narrative, the author's personal opinions surfaced clearly. "Treasury's Secret Service agents were furtively at work," wrote Weaver, "ransacking Brownsville for proof of what Roosevelt insisted had already been conclusively proved." Weaver does not mince words. He calls the Browne-Baldwin report "shameless forgery." He decries "the so-called 'confession' of Boyd Conyers and "the Administration sleuths with their threats and misrepresentations," who made up their "own version of a Company B conspiracy and put it forth as a 'confession' by this likeable, hard-working happily-married young Negro."[11]

"Oh, shame upon a Government that will employ all its power," he quotes Foraker, "every power that it commands, not for the purpose of protection of men in their right to be presumed innocent until they are proven guilty, but to prove men, who claim they are innocent, to be guilty of a heinous crime, and to do it behind the door and in the dark."[12]

If Weaver was outraged over the November 5 dismissal, he saved his harshest language for the ongoing harassment of the soldiers and the scurrilous work of Browne and Baldwin in trying to bribe and coerce testimony from them, years after their dismissal. He called it "a massive assault by two Presidents on the civil rights of one hundred and sixty-seven black Americans .... Alive, they were denied the equity of the white man's justice and, dead, the vindication of his Jim Crow history."[13] Weaver, who had seen innocent individuals persecuted in his own lifetime, takes aim at Roosevelt's two henchmen and their badgering of Private Conyers. "Browne and Baldwin, with the full weight of the White House and the War Department behind them, had done everything they could to trick, tempt, and terrorize a young Negro preoccupied with his work and his ailing wife. They had offered him money, confronted him with what they knew to be perjured testimony, promised him protection and tried to frighten him with the prospect of Texas noose."[14]

Weaver followed the story wherever the trail lead him – to the minute particulars (the brand of beer – *Schlitz* – being downed by Louis Cowen the night of the raid) border life in Texas, to Washington society, to political rivalries, military bureaucracies, disagreements among black leaders, and the intricacies of Congressional procedure. As he enters each new subject area, Weaver slows down long enough to give his reader enough background to appreciate the complex roots of the not only the initial incident but a protracted struggle played out on many stages. To set the stage for Foraker's entrance into the drama, for example, Weaver gives us Foraker's experience in the Civil War because the topic comes up in Roosevelt's Gridiron Club speech. We know going in of the Senator's background with the ICC and with Standard Oil – again, points he knows the reader will need later in the narrative. While these sidebars tend to weigh down Weaver's storyline, they are necessary for accuracy. "The interplay among local events in Brownsville, the politics of the army, and the national scene is one of the strongest parts of his story."[15]

His thirty chapters are divided into nine sections, each section with a focus on one aspect of the complex affair – the mystery, the soldiers, the townspeople, the investigation, the politicians, the hearings, the verdict, the face-saving, and the coda. A final section provides Weaver's documentation, including a chronology and a list of key witnesses.

Weaver theorizes that local vigilantes shot up the town, hoping to cast a pall on the black troops.

"Weaver demonstrates the extraordinary lengths to which Roosevelt and ... Taft, his secretary of war and likely successor, went to establish the guilt of the soldiers *after* they had been dismissed..." wrote one reviewer. "Weaver brings out of the historical shadows the crucial role of Senator Foraker," wrote another. "Weaver's book attacked the accepted version at all points," wrote Lewis Gould in his foreword. "As a piece of historical investigation, the book offered the first judicious and balanced appraisal of the case that had been mounted against the accused men." Gould called it "historical justice."

Truth, John Weaver could not help but feel, was on the march -- just as it was with Zola and Dreyfus -- and nothing could stop it.

CHAPTER 14

# A Reputation Cleared

Among historians, it is relatively rare for a single book to change the way that a past event is seen and interpreted. In the case of John D. Weaver's *The Brownsville Raid*, however, the book's publication in 1970 led to a reappraisal of the controversial events of August 6, 1906 ...

-- *Presidential scholar Lewis Gould*

**OCTOBER, 1971**

Three men took seats in a narrow triangle in the White House Situation Room.[1]

President Richard Nixon, at the apex, sat forward in his seat. He was eager to discuss the latest developments with two of his closest advisors, White House Chief of Staff Bob Haldeman and National Security Advisor Henry Kissinger. Kissinger had just returned from secret negotiations in Paris.

# Teddy's Tantrum

"You've got three for three, Mister President," said Kissinger excitedly.

"Really, Henry?

"Yes, sir. It's better than anyone could have expected. We have guaranteed a cease-fire by October. All our troops come out within 60 days of the cease-fire. And all our POW's will be returned within that same framework."

"Historic," exclaimed John Haldeman. "Super-historic."

"And Le Duc Tho has agreed to all this?" asked Nixon.

"Yes, sir," replied the Secretary of State.

"But the South Vietnamsese could scuttle the deal," Nixon worried.

"Yessir, but all indications are that they will go forward on these terms.

"All right. Excellent. This is excellent. Bob, let's serve the '57 Lafite-Rotschild tonight, shall we?"

"Yessir."

"Now, we need to keep State out of the picture." By this, Kissinger meant William Rodgers, the Secretary of State.

"Yes," agreed Nixon. "Rogers shouldn't know."

"There might be a leak," warned Haldeman.

"We do NOT need that," sad Nixon. "Not now, just before the elections …"

"Something could go wrong," said Haldeman.

"I can tell Bill that we had a breakthrough on *military* matters," offered Kissinger.

"Yes," replied the President.

"He's waiting for me now, with Al."

# A Reputation Cleared

"Al. Al Haig. Yes." The President seemed satisfied.

"We don't want to raise expectations," said Kissinger.

"No. No, we don't," agreed Nixon.

Kissinger smiled and clapped his hands.

"All right Henry," instructed the President. "Go ahead, meet with Bill now. Debrief Bill. Then come back and we'll plan out the next steps. I assume you're going to Saigon?

"Yessir. That's the hope."

"Now we can pull those poor men out of there."

"Overdue," said Haldeman. "Long overdue."[2]

Four years after Dwight Johnson lost his temper at Dak To, the situation in Vietnam had still not been brought under control. In the 1968 elections, Richard Nixon had promised At its peak, the Vietnam conflict included 543,000 American troops. The "Vietnamization" program was designed to extricate America from the collapsing walls of ethnic conflict in the vacuum that followed the fall of French rule in Indochina by turning over the conduct of the war to the South Vietnamese. Nixon directed that a "highly forceful approach" be taken by President Thieu to take more and more responsibility. Accordingly, South Vietnam grew its army dramatically. "Military schools were expanded to handle over 100,000 students per year. The Vietnamese Air Force (VNAF) was increased to 9 tactical wings, 40,000 personnel, and nearly 700 aircraft." By the end of 1971, almost 1 million men served in the ARVN.[3]

The tactic did not work.

The President turned to secret negotiations to resolve the disturbing imbalance in world power. That did not work, either.

# Teddy's Tantrum

The secret Paris accord between Henry Kissinger and Vietnamese leadership fell apart, and the lethal fighting in Vietnam continued.

The 25th Infantry arrived in Vietnam early and stayed late. During the Tet offensives of 1968 and 1969, they had defended Saigon.

During a three-month period, from April through June of 1972, the 25th Infantry – now re-formed and fully integrated – "participated in Allied thrusts deep into enemy sanctuaries located in Cambodia,"[4] incursions where the objective was to confiscate as many tons of the enemy's supplies and munitions as possible, lessening the pressure on American units.

During the war in Vietnam, 22 Medals of Honor were awarded to soldiers of the 25th -- more than any other division in the war.

Young Major Powell leaned out of the helicopter and looked down at the landing zone in the mountains west of Chu Lai. His tall frame was crammed into the Huey, so that he had to bend low to see.

It was a narrow landing zone. There was barely enough room for the chopper's blades to clear the encroaching trees.

Powell was escorting the division commander, General Gettys ("a rotund, amiable man") and the chief of staff, on the UH-1H helicopter. One of the 11th Infantry Brigade units had reported a large weapons capture by radio, and now they were flying into the jungle to help.

# A Reputation Cleared

But as the pilot lowered the helicopter into the narrow space, wind from the rotator blades hit the wall of foliage and blew back on them. The helicopter scudded sideways. The pilot could not correct his angle of descent fast enough and they veered dangerously.

Powell watched a blade strike against a tree and stop. That was it. "We ... went down like an elevator without a cable." Engines whining, the helicopter dropped eighty feet and crashed to the earth. Powell jumped clear, only to look back and see smoke pouring from the broken helicopter. He ran back into the smoldering wreckage to retrieve General Gettys: the division commander was barely conscious, his shoulder fractured. Powell dragged him into the woods.

Powell went back in for the chief of staff. He pulled the unconscious man clear of the downed helicopter. The pilot was pulled free by a private.

General Gettys' aide, Ron Tumelson, looked dead. His head was trapped between the helicopter's radio console and the engine. The man was bleeding badly, unmoving. Powell went back in, unbuckled the body, and dragged it out. He heard Tumelson groan. He pulled the bent helmet off the aide's head and found that the man was still alive.

Major Colin Powell, a black man from the South Bronx, "the best G-3 in Vietnam," made four trips back into the burning helicopter.

## Teddy's Tantrum

As the months passed, John D. Weaver grew increasingly frustrated.

What happened with the Dreyfus case was not happening here.

Where the French case of military injustice had mobilized students and intellectuals, eventually gripping the entire nation, America was going about its business with no further notice of the men of the Tenth. The Brownsville Raid was sinking back into the shadows, and Weaver could not seem to prevent it. The initial spate of publicity for his book, *The Brownsville Raid*, soon faded. Here had proven that the case against the troops was entirely manufactured, and ...silence. Nothing would change. Justice would not be forthcoming for the long-forgotten men of the 25th.

The people at William Morrow could not seem to stock the book properly. John would appear on a talk show only to find that local bookstores had no copies of the book. He appeared on a Chicago television show, Dr. Benjamin Mays "Black on Black." He appeared on cable television's *Book Beat*. A woman from Oklahoma who saw the show wrote to him: "How often I was told of this 'great tragedy' by all the elderly people who knew the story from hear-say…" Another letter said, "God bless you and in your effort to obtain justice." But sales of the book did not soar, or even climb. Worse, once the initial publicity faded, it was as if nothing had happened. Where were the other scholars to follow in his footsteps?[5] Weaver had hoped to see journal articles which expanded his research on the episode, now that he had revealed it, or perhaps a book or two to follow the path he had blazed. What about an official statement from the White House, or at least

## A Reputation Cleared

the Army? He had demonstrated clearly that the men had been railroaded.

Pamela Fiore, who was Weaver's West Coast Editor and then Senior Editor at *Travel and Leisure* described him as cheerful and trusting; she added that he needed very strong feedback, in the form of letters and phone calls. A lack of response was, to him, like death. "Nothing depressed him more." The injustice "consumed him" said his niece. "Brownsville brought out a passion in him. He never stopped talking about it, how it ruined the black soldiers' lives."

Then Gus Hawkins called.

A staff member of Augustus Hawkins, U.S. Congressman from California's 21st District (Los Angeles), had read the book and wanted to look into seeking justice for the long-forgotten black soldiers. Hawkins was an active proponent of civil rights who would go on to author 300 bills at the state and federal levels, among them the Humphrey-Hawkins Full Employment bill (co-authored with Hubert Humphrey of Minnesota). This was a powerful ally. Hawkins appointed a staff member to fact-check Weaver's work before submitting a bill to Congress which would exonerate the soldiers.

John Weaver was thrilled to have Hawkins' support. He pitched headlong into the process of finding survivors and sorting through communications with apparently endless number of claimants, the majority of which were mistaken in their claims. Weaver tracked down third and fourth generations of the Combe, Fernandez, and Hollomon families.[6]

They found two regiment members still alive: Dorsie Willis and Edward Warfield. Dorsie Willis, age 85, had worked in a downtown Minneapolis barber shop as a shoeshine for fifty-nine years. He had taken two weeks' vacation in all that time. He was a regular at the Zion Baptist Church and sponsored inner-city children at the Boys' Club Summer Camp every year.

The second surviving member was Edward Warfield of Company B, age 89. John Weaver visited Warfield in the ex-soldier's Los Angeles apartment and showed him a copy of the court of inquiry testimony, which Henry Weaver had recorded.

"It's like hearing yourself talk after you're dead," commented Warfield.

"To get ganged up on in something like that thing in Brownsville – it's just got to make you sorrowful," said Warfield in that same visit. He died shortly thereafter, leaving Willis as the sole surviving member of the 25th.

Working with Juanita Barbee, Doris Saunders, Fred Well, Alan Whitney, Tom Rees Frank Terry and Oliver Terry of the Veterans Affairs Committee, and Congressman James Corman, Weaver helped find Burkit Conyers, Burt's son, in Monroe, Georgia. They set up a committee to investigate the claims and called it the Brownsville Incident Survivor Identification Board (BISID). Weaver churned out letters for the cause. This less-than-subtle note to Hubert Humphrey reminded the Minnesota Senator:

> Mr. Willis is ill and his devoted wife should be at his side. Instead, she is working at a gruelling (sic) job to provide food and medication for her husband. This

## A Reputation Cleared

> *extraordinary man has suffered enough, and suffered it with exemplary dignity and grace. The "gross injustice' which the Army now admits was done him will continue to gnaw at the country's conscience until Mr. Willis and his family are placed beyond the reach of want and worry.*

Weaver's friend Ralph Martin urged him on, comparing Weaver's efforts to those of crusader Rachel Carson. Martin's Author's Guild Bulletin piece about Weaver refers to an appearance to testify before Congress. "How many authors get to see their book right a wrong?" wrote Martin.

Hubert Humphrey, Senator from Minnesota, joined the cause. Weaver was asked to come to Washington and help draft arguments for the bill to be presented to the House and Senate veterans' committees. There was opposition to such a bill, since it would set a precedent. There could be no precedent, argued Hawkins, since the mass punishment at Brownsville was a one-of-a-kind incident. President Nixon's administration was so beleaguered – the "Peace with Honor" announcement in January could not remove the bad taste of America's long engagement in Vietnam – that there was also hope that the army would see an opportunity for some positive news.

Humphrey proposed a bill that would "authorize a just recognition" of the wrong done to the regiment, as well as reimbursing Willis $100,000.

"The Brownsville veterans and their families have endured years of economic deprivation, denial of opportunity and personal anguish because of this tragic episode in American history," Humphrey wrote to Texas Representative Ollie Teague. "It was a ... mistake of the government which injured these men, and I hope we may right that wrong while ... Mr. Willis ... still live[s] to see it."

Weaver acted as a sort of one-man reconciliation squad, introducing Dorsie Willis to Harriet Lyon, daughter of his commanding officer, Captain Samuel Lyon. "Of the five white officers at Brownsville on the night of the shooting, only your father had the courage and the decency to stand up to the military bureaucracy from the outset," Weaver told her. She showed Weaver and Willis a photograph of her father. She asked Dorsie to sign a copy of *The Brownsville Raid* for her. "They were two wonderful people," he said of Captain Lyons and his wife, as Weaver describes it, "tears came to his eyes as his crippled hand slowly and painfully forced his name, letter by letter, onto the title page."[7]

The Army said the matter was brought to Froehlke's attention during a review of administrative and judicial policies. On that point, Weaver disagreed. "They didn't just stumble onto it," he said. He pointed out that after his book was published, a young black intern in the Washington office of Augustus F. Hawkins (D-Calif.) read it and passed it on to the black Los Angeles congressman. Hawkins then introduced legislation to clear the records of the soldiers. "The only reason that the Army acted today was that I spent nearly three years studying the records and discovering that injustice had been done," Weaver said.[8]

## A Reputation Cleared

Robert Hollomon, son of the Company B entrepreneur, wrote on his late father's behalf. "It was his feeling that the opening of the saloon and the subsequent economic loss to the white community was the real cause behind the false charges and the expulsion of the soldiers." As for himself, Robert Hollomon wrote that he was disillusioned by America's treatment of its black soldiers. "I have been a permanent resident of Canada for the past twenty years, and a Canadian citizen since 1960. My father's experience at Brownsville and my personal experience in World War II convinced me that the U.S. was unable or unwilling to defend the rights of the black people who go forth to defend it."[9]

On March 29, 1971, Congressman Hawkins introduced a bill, H.R. 6866, directing the Secretary of Defense to rescind "the effect of Special Order Numbered 266 issued by the War Department on November 9, 1906, and to rectify the injustice caused by such order with respect to all members of Companies B,C and D, First Battalion, Twenty-fifth United States Infantry." Hawkins added, "This grievous injustice will continue to gnaw at the nation's conscience until we correct it.

The Army opposed the bill.

Reiterating its sixty-year old conclusions, the Army was satisfied that the proper action had been taken and saw no reason to re-open the investigation.

Hawkins and Humphrey sent the Army report to the White House. President Nixon's advisors in the Office of Management and Budget passed it to the Department of Justice. Acting Attorney General Richard Kleindienst noted that the Army had missed the point: no one wanted a new investigation, but "to rectify the gross injustice involved in the mass discharge of 167 soldiers."[10]

On September 28, 1972, John and Harriett Weaver stopped on Sunset Boulevard to buy four copies of the *Los Angeles Times*. There on the front page was the headline:

*Army Clears 167 After 66 Years*

"John D. Weaver is an author known to his friends as a fanatical stickler for accurate details," began the article. "Because of this, 167 black soldiers stand exonerated of a crime that had tarnished their names for 66 years."[11] The article went on to chronicle the efforts to bring the injustice to light. On the day the newspaper articles appeared, Clifton Fadiman wrote Weaver a note suggestive of the good wishes aimed at Weaver from the writing community:

> *Dear John,*
>
> *Few writers live to see any of their words accomplish something. And something good, no matter what the government public relations motives may have been. You should take great pride in the Brownsville Affair; and your fellow-writers take pride in you.*
>
> *Kip*

In February of 1973, General De Witt Smith rose at a banquet table in the basement of the Zion Baptist Church in Minneapolis to address a small gathering of friends and family in tribute to Dorsie Willis.

## A Reputation Cleared

"Tonight, we gather to right a wrong comitted many years ago. To subsitute justice for injustice," he began. "The concept of mass punishment is repugnant to the American concept of justice."

"Tonight, we welcome the lone survivor of the dismissed company. A man who will have to represent the one hundred and sixty-seven men who lived out their lives under the cloud of a dismissal without honor."

"Private Willis, I want to say how much we of this generation – black and white – regret the injustices of an earlier generation."

"You honor us by the quality of the life you have led, by your outstanding citizenship, by the faithful service you rendered the United States Army."

Dorsie's wife, Olive, began to cry. It had been a long, long wait for someone to say that.

General Smith held up a letter and then read from it.

"The letter I am holding is signed by Secretary of the Army, Robert F. Kroehlke. "After our own investigation of the circumstances surrounding the 1906 Special Order 266, The United States Army hereby orders the records of the soldiers affected by Special Order 266 changed from 'discharges without honor' to 'honorable discharges.'"

Dorsie Willis stood to acknowledge the honor, and applause turns into an ovation

"Let all present take notice," said the General.

The Zion Baptist Church choir sang *The Battle Hymn of the Republic*.

Dorsie Willis smiled and shook the General's hand. He posed for pictures.

# Teddy's Tantrum

In June of 1973, the House Veterans Committee received a promising letter from the Department of the Army. "The Department of the Army believes that some compensation to surviving members of the Brownsville Incident or their widows is a fair objective through legislation," it read, adding that the President's advisors so far had no objection to the idea.

On December 7, 1973, Gus Hawkins wrote a note to John Weaver:

> *Dear John:*
>
> *I have just been informed that the President is today signing the bill which includes the Brownsville provision. This by no means is the end of the battle, but it is at least partial completion of the things you and I started years ago.*
>
> *Gus Hawkins*

In December, President Nixon signed a compromise version of the bill which Hawkins and Humphrey had proposed.

On January 10, 1974, General De Witt Smith returned to Minneapolis to award Willis a check for $25,000. Here is how *The New York Times* reporter Andrew Malcolm described this second ceremony:

> *Mr. Willis, his eyesight, hearing and lungs failing, donned his best blue suit ... and came downtown to receive a check from an Army general about half his age.*

## A Reputation Cleared

*After a meal of veal cordon bleu, peas, potatoes, salad and chocolate sundaes, John Cornelius, a longtime family friend spoke.*

*Mr. Cornelius, whose shoes Mr. Willis shined for many of the 50 years he worked at the Northwestern Bank Barber Shop, recalled how every six months Mr. Willis quietly handed him a paper bag full of quarters to help support one youth in the Minneapolis Boys Club.*

*"The money totaled $50 a year," said Mr. Cornelius, "and the way I figure it, that's 200 shoeshines every 12 months." So he gave Mr. Willis the Club's Man and Boy Award, a gold statuette.*

*"It's wonderful," said Mr. Willis, "It's wonderful. It's wonderful."*[12]

## CHAPTER 15

# Jalester Lincoln

> I [am] a direct descendant of those Buffalo Soldiers and the Tuskegee Airmen and all the black men and women who have served the nation in uniform. I will never forget my debt to them.
>
> -- *General Colin Powell*

In September of 1981, Colin Powell, the young officer whose helicopter had crashed in Vietnam, now a Brigadier General, walked into a barber shop in Leavenworth Kansas.

His wife had told him that morning that he needed a haircut, and he "had not done that well" at the barbershop on the Army post, Fort Leavenworth, so he drove into town thinking he might find a barber shop in the black section of town he remembered from a visit over a decade earlier.

During his two tours in Vietnam, Powell had seen both sides of the armed forces. He was inspired by the good men under his command, "the same kind of young Americans who had fought, bled, and died winning victory after victory throughout the country's history." But he was also aware of incompetence at higher levels, of "a war so poorly conceived, conducted, and explained by [the] country's leaders," of an Army that often did not face its own failures, an Army which sometimes rewarded short-term indicators of success and disregards or discourages the growth of long-term qualities of moral strength." He called the body-count metrics of how the war was being won "nonsense" and "flabby thinking" and worse.[1] He worried that "a corrosive careerism had infected the Army," and that he was part of it.[2] He became convinced that "War should be the politics of last resort. And when we go to war, we should have a purpose that our people understand and support…you do not squander courage and lives without clear purpose, without the country's backing, and without full commitment."[3]

Black soldiers faced challenges. "Less opportunity, less education, less money, fewer jobs for blacks equaled more antisocial behavior in the States, and these attitudes traveled. I also observed that black soldiers were less skillful at manipulating the system than white troublemakers. The blacks tended to be defiant, as if breaking the rules were a badge of black pride. Their attitude seemed to be 'Take that,' whereas the white offender's attitude was 'Who? Little me, sir?'"[4]

While he had been patrolling the A Shau Valley for Viet Cong, he found out later, his father had been sitting up all night on the porch of his Birmingham, Alabama home, a shotgun across his lap, protecting Powell's pregnant wife. Martin Luther King had marched on the Birmingham city hall.[5]

He had come to deeply admire not only his predecessors, but the Southern blacks who had grown up with intolerance and "refused to carry the baggage that racists tried to pile on their backs. The day they put on the same uniform as everybody else, they began to consider themselves as good as anyone else. And, fortunately, they had joined the most democratic institution in America, where they could rise or fall on merit."

As he described it in his autobiography, that morning in Fort Leavenworth, Powell drove downtown and found the little barber shop, "just as I remembered it, down to the striped barber pole in front. Inside, faded pinups advertising ancient hair tonics covered the wall. Dog-eared magazines littered a rack, and the place had that unique barbershop fragrance. The shop was empty except for a barber older than his posters.

"He put the newspaper down and waved me to a chair. 'Welcome, General,' he said, introducing himself as 'Old Sarge' and draping a striped sheet over me. I studied the photographs over the mirror, black generals, including Rock Cartwright, Julius Becton, Roscoe Robinson, Emmet Page, and Harry Brooks, all from the generation just ahead of me.

"The barber handed me a small red-covered diary. 'I'm going to ask you to sign my book where we're done,' he said. The cover was stamped '1959.' I started thumbing through it, studying the signatures, caught up in the parade of familiar names. His little red book read like black military history. Early signatures were mostly of majors, then a few lieutenant colonels, and in more recent years, a comforting number of more senior officers. And then I stopped short. There, in 1968, I found 'Colin Powell, Major, USA.' I had no recollection of signing the book.

"'You don't remember me, but I remember you.'

"He held up a hand mirror so I could see the back of my head. I nodded my approval. He removed the sheet and shook it out. I fished out a pen and signed the book, this time as 'Brigadier General Powell.' 'What's your name again?' I asked.

"Jalester Lincoln," he said. "Tenth Cavalry, Buffalo Soldiers."[6]

# CHAPTER 16

# A Second Book

> The greatest historian should also be a great moralist. It is no proof of impartiality to treat wickedness and goodness as on the same level.
>
> -- *Theodore Roosevelt, History as Literature*

ON THE SUNNY MORNING OF July 25, 1992, a tall black man on the raised stage stood upright and approached the podium.

The plains of Kansas stretched out beyond Fort Leavenworth. "A crowd of thousands engulfed the heart of the post ... Flags snapped and bands played."[1] A color guard paraded by on horseback.

Brigadier General Colin Powell, the highest-ranking black man in the history of the U.S. military, was ready to dedicate a monument to the Buffalo Soldiers.

The encounter with Sergeant Jalester Lincoln had sparked a desire in Colin Powell to remember those who had come before him. With help from others, he had raised the money and, over the course of a decade seen the project come to completion.

Applause broke out as the crowd recognized him, and the clapping sustained as he waved.

## Teddy's Tantrum

"There he is, the Buffalo Soldier," said Powell, revealing a "magnificent eighteen-foot statue of a black soldier ... on horseback, in his coat of blue, a soldier of the nation, eagles on his buttons, crossed sabers on his canteen, a rifle in his hand, a pistol on his hip,

iron- willed, every bit the soldier that his white brother was.

"Beginning with the Buffalo Soldiers in 1866, African Americans would henceforth always be in uniform, challenging the conscience of a nation, posing the question of how they could be allowed to defend the cause of freedom, to defend the nation – if they themselves were to be denied the benefits of being Americans.

"The great liberator Frederic Douglass made the same point. Douglass said, 'Once let the black man get upon his person the brass letters of "U.S.," let him get an eagle on his buttons, and a musket on his shoulder, and bullets in his pocket and there is no power on earth which can deny him his citizenship in the United States of America.'

"So look at this statue. Look at him. Imagine him He was every bit the soldier that his white brother was. He showed that the theory of inequality must be wrong. He could not be denied his right. It might take time – it did take time. But he knew that in the end he could not be denied.

"The Buffalo Soldiers were not the only ones in this struggle: the 24th and 25th Infantry regiments; the 92nd and 93rd Infantry divisions; the high-flying Tuskegee Airmen; the parachuting Triple-Nickels; our Navy's Golden Thirteen; the Montfort Point Marines; and thousands of other brave black Americans have gone in harm's

## A Second Book

way for their country since the days of the Buffalo Soldier. Always moving forward and upward, step by step, sacrifice by sacrifice.

"But we are not here today to criticize an America of a hundred and fifty years ago, but to rejoice – to rejoice – that we live in a country that has permitted a spiritual descendant of the Buffalo Soldier to stand before you today as the first Afro-American Chairman of the Joint Chiefs of Staff.

"And I am deeply mindful of the debt I owe to those who went before me. I climbed on their backs. I will never forget their service and their sacrifice. And I challenge every young person today: don't forget their service and sacrifice. Don't forget our service and sacrifice and climb on our backs to be eagles.

"And so the powerful purpose of this monument must be to motivate us. To motivate us to keep struggling until all Americans have an equal seat at our national table. Until all Americans enjoy every opportunity to excel, every chance to achieve their dreams, limited only by their imagination and their own ability.

"We will leave this beautiful monument site today knowing that caring Americans made a modest dream come true. But let us also leave, my friends, determined that the most important dream in the world – the American Dream – of progress and full equality has gained today with this monument a new vision. A new strength. A new tomorrow."[2]

The bronze statue gleamed. The crowd spread across the lawn to admire it.

# Teddy's Tantrum

The controversy over the Korean War battle of Yechon was resolved in 1992, but inconclusively.

In 1961, the U.S. Army's official version of the Korean War had been published, reigniting the controversy over Yechon by ignoring the battle, as though it never happened. In 1987, Secretary of the Army John O. March, Jr., directed that the U.S. Army Center of Military History undertake a study of the subject. In 1992, that study was published. Here are excerpts from the study:

"Few historical problems are more demanding than those that accompany an attempt to reconstruct the performance of a military unit in combat.

"In World Wars I and II, the African-American soldier seemed destined for failure from the beginning ... the Army's commanders used them mainly to perform menial tasks, such as unloading ships and digging ditches. Even when finally constrained by political pressure to form all-black regiments and divisions and to allow African-Americans to enter combat, they tended to employ them in areas would little would be lost if they failed. When black Americans performed well, as they did when they fought under French command in World War I, white America made little of their successes, but when they failed, as some did, the news was well circulated. Over all, few in positions of authority were willing to admit that the system of racial segregation was at fault or that a lack of mutual confidence and respect between the black soldier and his white commanders had all but destroyed the sense of oneness, mutual dependency, and self-worth in black units that are the chief constituents of good military performance.

# A Second Book

"The Third Battalion of the all-black 24th Infantry performed well in the initial fighting at Yechon," the report notes. But it refers to "disturbing trends" among the 24th which appeared almost immediately in combat at Sangju and continued at Masan. "In the fight for Battle Mountain, Company C was reduced to a shell and other portions of the regiment suffered heavily. Misfortune … continued to dog the regiment … the unit was unprepared on 1 September when the enemy attacked through the center of its position and the 2nd Battalion collapsed." Replacements "reported for duty unable even to load and fire their rifles … casualties among officers reached critical levels. …" It also refers to "a heroic bayonet and grenade assault" by Company F of the 2nd Battalion on 15 September.

Excerpts from the report's conclusion:

"…If American history shows anything, it reveals that racially segregated combat units have succeeded in battle.

"What happened to the 24th Infantry in Korea was a product of injustices that afflicted black Americans prior to the integration of the Army.

"The whole story … reflects lapses of command and deficiencies in leadership, training and equipment …. it also contains displays of honor, commitment, selflessness and heroism that are in keeping with the best traditions of the United States Army."

Louis Untermeyer died in 1977. John Cheever died in 1982, at the age of 70, of bone cancer, "peacefully at home in bed surrounded by his children." Late in life, he had battled alcoholism and other personal complexities chronicled in his daughter Susan's memoir, *Home Before Dark*. Cheever mentioned in his diaries that he had once been diagnosed with Narcissistic Personality Disorder.

In addition to hundreds of boxes of material at UCLA, you can find evidence of John Weaver's prodigious work ethic during this period in the University of Maryland's Louis Untermeyer - John D. Weaver Collection, which spans the years 1938 through 1995. There you can find Weaver's advice to fellow author Gil Fates on his *What's My Line* book, his articles, his voluminous correspondences with librarians, friends, magazine editors, curators, letters to Untermeyer's son, Untermeyers's widow, Bryna, and the occasional birthday sonnet.

Weaver wrote a long article breaking down the events and personalities involved in the 1932 Bonus March for *American Heritage* magazine, seeking to amend the historical record, much as he had in the Brownsville matter. "The crimson glow of the burning camps had hardly faded from the midnight sky before a dispute arose as to who these people were, why they had come to the capital, and under what circumstances they had been expelled. After a generation of impassioned and often inaccurate oratory, the Bonus March remains one of the most controversial and grotesquely distorted episodes of recent American history."[3]

For the better part of that decade, cancer was sapping Harriett Weaver's strength.

"As a result of the radiation therapy, the bones in Harriett's hip have deteriorated to such an extent that she moves about on a cane with some difficulty and … considerable pain."[4] Her husband records that "we had lived with cancer since 1969," when melanoma cancer was found on Harriett's left leg.

Harriett Weaver lost her will to live when the disease incapacitated her. John did not enjoy the role reversal, which now cast him as the caregiver. A July, 1986, letter to Pamela Fiore gives an indication of the strain it took on the both of them:

> *When I slipped out of bed around 5 o'clock this morning she was in pain and tears. I gave her a Darvocet for the pain and Ativan for the tears, then sat with her for an hour until she fell asleep.*
>
> *Now, four hours later, she's had her breakfast and is sitting up in bed reading the morning papers, quite cheerful and very pretty with her hair done in preparation for the speech therapist's visit. It's a little after 9 and I feel as though I'd put in ten hours at the local jute mill. But the beds are made, the cat fed and the breakfast dishes done ... At this point, the therapist arrived and when I took her into the bedroom, Harriett broke out crying, so I got her up, wheeled her into the living room, helped into her armchair and came back to what I hope will be an uninterrupted half-hour with the PC. I no longer sit in on the speech therapist's sessions, not since the first one when she asked Harriett to name five dogs, then five cats of different breeds. Harriett smiled helplessly up at her and the therapist asked for the names of five favorite*

> *writers. Harriett said, "John Weaver ... John Cheever ..." Then, after an embarassed pause, she came up with two other names, Louis Untermeyer and Ralph Martin. She never made the fifth name.*

In the same letter he refers to renewing a film option on the Brownsville book in order to extend his health coverage with the Writers' Guild. "If Brownsville ever reaches the screen and I'm given story credit, we'll get an extra year of free coverage."

Just before Thanksgiving, 1988, Harriett's "long ordeal ended gently." Her extended illness had been difficult for John, and one friend saw relief in John's face at her funeral.[5]

His writing had taken a back seat. He had planned to write a second book on the Brownsville incident, but had not been able to free the time.

Living in Encino, he seemed to friends to be adrift.[6] A mutual friend introduced him to a bright, attractive woman named Chica Nimocks. The two met and "laughed a lot," as he recalled in a letter. "She is a pretty," as Weaver described her to a friend, "beautifully groomed, intelligent, caring, politically liberal, generous woman with a terrific sense of humor." John and Chica married on October 7, 1989.

Meeting Chica, brought him back to life and generated a new spate of writing. He rose early and walked six miles every day. From John's September, 1992 letter:

> *I got a call the other day from one of Harriett's old friends in Los Angeles who had met Chica for the first time last June. She*

## A Second Book

> *called to tell me how lucky I am to have her. When I passed this on to Chica, I said, "I hear that all the time." Then I said, "I suppose you do, too." She smiled. She didn't say anything. Just smiled.*

Where Harriett allowed John his freedom from all worldly tasks, Chica asked more – that he look at a map while they drove, for example. Chica, too, experienced Weaver's "aboriginal" fear of electricity. He would warn her of life-threatening consequences if she tried to changing a fuse in a fuse box. His Mother had cautioned that "You never pick up the paper without reading about those things electrocuting somebody," and John had never shaken the idea. Chica was less lenient than Harriett, and urged him to get over his superstitions and pitch in.

He compiled *Glad Tidings: A Friendship in Letters*, a book collecting letters from his forty-year correspondence with John Cheever and dedicated to Chica, "who made the lights come back on." *The New York Times* review wrote that the book "completed the oeuvre of John Cheever." *The Los Angeles Times* wrote that *Glad Tidings* represented "a treasury of private letters that allow us to glimpse the rich and sometimes troubled inner life" of Cheever. *The Brownsville Raid* fell out of print and was re-issued by the Texas A&M University Press. Weaver assembled a collection of his correspondence with Untermeyer, a collection which is currently at the University of Maryland.

He began work in a second Brownsville book. In it he would dramatize the human cost of the raid and its aftermath. Weaver turned to other writing projects, notably a history of Los Angeles, and fanned the occasional interest in the Brownsville matter. A September, 1997, letter refers to a phone call from John Warren (Earl Warren's grandson), a film producer. "He said he had been talking to Denzel Washington about the Brownsville story and asked what I might have to show him. I am sending him my recently revised text of a the 4-hour TV miniseries script I worked on with playwright Robert Anderson ten years ago."

He called the second Brownsville book "The Senator and the Sharecropper's Son," referring to Joseph Foraker and Dorsie Willis. In it, he uses the two men as bookends through which he traces the progress of the Affray. From his September 26, 1996 letter to Pamela Fiori:

> *I'm in the final editing process with A&M and have run into a bureaucratic mares nest in Editorial. As I have done in all of my books except the first, I wrote jacket copy which was translated into the tapioca prose of academia by two women who may be a credit to their gender, their country and the Great Republic of Texas, but they aren't writers.*

Weaver did his own indexing, as well as the flap copy, the catalogue copy. His first draft of the manuscript for *The Senator and the Sharecropper's Son* was 130,000 words, from which he cut 40,000 words.

In 1997, John D. Weaver's *The Sharecropper and the Senator's Son* was published by the University of Texas A&M Press. Here is his report on the book's progress:

## A Second Book

> *The book is finally in print, but in Texas "spring publication" seems to mean delivery in time for Fourth of July beach parties ...*
>
> *I expect a summer sale of two copies. In whatever bookstore my sister Jane is using these days.*

This book has none of the storytelling ease of his short stories, nor any of their easy sentiment. Weaver's problem was not so much his own storytelling skills, but that his material lacked the essentials for a good story – namely, something approaching a happy ending, or any ending at all. While the book fills in some significant details of the episode, Weaver's narrative powers are not shown at their best in *Sharecropper* as he follows his two protagonists through a literary terrain that is too sweeping.

Weaver was particularly moved by the response from a handful of relatives and descendants of the men of the 25th Infantry. "My family and I do not have the words to express our gratitude," wrote Ira Warfield, Private Edward Warfield's brother. "It is not often that the black race has such a champion of our cause." A letter from King D. Collins, Jr., of Oakland reports an unfortunate aftereffect of Special Order 266 at John Hollomon's Louisville funeral. "At the last moment, when the funeral party arrived at the ceremony, permission to bury Mr. Hollomon was denied because of the dishonorable discharge."

John celebrated his 80th birthday with a party themed "doing 80 and 80." According to Simon Elliott, librarian at the UCLA Special Collections, John "spent years" during the 90's arranging and re-arranging his UCLA collection of papers

217

and correspondence – five hundred boxes in total, much of it ephemera regarding the history of Los Angeles. "He would look for something in Box 42, and find that it wasn't there." He would decide that certain boxes were "on deposit" – that is, they were in the collection, but he had not yet given them to the university.

He felt his work on Brownsville was not taken seriously. Perhaps it was because he had no academic degree, he worried, that scholars and historians were slow to absorb the clear truth about the incident. Why were there not other scholars following in his footsteps? The question haunted him. Maybe, he told Chica, he should have written it as an historical novel. Or, had he been black, he said, *then* it would have made a bigger splash.

John cared less and less for travel, and when his brother Bill invited the couple to Italy, he declined. He was due royalties in Russia, but he would not travel to collect them.[7] Light bulbs and garage door openers remained objects of mystery and danger, and he would not deal with them. When a car mechanic offered to teach John how to change a tire, he answered, "Why would I want to do that?"

"He never quite got over Brownsville," Chica says, because he was hoping for more. Yet for all the darker emotions in these waning years, perhaps there were also moments when he felt he had settled the score in a small way, or at least put some points on the board, for Louis Untermeyer and for Carl Foreman as well as for the men of the 25th Infantry. According to Harriett's niece, Weaver especially basked in the good company of the black families, descendants of the men of the 25th Infantry, who kept in contact with him and appreciated his efforts.

## A Second Book

John Weaver died on December 4, 2002.

CHAPTER 17

# More Lost Stories

*The fame of other men may fear the onslaught of time; but the fame of Roosevelt need not fear it.*

*-- Calvin Coolidge*

IN THE LATE 1990's, A young lawyer in New York City attended a Christmas party.

The lawyer's name was Ovidio Diaz Espino, he was Panamanian, and he worked for Morgan Bank. The J.P. Morgan Bank.

At the party, he met "a witty and animated young man" who, upon hearing where Espino was from and where he worked, "threw up his arms in the air."

"Are you aware that J.P. Morgan was the treasurer of Panama during its first decade?" asked the animated young man. "Did you know that your country was conceived in Room 1162 of the Astoria Hotel?"[1]

# Teddy's Tantrum

Much as John Weaver's mother sparked a one-man chain of inquiry, so did the comment from Espino's witty young acquaintance. Espino spent the next eighteen months camped inside the New York Public Library doing his own detective work. He realized that the official version of his country's birth was "idealized but false … The official story written in schoolbooks made our liberators to be heroes who won a war of independence." He quickly concluded that such a war had never occurred, and that he "had the outlines of a story hidden for almost a century."[2]

Theodore Roosevelt had found a way to reward J.P. Morgan for his good deeds in saving the nation from financial chaos on three occasions: the Panama Canal. Through his colleague, William Cromwell, Morgan had been granted a hugely profitable tropical fiefdom. Espino's tale is a twisted, fascinating one. Cromwell lobbied for Morgan to be the agent for all payments for the Canal and its construction. So when the time came to pay $40,000,000 to the French liquidator and $10,000,000 to Panama, it was Cromwell who received the money and distributed according to who owned the stock certificates – many of which were in the possession of himself and Morgan. It was scarcely an accident that Cromwell compared himself to the Romans in their foreign wars. Roosevelt was doing what every emperor must do: reward his nobles for their service by granting them territories. Cromwell wisely couched his sentiments in Rooseveltian terms, referring to himself as "a humble soldier in the Panama cause" battling on behalf of "the Canal – the hope of the Isthmus … upon the fate of which, hung its very existence."

# More Lost Stories

While the general outline of Espino's version was known (and can be read in the incomparable *The Path Between the Seas*, by David McCullough) the level of detail and depth in his account was certainly new. As with Brownsville, the press had cried foul from the sidelines as the Roosevelt steam engine forged ahead, to little avail. "Isthmus Coup D'Etat Planned in New York," the *New York Times* had announced in November, 1903. "Men Who Figure in Rumors about Great Panama Canal Deal – Candidate Taft's Brother and Douglas Robinson, President Roosevelt's Brother-in-Law Alleged to Have Been in Syndicate," screamed *The World* in October, 1908. The sardonic Elihu Root's famous comment after one of Roosevelt's spirited defenses of his action on the Isthmus perhaps reflected a consensus: "You have shown that you were accused of seduction," he told the President, "and you have conclusively proved that were guilty of rape."

Unlike Harriett Weaver, Espino's family resisted the uncovering of century-old incidents. "My father ... warned me that my book diminished not only the Americans, but our own patriots, and begged me to suppress the truth about the corruption and the Wall Street ties."[3]

Espino's 2001 book, *How Wall Street Created a Nation: J.P. Morgan, Teddy Roosevelt, and the Panama Canal* looks with great detail into a single question: What really happened in Panama in 1903? That was the year found an account in the *World* describing how Cromwell, on J.P. Morgan's behalf, had bought the shares of the bankrupt French Canal company and sold it to Roosevelt for $40 million, far above its worth.[4] American investors like Charles Taft (William's brother) and Roosevelt's brother in law Douglas

# Teddy's Tantrum

Robinson bought the French shell company in the full knowledge that the American people were about to pay them a huge profit for it. Cromwell then lobbied to become the agent for all Canal payments: overt Elihu Root's objections, Roosevelt appointed J.P. Morgan "Special Disbursing Agent." Espino writes that "Cromwell and J.P. Morgan now had control over the disbursement of the single largest payment ever made," dwarfing the Louisiana Purchase and payments for Alaska. Espino reports that Cromwell's "law offices at No. 41 Wall Street were … regarded by many as the real executive offices of the Panama Canal."[5] Aware of these same circumstances, *The New York Times* concluded at the canal's inception that "The Canal was stolen property" and that "The history of the Panama Canal is one long track and trail of scandal."

Wall Street's accomplice in the swindle was Philip Banau-Varilla, a "soldier of the 'Idea of the Canal'" and an engineer for the French, who made a small fortune as a sub-contractor for the French effort (thanks to his brother, who gave him the contract)

Notes of particular meetings reflect detailed accounts of the unorthodox process by which Colombian interests were ousted ("This uncle of our can settle it all with a single crunch of his jaws," noted one Colombian diplomat) and a small cadre of aristocratic Panamanian "patriots" who rebelled and instantly signed a lucrative contract with America. Roosevelt claimed the Isthmus to be "international eminent domain." He also claimed that, by virtue of an 1846 treaty with Colombia, the U.S. was entitled to take the Isthmus by force. Those familiar with Roosevelt's hunting trips surely saw the clear intent in his statement on negotiations with the Colombians "I fear we may have to give a lesson to those jack rabbits."

Espino concludes that the Panamanian patriots received between $25,000 and $100,000 each; Colombian military officers who aided in the rebellion were also paid, as were the Panamanian diplomats who helped negotiate the treaty with America. Espina found memoranda of the Cromwell syndicate as well as detailed records of the bonds paid to the Wall Street speculators

Just as in the Brownsville episode, lengthy Congressional hearings on the charges came to nothing.

Espino calls the Hay-Banau-Varilla Treaty "the offspring of Banau-Varilla's treachery."

In the Spring of 2002, one of Theodore Roosevelt's biographers, Edmund Morris, published an article in the *Naval War College Review* entitled "A Matter of Extreme Urgency: Theodore Roosevelt, Wilhelm II, and the Venezuelan Crisis on 1902."

Morris had uncovered secret memoranda revealing that a minor incident had actually been far more serious than anyone knew: war between America and Germany was narrowly averted. Roosevelt's cryptic allusions to the true nature of "the Venezuelan business" have, Morris concluded, misdirected historians. Here was even more evidence that Roosevelt had "accomplished much of his grand strategy in silence and secret."

# Teddy's Tantrum

On June 14, 2004, the 25th Infantry stepped on the sands of Iraq. American forces launched a raid campaign in the area of *Al-Ishaqi* in southern Samarra, north of Baghdad, at dawn.

"Our mission in Iraq is clear," President George W. Bush had declared two years earlier. "We are hunting down the terrorists. We are helping Iraqis build a free nation that is an ally in the war on terror. We are advancing freedom in the Middle East. We are laying the foundation of peace for our children and grandchildren."

That same day, a small crowd in the White House applauded politely.

"Thank you, thank you very much."

The 42nd United States President, William Jefferson Clinton, smiled and showed the palms of his hands as if to say, "Enough." Out of office 22 months, he was pleased to be back in the White House. He was flanked by his wife and daughter, his predecessor, George H.W. Bush, and his successor, George W. Bush, on the occasion of the unveiling of the official Clinton presidential portrait. He held up his hand and the applause quieted.

"I was thinking of, President and Mrs. Bush, on the way over here today, which ones of these pictures I liked the most, and in the darkest days, which ones helped me the most." Clinton's familiar raspy voice filled the room.

"I like John Singer Sargent's portrait of Theodore Roosevelt over there. But there's one over in the Cabinet Room by a man named Laszlo of Theodore Roosevelt. I used to look at it all the time when I felt bad …"

"Because if you look at that picture, Theodore Roosevelt, who was known as our most macho, bully, self-confident president ...

"You look at that picture and you see here's a human being who's scared to death and not sure it's going to come out all right. That's what I saw in that picture."

He removed the cloth.

Applause and cheers broke out as Clinton unveiled his own portrait.

As Bill Clinton admired his portrait, Colin Powell was backpedaling.

For the second time in a month, the Secretary of State was forced to address an erroneous report on terrorism.

Stuck as the lead spokesman for an administration whose actions he did not condone, Colin Powell acknowledged that an erroneous terror report was a mistake and insisted politics did not lead to the report's omissions. Released in April, the State Department's annual report on global terrorism had incorrectly declared that terrorist attacks declined in 2003. But figures from a corrected report "will be up sharply," State Department spokesman Richard Boucher has said. According to CNN, The inaccurate report said 190 acts of international terrorism occurred in 2003 -- a slight drop from 198 attacks the previous year and the lowest total since 1969. The report found that 169 of those were "significant" attacks, which involved death, serious injury or major property damage. However, researchers Alan B. Krueger of Princeton University and David Laitin of Stanford University reported in May that the number of significant attacks represented a 36 percent increase over the 124 events in 2001.

Powell, the White House sole advisor who had ever seen combat, had harbored the gravest doubts about sending U.S. armed forces into a cauldron of crossfire to solve a problem he saw as too vast to have a military resolution. He had been outvoted. His warnings went unheeded. The thick documents which detailed the State Department recommendations had been tossed aside. Over the past twenty months, as exhilaration over the easy military victory had curdled as no weapons of mass destruction were found, as the populace descended into sectarian violence, General Powell had stoically defended a policy he felt was fundamentally flawed. Loyal to his commander, he tried to explain to an interviewer[6] the broad picture. "What we would like to see is a greater understanding of power, of the democratic system, the open market economic system, the rights of men and women to achieve their destiny as God has directed them to do if they are willing to work for it. And we really do not wish to go to war with people. But, by God, we will have the strongest military around. And that's not a bad thing to have. It encourages and champions our friends that are weak and it chills the ambitions of the evil." Coming from Colin Powell, this strong statement of mission showed purpose and integrity. It masked a strategy in Iraq that had little coherence, military or otherwise.

That Sunday in June, 2004, Powell said on NBC's "Meet the Press" that the disputed report "doesn't downplay terrorism in the slightest. But unfortunately, the data that is within the report -- the actual number of incidents -- is wrong." Powell said the information was compiled by the CIA and the Terrorist Threat Information Center, which includes officials from the Pentagon, the Department of Homeland Security, the FBI and CIA. He said State Department officials were working during the weekend to find out how the mistakes occurred, and he said he would meet Monday with officials from those agencies to discuss the errors.[7]

"All sorts of alarm bells should have gone off" when the data were being compiled," Powell said, but he denied that the figures were skewed for political purposes.

"I am not a happy camper over this," he said. "We were wrong."

Within six months days, Colin Powell would announce his resignation as U.S. Secretary of State.

PART THREE

# HISTORY AND LITERATURE

In 1492, upon being presented with a Castilian grammar book, the first grammar of a modern European tongue, Queen Isabella of Spain asked,

"What is it for?"

"Your majesty," answered the Bishop of Avila, who had helped compile the book, "language is the perfect instrument of empire."

-- J.H. Elliott, *Imperial Spain*

CHAPTER 18

# The Anger of the Legions

> The Spanish American was not the last war this country is going to be involved in, there will yet dawn a day when this country will be glad, yea, will court and beg the services of the Negro in time of warfare.
>
> *-- Reverend William Decker Johnson on Roosevelt's treatment of the 25th Infantry*

ONE STRAND RUNNING THROUGH THE Brownsville saga is the flawed nature of the U.S. military command. Like many military histories, it is a performance with its share of mistakes and missteps.

First, the 25th Infantry was part of an ill-conceived war against Indian tribes. The U.S. Army command mistook the nature and seriousness of the campaign in the West, grossly underestimating the extent and ferocity of Indian tribes' resistance to new settlements.

Second, the U.S. Army employed four black regiments to serve in the Spanish-American War, the 9th and 10th Cavalry along with the 24th and 25th Infantry on the mistaken assumption that black men were immune to tropical disease. "Assumptions of racial immunity to disease pervade nineteenth-century medical and social theory," writes Warwich Anderson in his article "Immunities of Empire" in the *Bulletin of History of Medicine 70.1 (1996) 94-118*. The 7th, 8th, 9th and 10th U.S. Volunteer Infantry later came into existence in response to Congress' need for more soldiers, preferably "immune" to tropical diseases.

Third, black regiments were often commanded by inept or prejudiced officers. White officers vigorously avoided command of black regiments. *"Command niggers?"* wailed a white officer assigned to the 25th. Black officer candidates were unwelcome at West Point. One of the first black cadets, Johnson C. Whittaker, after two years of academic success at the Academy, was found tied to his bed on April 6, 1880, his ears slashed and his hair cut. He was court-martialed after being charged with inflicting the injuries on himself.[1] One element, however large or small, of the original raid has nothing to do with race, and that is the resentment in all cultures between the citizens and the soldiers who guard them.

As Harold Lasswell demonstrates over and over in his wide-ranging 1997 book *Essay on the Garrison State*, there is a permanent mistrust between military and civilian societies because their values are so different. The military virtues of teamwork and hierarchy are at odds with "civilian society," which values compassion, equality and individuality. This military-civilian schism has not gone unnoticed: Roman garrisons were stationed far away from the towns they protected. In American society,

# The Anger of the Legions

the schism has often taken on a moral element. Eschewing mercenaries, we have taken our citizen-soldiers from our own farms and villages. "From the beginning," writes Lasswell, "career soldiers perceived themselves as occupying a somewhat hostile environment, distrusted by American civilians – which indeed they were, because American civilian culture had absorbed an English tradition inimical to standing armies ... The soldiers reciprocated civilian distrust with ill-feeling of their own, often fortified by their sense that they themselves represented an ethos of discipline and manly virtue superior to the easygoing values of civilian society ..."[2]

Military historians Gronke and Feaver refer to an "uncertain certainty" that has always existed between civilian and military cultures. In the garrison state, there is a latent alienation between the two. "We live in a world that has walls. And those walls have to be guarded by men with guns," warns the antagonist, Colonel Nathan R. Jessup, in Aaron Sorkin's 1981 stage play, *A Few Good Men*, and "...deep down, in places you don't talk about at parties, you want me on that wall. You need me on that wall." Sorkin's message may play a small role in the Brownsville Raid's drama: polite society is not always comfortable with the savage men who defend it.

Two examples from our story – the Russo-Japanese War and France's Dreyfus Affair – show that ours is not the only nation which has encountered turmoil in assembling armed forces from among its various tribes. All empires seem to go through the same process, and America's armed forces handled it better than most.

Tribal and racial loyalties were factors in the Russo-Japanese War, not only in the enmity between the two nations but in the performance of their armies. Russia had taken Darwin's ideas about survival of the fittest species and mixed them with Tsarist arrogance to concoct a highly-charged atmosphere of national destiny. It has been called imperialism, a term which does not seem adequate to conjure up the deluded self-confidence with which Russia entered into this war. The facts turned out to be the opposite: because of conflicts between ethnic groups within the Russian forces, the Japanese out-fought them at almost every turn. Tsar Nicholas did not have the luxury of choosing soldiers who liked one another and so assembled a fighting force that fought itself. Two hundred thousand young men were conscripted by Tsar Nicholas to travel thousands of miles across the continent to protect the empire's eastern flank, Finnish troops, and Poles, who hated one another, and hated the Russians who led them. "Desertions were common. Non-Russian soldiers needed little incentive to desert the cause, and were often quick to surrender."[3]

As the Dreyfus Affair -- to which John Weaver liked to compare the Brownsville Affray – demonstrated, tribal tensions within the French army cracked during the decades France tried to defend its waning empire. After the Napoleonic Wars, the *Grande Armee* was over half comprised of non-Frenchmen, regiments of colonial minorities who often out-performed French troops. To avoid the troops fragmenting into factions, in 1831 King Louis-Philippe formed the French Foreign Legion, a battalion created for non-Frenchmen.

# The Anger of the Legions

Algerian, Tunisian, and Moroccan soldiers served in French cavalry regiments called Spahis. A squadron of Spahis mutined in 1871 rather than fight in the war against Prussia. Anti-semitic tensions within the French army erupted into the Dreyfus case at the turn of the century. Unfortunately for Weaver, the similarities between Dreyfus and Brownsville are limited. Weaver liked to compare the affray to the Dreyfus affair, but the two incidents may hold more differences than similarities. First, the unfairly accused was Jewish, not black. Dreyfus' family had considerable resources with which to fight back. The case spent twelve years in the French legal system. Second, Zola was put on trial for his editorial in defense of Captain Dreyfus, so the matter received a full and relatively fair treatment in French courts. Roosevelt was able to cut off the men of the 25th from any such day in court, and the outcry among the black press did not match Zola's. While there was public outrage, critical mass was never reached. If Mark Twain or Henry Adams (to name two anti-Roosevelt writers) had written an open letter to the President entitled "I Accuse," and if the *New York Times* had published it on its front page, events might have played out differently. Third, the Dreyfus affair opened a fissure in a government and a society that was badly cracked. The intellectual community seized upon the railroading of Dreyfus as a lever to crack open an already divided Third Republic. The Brownsville Affair, while equally egregious, struck no such chord in American society. The Dreyfus affair was an ideological campaign against the army as a whole, against nationalism, against the church. Waving the bloody shirt—or torn epaulets—of Captain Dreyfus, generations of French liberals of all shades inveighed against "militarism" or "clericalism." The Dreyfus incident was mixed up in a very different stew of issues -- anti-Semitism, Zionism, the new-found power of an intellectual class, resentment against the third Republic as a whole – than was the Brownsville Raid and its aftermath.

Another imperial corollary to the experience of the 25th Infantry lies in Africa. A century earlier, the great-grandfathers of the young men at Fort Brown were guarding the grasslands of Ghana and Mali in tightly disciplined bands, protecting their villages from rival tribes. The Kingdoms of Benin in 19th century West Africa fought a brutal war against the competing coastal states of Ghana and Mali. This region supplied as many as 15,000 slaves to America per year during the high years of the slave trade, and the warriors who patrolled the borderlands of the savannahs bear a striking similarity to the men of the U.S. Army's 25th Infantry who patrolled the borderlands of Texas. "Several large political groupings emerged [in the early 1800's] to control the area between the Thukela and Black Mfolozi rivers. The Zulus … were initially no more than subordinate allies to one of these groups, but their rising commenced with sometime between 1816 and 1818, when a minor son of the ruling chief [ShakakaSenzangakhona]… was raised up to control of the clan… by 1824, the Zulus had eclipsed all their rivals," writes Ludwig Alberti in his book *Account of the Tribal Life and Customs of the Xhosa in 1807*. Shaka, called by European historians the Napoleon of his day, trained an army so swift and savage that they "… shocked even the hardest professional soldiers … who opposed them …" according to Alberti. Once the main army was mobilized,

# The Anger of the Legions

its explicit objective was to 'eat up' the enemy. "The Zulu army was committed to the concept of aggressive action ... [Shaka's] military philosophy ... was always to attack whenever possible." As a result, the men of the African patrols were filled with tension. "The Zulu army in the field was like a spring that had been wound to breaking point by days of psychological preparation, and it required only the presence of the enemy for it to snap."[4]

So did the men of the 25th Infantry attack whenever possible. They had learned the lesson of San Juan Hill: charge or die.

Shaka's Zulu army was built on basic units called *amabutho*, or guilds, bands of youth who had just entered puberty. He would summon all the 18- and 19-year olds to attend a sort of training camp, "regardless of their origins or local allegiance. These were then formed into an *ibutho*, and given a name, and a distinctive group uniform ... the common age of these young men in the *amabutho*, and their shared experiences, tended to foster close ties between them, to the extent that many came to refer to themselves by their regimental, rather than their clan, names."[5]

So was Company C a collection of young men separated from their families, taken randomly from cities like Philadelphia and Chicago as well as tiny towns in Oklahoma and Virginia and Georgia. Their common age and common experience forged the bond that saved them in The Brownsville Incident: without the most powerful loyalty to the Regiment, any number of these young men would have taken the money Roosevelt offered through his henchmen, Browne and Baldwin. If the young men of the 25th Infantry had not considered themselves part of the regimental society, they would have favored their own families and traded their friends' reputation for good jobs, with salaries that would send their children to good schools and good doctors. Instead, they kept the pledge, said nothing, and suffered for it. The following description by Alberti could be written about the 25th Infantry as well as Shaka's *amabutho*:

> "... by the time a warrior had undergone the preparatory rituals for combat, he was set apart from peaceful society, bound to his fellows by the tightest emotional bonds, and the powerful taboos that surrounded him could only be expiated in the terrible excitement of combat.")

Here is an American version of what is very much the same process, taken from James Utley's essay in Bradford's *Crucible of Empire*:

> *The common soldier very often was recruited territorially, and usually he was linked to his buddies in his unit by ties of home locality, schooling, language, customs, tradition and military specialty ... being in the military, moreover, created a new and special bond. Soldiers become professionals with their own language, food, clothing, shelter, support forces (including, at times, women), arms and accoutrements, and mobility ...*[6]

W.E.B. Du Bois pointed out that during the Civil War black troops were "repeatedly and deliberately used as shock troops, when there was little or no hope of success."

# The Anger of the Legions

After the Civil War, the army was reorganized in 1886. Six Black regiments were for formed by law to be a part of the regular army for their valor during the Civil War. In 1866, Congress passed an act creating four regiments: the Twenty fourth and Twenty-fifth Infantry and the Ninth and Tenth Cavalry. These regiments were to be permanent army regiments. Of these four regiments, the Ninth and Tenth Cavalry distinguished themselves during the Indian Wars in the West between 1870 and 1900.

Professor Gerstle points to the day on Kettle and San Juan Hills as a watershed opportunity to mend fences between the races, an opportunity that was missed. "Something extraordinary had happened during those battles, as black American soldiers had fought alongside and intermixed with white ones, demonstrating that racial division could be overcome and that a fighting force including all Americans, not just those of European descent, could operate effectively. [Roosevelt] was not prepared for the opportunity that the victory at Kettle Hill and San Juan Hills had handed him."[7]

No African American soldier was awarded the Medal of Honor for service during World War II. In 1993, the U.S. Army contracted Shaw University in Raleigh, North Carolina, to research and prepare a study "to determine if there was a racial disparity in the way Medal of Honor recipients were selected." Shaw's team researched the issue and, finding that there was disparity, recommended the Army consider a group of ten soldiers for the Medal of Honor. Of those ten, seven were recommended to receive the award, and Fox was among them.

# Teddy's Tantrum

# CHAPTER 19

# Mosaic

> Each picture is like an individual mosaic, indeed almost like the proverbial picture puzzle, for it is difficult to put together clearly such divergent characters as these sketches portray.
>
> -- *Corinne Roosevelt Robinson, Theodore's sister, on her brother's many aspects*

"Your excellency knows the vehement character of the President," warned Colombian diplomat Tomas Herran in a letter to his superiors, "and you are aware of the persistence and decision with which he pursues anything to which he may be committed."

Roosevelt's "vehement character" was noted by many of his contemporaries. Mark Twain wrote that Roosevelt was "clearly insane ... and insanest upon war and its supreme glories." "I see nothing for him but the asylum," added historian and Roosevelt contemporary Henry Adams.

In the thirty-seven years since Weaver's Brownsville book appeared, a new crop of Roosevelt books has enriched our appreciation of Theodore Roosevelt, not so much reconsidering him as exploring his lesser-known aspects. The richest of all presidential subjects, Roosevelt has attracted some of our finest writers.

One of the most ambitious is Gary Gerstle's 2001 book *American Crucible*, which combines a psychological consideration of Roosevelt with the formation of the idea of an American nation. At the time of the Brownsville incident, writes Gerstle, a "Roosevelt nation" was taking shape, one that combined both liberal ideals of inclusion and progress and less-admirable ideals of racial castes – what Gerstle calls "civic nationalism" and "ethnic nationalism." War was the crucible which would forge these disparate concepts into a new nation.

Another insightful Roosevelt study is Kathleen Dalton's *Theodore Roosevelt: A Strenuous Life*, was published in 2002. "The trend toward accepting Roosevelt's heroic interpretation of his own life has not abated in our own time," she writes.[1] "To see TR anew ... we have to look beneath the heroics."[2] Dalton looks at his tendency to always have one eye on the mirror. "...His presentation of himself was shaped by his awareness of public scrutiny." Even his children were aware of it, referring to certain of his letters as "posterity letters" which would one day be published (as all of them were). He had help in preserving the legend. "Family and friends edited or destroyed embarrassing letters and hid family secrets in order to keep the story of Roosevelt's life and times presentable."[3] Dalton points to the Civil War as a powerful influence in Roosevelt's childhood, an event "full of loss, grief, shock insecurity and conflict" which became the model for the apocalyptic world which was so vivid in his adult mind.

She identifies Roosevelt's mother, Mittie, as the source of his extravagant idealism.

Of the many excellent books delving into this topic, Sarah Watts' *Rough Rider* is one of the very best. "Roosevelt was the first president to articulate the shared anxieties of his generation," Watts writes, "and he provided its first seemingly coherent response to the cultural dislocations of modern society."[4] To Watts, Roosevelt's effort to remake the image of the American male was at the heart of his mission, and at the heart of his popularity. He exhorted each man to have "thorough command over himself and over his own evil passions." He set an example with his own life and deeds, pointing the way to a strenuous life that could overcome the dangers of civilization. "Thus locked together. Race, manhood and nation stood in polar opposition to all elements of modern life that could threaten individual white men – moneyed Jews, dangerous women, wild Indians, or defiant Negroes. That any one danger might challenge 'our mighty manhood,' in Roosevelt's parlance, meant that it threatened all white men of 'our' social class, as well as 'our' nation and the trajectory of 'our' civilization."[5] William Allen White, a Kansas editor and Roosevelt's friend, estimated that of the four million votes Roosevelt received in his second and last campaign for president in 1912, approximately one million were cast by men "for no particular intelligent reason" other than "you were a masculine sort of a person with extremely masculine virtues and palpably masculine faults."[6]

"He targeted men who had 'certain dreadful qualities of the moral pervert.' He denounced the 'soft, swollen eunuchs,' those 'men who were not men' who refused to father children, and the 'sinister opposition,' those congressmen who voted against naval appropriations."⁷ Watts describes Roosevelt as "a man driven by foreboding and a deep fear of social disorder." This explains his antipathy for anarchists, and for organized labor and their demands, which "strike at the foundations of society." Rebellious soldiers of any color, soldiers who take the law into their own hands and then refuse to talk, might fit this same category. For Roosevelt, "treason, like adultery, ranks as one the worst of all possible crimes."⁸

Writing like Watts' and Dalton's helps explain Roosevelt's extraordinary vindictiveness -- the length to which he was willing to go rather than back off his initial mistake in prosecuting the black soldiers of Fort Brown, against whom he had no credible evidence. This recent work enriches and informs Weaver's portrait of Roosevelt as a man driven by internal conflicts. Weaver uncovered what Roosevelt did to ensnare men of the 25th Infantry; these works help fill in our understanding of why he did it.

If the principles of psychoanalysis had not invaded the mainstream of presidential history by 1976, it certainly did in that year with the publication of Doris Kearns Goodwin's biography of Lyndon Baines Johnson.

Two Texas psychologists took Goodwin's approach one step further. Steve Rubenzer and Thomas Faschingbauer assembled a panel of over 100 experts in presidential history to give a psychological profile of each of the presidents.⁹ Their results are given in their 2002 book, *Personality, Character and Leadership in the White House*. They found in general that straightforwardness is not necessarily a good thing in presidents. "Straightforward people tend to be very honest and sincere and ingenuous, but they don't tend to make good presidents. Candidates with a solid character--straightforward, dutiful and disciplined--often run into trouble being an effective president," says co-author Steven J. Rubenzer, Ph D.[10] "We don't hear too many candidates touting that they are a better liar than the others," says Rubenzer. "But it seems to increase their chances of putting their policies in place."

By the same token, narcissism is not a bad thing among presidents. Narcissism is characterized by a self-centeredness that makes one oblivious to the emotional existence of others. In its extreme, narcissism is "a pervasive pattern of grandiosity ... a need for admiration, and lack of empathy." The narcissist "has a grandiose sense of self-importance .... is preoccupied with fantasies of unlimited success, power, brilliance, beauty, or ideal love ... lacks empathy: is unwilling to recognize or identify with the feelings and needs of others."[11] Several presidential types emerged from the profiles. Theodore Roosevelt landed in two categories, "extraverts" and "dominators." The extravert category also includes FDR, John F. Kennedy, Bill Clinton, Ronald Reagan, William Harrison, Warren Harding, Andrew Jackson and LBJ and is described as follows:

> *Extroverted presidents are enthusiastic, spirited, vivacious, and zestful; they call attention to themselves. They are impetuous, uninhibited, unrestrained, are not consistent,*

> *predictable, or steady. They don't take pride in being rational or objective.*

The presidential "dominators" include Lyndon Johnson, Richard Nixon, Andrew Johnson, Andrew Jackson, James Polk, and Chester Arthur.

> *They are prone to bully others and to disregard the feelings and rights of those not on their side. They are bossy, demanding, and domineering; they flatter or manipulate people to get their way. They bend or break rules, and as presidents, stretch the constraints of constitutional government. They are not religious or spiritual, and tend to be prejudiced.*

William Howard Taft is grouped with Warren Harding and U.S. Grant in the category of presidential "Innocents."

> *Submissive and accept domination easily gullible, naive, suggestible. Not autonomous, independent or individualistic, they sometimes don't assert themselves when they should. Compared to other presidents (who are an industrious lot), they have trouble getting motivated and down to work, and are lethargic, sluggish, lazy, and slothful.*

In the tantrum episode, we see Roosevelt's personal demons became the demons of his politics. The tight control he held over his own urges became the tight control America held over its collective urges. "Real virtue requires enemies," wrote early psychologist (and eugenicist) G. Stanley Hall, and in striking down these armed black men, these new members of the imperial forces, these former slaves, Roosevelt was striking a blow for civilization. This was the very treachery from within that the white man so feared. The Brownsville tantrum erupted in some part because it was part of a combat tableau, a desperate, daily struggle, which Theodore Roosevelt fought in his imagination. His inner landscape was a battlefield in which virile American white men fought off the pernicious elements of modern life that threatened civilization – foreign cultures, moneyed Jews, dangerous women, wild Indians, and defiant Negroes.

Today, Theodore Roosevelt would no doubt be diagnosed as a narcissistic personality. The narcissistic personality disorder displays "an all-pervasive pattern of grandiosity ... need for admiration or adulation and lack of empathy, usually beginning with early adulthood and present in various contexts," as described in *The Diagnostic and Statistics Manual*,[12] the narcissist is "firmly convinced that he or she is unique" and "feels entitled ... expects unreasonable or special and favorable priority treatment. Demands automatic and full compliance with his or her expectations."

It would not be too farfetched to connect the onset of this disorder to his childhood moment of reckoning. "A person undergoing a ... crisis brought on by an insurmountable obstacle will ... revert to excessive and compulsive behavior patterns." Psychological theory also indicates that the mother is a key figure in the development of the trait. "If the mother does not 'let go' – the child will not go. If the mother herself is the dependent,

Narcissistic type – the growth prospects of the child are, indeed, dim," writes psychologist Sam Varnick. The narcissist has a black-and-white view of all things. "Narcissism is fundamentally an advanced version of the splitting defense mechanism. The Narcissist cannot regard humans, situations, entities (political parties, countries, races, his workplace) as a compound of good and bad elements. He is an "all or nothing" primitive "machine" (a common self-metaphor among narcissists). He either idealizes his object – or devalues it."

Here is Roosevelt's fantasy world, richly charged and brilliantly articulated as perhaps only a severely disordered mind could do:

> *Often the white man and red fought one another whenever they met, and displayed in their conflicts all the cunning and merciless ferocity that made forest warfare so dreadful. Terrible deeds of prowess were done by the mighty men on either side. It was a war of stealth and cruelty, and ceaseless, sleepless watchfulness. The contestants had sinewy frames and iron wills, keen eyes and steady hands, hearts as bold as they were ruthless ... The dark woods saw a myriad lonely fights where red warrior or white hunter fell and no friend of the fallen ever knew his fate, where his memorial was the scalp that hung in the smoky cabin or squalid wigwam of the victor.*[13]

Roosevelt's narcissistic fantasy universe, with its "terrible deeds of prowess" and "men of sinewy frames" and "dark woods" is perhaps one of the most successful narcissistic creations of all time. All of us – from poor Taft, sitting in his office listening to TR urge him to spear Foraker, to the current editors at *Time* magazine – have bought into it.

A 1999 study by Elmes and Barry of narcissism and its contribution in the May 1996 article "Everest Climbing Disaster" distinguishes between healthy ("high self-esteem based on predominantly ... pleasurable self-representation linkages") and unhealthy ("self-centeredness ... utilized as a defense against underlying unpleasurable linkages") narcissism, and certainly Roosevelt can be seen in the former category. Sarah Watts makes no such distinction in her book *Rough Rider*, citing Roosevelt's girly childhood as the direct motivation for his re-invention of himself as a warrior and frontiersman. Elmes and Barry also refer to "the so-called 'narcissistic vulnerability,' the tendency to register with oversensitive antennae the least sign of challenge ..." and "a tendency towards uncontrolled rage when feeling slighted," descriptions which sound at least a little like Roosevelt's reaction towards the "conspiracy of silence" by the black troops as well as his savage response to Foraker the night of the Gridiron Club dinner. It was not just that Roosevelt was angry at his opponents, but that he felt they had no right to their opinion: he did not want to disagree with them, he wanted to destroy them (which he did).

A 2006 book called *The Productive Narcissist* demonstrates that the narcissistic personality can also account for innovative leadership, and certainly that might apply to Roosevelt. Author and anthropologist Michael Maccoby replaces the negative stereotype with the depiction of bureaucracy-shattering innovators

# Teddy's Tantrum

who, through strategic intelligence, are capable of visionary leadership in times of rapid economic and social change. Narcissists experience a fragmented reality, even as they attempt to create one.

There was a larger context to the Foraker – Roosevelt fight over Brownsville. The two men had opposed one another over anti-trust legislation and the Cuba intervention. Political rivalry was also at stake, with each positioning himself for the 1908 Republican convention. A number of Roosevelt biographers attribute Foraker's involvement in the Brownsville Affray almost entirely to his desire to oppose Roosevelt. If Foraker could embarrass Roosevelt on Brownsville or any other matter, it would lessen Roosevelt's power to name his own successor, and clear the way for Foraker to run for the presidency. "There is more in this contest than a mere discussion of the Brownsville incident," wrote the Washington *Post*. "A far greater stake is being played. Should an investigation by the Senate show that a grave injustice has been done the members of this battalion, the outcome would lessen the great prestige the President now has before the country, and would necessarily cause Senator Foraker to loom as a much greater political factor politically than he is today."

If the initial discharge of the soldiers can be seen as a sort of temper tantrum, the ensuing vendetta cannot. This was a coolly calculated war to destroy lives and reputations, and keep them destroyed, never letting his foot off the opponents' neck. The persecution of the black troops can also be seen as part of Roosevelt's campaign against the enemies of civilization in general. Greed, soft character, low birth rates, Africa, Jews, unmanly conduct, negroes, salacious women and their depictions, oil monopolies, Irishmen, reporters, encroaching modernity, railroad monopolies, corruption, lesser races of all kinds – it was a constant battle, on all fronts. It is the source of his great energy and certainly the source of his great accomplishments. It is the myth or the story of his life, and provides his reason for fighting so hard through a life beset with the deepest conceivable heartbreak. These same convictions caused him to build the Panama Canal, and trot the French Ambassador into rags; they propelled him to treat humble visitors as he would royalty, it motivated him to fight corruption as Police Commissioner, as Governor, and as President; and it caused him dismiss 167 fellow soldiers against whom he could not produce any credible evidence.

Theodore Roosevelt's moment of reckoning had come early in his life, sometime in 1872[14] He was "a slender, pale-haired boy, costumed in infant dress," when chronic asthma brought his delicate health to the brink. "Nothing seemed to relieve him from its strangling grip."[15] A neurologist diagnosed Theodore as suffering from "the handicap of riches ... excessive upper-class refinement."[16] This "wretchedness of extreme civilization" was brought about by the advances of modern life. Theodore's father confronted him. He had to make a decision: either cast off his invalidism, or he would succumb to the world's corruption. "Sickness is always a shame, and often a sin," the father warned the 14-year-old boy. "Theodore, you have the mind but you have not the body." He demanded that his son make himself strong by force of will. From that point, Theodore began to transform himself, both in body and in identity, from a "nervous and timid child" and "foreordained and predestined victim" into a mighty man of valor.[17]

As an adult, Theodore Roosevelt played a game with his children, and with any visitor unfortunate to be present at the game's inception: they would advance in a straight line until it pleased the President to stop. They would never stop for any obstacle, or go around it: they would climb over or through it by whatever means possible; if it was a stream they must ford it; if it was a log cabin, they must climb up the walls and scale the roof and down the other side; if it was a canyon, they must descend it and then mount the other side; if it was a wall of thorny shrubs they must break through it, suffering what punishment they might need to endure for their boldness. "Following neither road nor path, always on, on, straight ahead!" as the French Ambassador described it.

Senator Joseph Foraker, while an excellent lawyer and a more than competent politician, was perhaps not fully mindful of the deeper meaning in this game. Roosevelt did not relent in the matter of the Brownsville soldiers, not in the episode's immediate and unpleasant aftermath; not while the withering rhetoric of the black and northern press rained down; not during the extended Congressional hearings, when the flimsy evidence was shredded by Foraker; not when dismissed soldiers like Mingo Sanders came to the nation's capital to beg for reinstatement, or at least an honorable discharge so they could find employment; not when he had left office and embraced more progressive policies; not on his deathbed; not ever.

CHAPTER 20

# Imperial Grunts

> The great error of nearly all studies of war ... has been to consider war as an episode in foreign policies, when it is an act of interior politics.
>
> -- *Simone Weil*

MASTER HISTORIAN NIALL FERGUSON ATTRIBUTES the violence which dominated the 20th century to four root causes: the rise of Eastern empires; the fall of eleven Western empires; economic volatility in the wake of the fallen Western empires; and ethnic conflict. In four remarkable books -- *Colossus: The Price of America's Empire, Empire: The Rise and Demise of the British Empire, The Pity of War: Explaining World War I*, and *The War of the World: Twentieth-Century Conflict and the Descent of the West* – he sets out a comprehensive design that asserts empires as the grand engines of world history. To misunderstand them and the common elements which cause their rising and falling, he warns, allows terrible savagery to accompany even the greatest progress, as it did in the 20th Century.

In this excerpt, Ferguson compares the modern American empire which Roosevelt helped shape to others:

# Teddy's Tantrum

> *Like the ancient Egyptian, [the American Empire] erects towering edifices in its heartland, though these house the living rather than the dead. Like the Athenian Empire, it ahs proved itself adept at leading alliances against a rival power. Like the empire of Alexander, it has a staggering geographical range. Like the Chinese Empire that arose in the Ch'in era and reached its zenith under the Ming dynasty, it has united the lands and peoples of a vast territory and forged them into a true nation-state. Like the Roman Empire, it has a system of citizenship that is remarkably open; Purple Hearts and U.S. citizenship were conferred simultaneously on a number of the soldiers serving in Iraq last year, just as service in the legions was once a route to becoming a civus romanus.[1]*

In this excerpt from *Colossus*, Professor Ferguson identifies one method which presidents like Roosevelt used to circumvent the constitution's limits on acquiring new territories:

> *Actual annexation of territory beyond the shores of the continent was another matter. Was it even constitutional? Chief Justice Roger Brooke Taney's opinion in the notorious Dred Scott decision (1857) stated that there was "certainly no power given by the Constitution to the Federal Government to establish or maintain colonies bordering on the United States or at a distance, to be ruled*

*and governed at its own pleasure; nor to enlarge its territorial limits in any way, except by admission of new States." This seemed to make it plain that there could be no colonies or other forms of dependent territories, only new states...Thirty years later, however, A. Lawrence Lowell could argue quite differently. "Possessions may also be so acquired," he wrote in the* Harvard Law Review, *"as not to form part of the United States, and in that case constitutional limitations such as those requiring uniformity of taxation and trial by jury, do not apply."*[2]

Roosevelt saw the modern age coming, and did everything it his power to station himself, America, and the English-speaking white race at its fulcrum. His involvement in the cessation of the Russo-Japanese War was, in Ferguson's context, the management of a peaceful change in world order: the rise of an eastern power at the expense of a declining western power. Roosevelt's desire to balance world order in the turbulent rise and fall of empires explains all his priorities: the Panama Canal, the building of which "affected the lives of tens of thousands of people at every level of society and virtually every race and nationality. Great reputations were made and destroyed...";[3] his courting of J.P. Morgan and his Wall Street chieftains, who provided the capital for expansion and economic stability (if not prosperity) for the workers; even the Perdicaris incident. "These two events," writes Dennett, referring to the Moroccan crisis and the Russo-Japanese conflict, "were integral parts of world politics, which already enfolded the malodorous embryo of what became ten years later the world's pestilence," by which he means World War I. Roosevelt felt war on the scale of Armageddon scale was imminent, if any one or two elements fell out of balance, and he was not far wrong. World War I broke out les than a decade after Roosevelt left office: it was warfare merged with modern technology, and brought death on a scale never seen before.

In the brutal, piston-driven world of upheaval which Ferguson imagines, we can see that the men of the 25th Infantry were caught up in the machinery of empire, and that they were neither the first nor the last troops to be so caught up. While local racial bigotry was a proximate cause of their treatment, the Panama Canal was a distant cause; the push to take a place on the world's stage, and the unseen forces of economic growth were bundled together in Roosevelt's impatient drive. Where McKinley was catching up to events, Roosevelt was racing towards a very specific vision of the future, and made use of events as they arose. From another angle, Roosevelt seemed to see this same, Ferguson-style era of upheaval coming just over the horizon, a violent modern century of toppling and rising empires, and he constantly expressed urgency to his fellow citizens. That urgency contributed to Roosevelt's short temper in the Fall of 1906.

The men of the 25th Infantry were what author Robert Kaplan calls "Imperial Grunts." In his 2003 book by that name, Kaplan documents the gap between our mainland nation and the caste of working-class men and women who live on the frontiers of the

## Imperial Grunts

American interests, in borderlands from Zamboanga to Alaska to Firebase Gardez, in southern Afghanistan, a mud-walled fort over which fly the flags of the United States, Texas and the Florida Gators. Kaplan's writings remind us that the men of the 25th Infantry are part of a large, historical brotherhood of loyal troops facing adversity in isolated borderlands. "Welcome to Injun Country" is the catchphrase Kaplan hears from all the U.S. soldiers, marines, airmen, and sailors he meets, a phrase which must have been familiar to Burt Conyers and Mingo Sanders a century ago.

Another contemporary writer whose work casts light on the Brownsville saga is the late literary critic Edward Said. Published in 1972, almost concurrent with *The Brownsville Raid*, Edward Said's slim book *Orientalism* introduced an influential theory of literature based on the idea that a dominant culture captures and dominates its conquered cultures in its language and images. As Europe conquers foreign lands, so does the West capture the East (the East, or the "Orient" in this case includes all Asian and African cultures) in its language, portraying it in terms the Western mind finds acceptable. The building of empire requires the subjugation of the defeated as well as the depiction of an identity among the conquerors. To truly "conquer" a people, the imperialist has to understand it, and Said finds that 19th century colonial culture conquered but did not absorb certain subcultures. "The Other" is his term for the un-understood, conquered culture. Novelists like Toni Morrison relate this directly to black America, a people and a culture which has been conquered but never properly absorbed.

Here is the crux of the matter, as outlined by Edward Said in his Introduction to *Orientalism:*

> *The French and British ... have had a long tradition of what I shall be calling Orientalism, a way of coming to terms with the Orient that is based on the Orient's special place in European Western Experience. The Orient is not only adjacent to Europe; it is also the place of Europe's greatest and richest and oldest colonies, the source of its civilizations and languages, its cultural contestant, and one of its deepest and most recurring images of the Other ... The Orient has helped to define Europe (or the West) as its contrasting image, idea, personality, experience.*[4]

In this excerpt, Said describes a specific encounter which describes the larger relationship between Oriental culture and its Western interpreters:

> *Flaubert's encounter with an Egyptian courtesan produced a widely influential model of the Oriental woman; she never spoke of herself, never represented her emotions, presence, or history. He spoke for and represented her.*[5]

Because the French writer was wealthy, and from the West, and male, he was able to "speak for her and tell his readers in what way she was 'typically Oriental.'"[6]

# Imperial Grunts

The Egyptian woman had no access to Western readers. She could not define herself or explain that she was not merely a mysterious courtesan but also someone's daughter, or a musician, or a good horseback rider, or anything else.

While the main battle in imperialism is over land, a second battle is waged over narrative. Narrative, writes Said, is not only the instrument by which explorers and novelists capture "the strange regions of the world," but also the weapon which allows the colonized tribes to fight back.

> *The power to narrate, or to block other narratives from forming and emerging, is very important to culture and imperialism ...The grand narrations of emancipation and enlightenment mobilized people in the colonial world to rise up and throw off imperial subjection ... "*[7]

In the framework of our story, Edward Said would certainly welcome Haroun Al-Roosevelt's attentions to the Other, while calling our attention to the inaccuracies and stereotypes of which it consists. America's identity, like that of any empire, has been formed largely in opposition to this alternate identity. In its poetry and stories, Said suggests, the dominant western order seeks to subjugate and devour the Oriental (by 'Oriental,' Said includes Asian, African, Arabic and perhaps all non-English-speaking peoples). What you see in Coleridge's poem *Kubla Khan* and Shelley's *Alastor* is a clash of philosophical orders, Western logic and Puritan restraint versus Oriental paganism and unleashed sensuality. When Keats mentions Ozymandias, he means to summon all those rival empires which have ever encroached on England's; when Blake mentions Bedouins, he is conjuring a darkly mysterious, unknowable anti-Christian world order that he wants to understand, to see what it's made of and where it fits in his universe. Said looked at Shakespeare's Othello as representative of a cultural domination. What Iago did to Othello, England did to Africa: Iago imposed an Occidental (that is, Western) way of thinking on the Moor, a set of logic and symbols that worked against his natural instincts. His thinking clouded by European logic, Othello assigns the wrong meaning to the signs around him and comes to doubt and then murder his loving wife, Desdemona.

What is Said's message for us? What would Said tell us about the story of the Brownsville dismissal, which went underground for sixty years and then re-surfaced?

Edward Said would surely hold that the exoticism of the black warrior threatened first the townspeople of Brownsville and, second, the fragile identity of turn-of-the-century America.

A Saidian might say that the idea of Otherness lies at the heart of the Brownsville episode: Americans are rational and temperate, but Negroes are irrational and given to savage outbursts. Roosevelt struck down the avatars of a dark army of Others, and in doing so affirmed the foundations of Western civilization. No figure stands at the juncture of the two cultures so prominently as Teddy Roosevelt. He is the poster boy for Orientalism, and his political and literary careers owe much to his forceful opinions about "the general smash-up of civilization." He vilified the loyal men of the

25th Infantry in part because they had reached the highest rung of the Other ladder.

Edward Said might also point out that John Weaver was white. John Weaver had a Park Avenue literary agent (the Harold Ober Agency). Weaver was a member of the literary class, that section of society with access to the written word, and with the access to change the record. James Tinsley, the graduate student who wrote a scholarly piece on Brownsville in 1943, was no less aware of the truth about Brownsville, but he was much further from the offices of William Morrow than was Weaver.

*The Brownsville Raid* and *The Senator and the Sharecropper's Son* seem to be out-of-the-ordinary but authentic examples of literature about the discourse between East and West, literature produced by a highly charged social and political context. (They are out of the ordinary because most literary theory is applied to literary works, not historical.) *The Brownsville Raid* is rich in underlying imagery, and its events act out both Roosevelt's and America's inner emotional struggles – very much the product of a disturbed social world. The men of the 25th did not have "the power to narrate," and their nemesis Roosevelt had the overwhelming skills to tell his own story, and in so doing to block theirs from emerging; John Weaver's narrative power was somewhere between the two, and if the story he tells is not "a grand narration of emancipation and enlightenment," then it is certainly an intricate and resonant passage within the grand American narration.

## CHAPTER 21

# Tribal Loyalties

> All the great masterful races have been fighting races, and the minute that a race loses the hard fighting virtues it has lost its proud right to stand as the equal to the best.
>
> -- *Theodore Roosevelt*

THEODORE ROOSEVELT SOUGHT THROUGH BREEDING and vigorous exercise to build up the white race. But it was not for any kind of exultation, rather for the comprehensive and deadly serious task of saving the rest of civilization. "If we refrain from doing our part of the world's work," wrote Roosevelt, other races will not, and "we will have shown ourselves to be weaklings." Roosevelt held the "dream of war as the crucible for forging a superior white race."[1]

History had shown Roosevelt that superior races had a responsibility to civilize the barbaric races, bring benefits to the conquered tribes, and guard against their own descent into weakness and decadence. The penalties for breaking this third rule were harsh: the Romans, for example, had gone soft, and been conquered by the Teutons, a race Roosevelt greatly admired. "These Teutons possessed the intelligence, the independence, the love of liberty and order, and the intense tribal loyalty (patriotism) necessary to push civilization forward."[2]

In his balanced 1980 study, *Theodore Roosevelt and the Idea of Race*, Thomas Dyer considers the "complexity and variety" of Roosevelt's racial views, and looks squarely at the question of how those views affected his policies. Was Roosevelt a racist? Scholars, writes Dyer, disagree. "Because Roosevelt used the term race and nation interchangeably," writes one of TR's biographers, William Harbaugh, "many of his harsh judgments about ethnic groups have been incorrectly characterized as racist." Dyer cites a sociologist, Pierre van den Berghe, as an example of the contrary view: "Western racism had its poets like Kipling, its philosophers like Gobineau and Chamberlain, its statesmen like Hitler, Theodore Roosevelt, and Verwoerd."

Theodore Roosevelt's views on race are, Dyer holds, an important topic for us to understand. That TR was "the most effective racial educator" of his times. "Roosevelt said and wrote much about racial theory and racial beliefs that helped to set the tone for the American understanding of the concept."[3]

He is careful to set Roosevelt in the context of his times. "In the intellectual ambience of the late nineteenth century, it would have been remarkable if any individual with Roosevelt's interests and inclinations had not developed a fondness for the discussion of race and race theory."[4] Dyer picks apart Roosevelt's childhood and education to trace the antecedents of specific ideas such as evolution, race suicide, and phrenology. Dyer also notes that Roosevelt's theories as well as his uses of the term "race" change over the course of his lifetime. Roosevelt used the term "race" in five ways: as a broad designation when discussing any human group; as a national label; as a language-based grouping; as a color-based grouping; and as "representing the principle ethnic divisions of mankind." While he rarely used racial epithets in public, he "seemed to derive considerable pleasure from the frequent private use ... He used a variety of terms with respect to blacks ... 'colored people,' 'mulattoes,' 'darkeys,' and on rare occasions 'quadroons' and 'octoroons.'"

As the part represents the whole, the Raid might be considered to be a milder part of the larger wave of racial violence and lynchings going on in this same period. If the Brownsville Raid has taken us a century to process, the Atlanta Riots may take two. This episode dwarfs the Raid – none of the 25th Infantry were lynched -- and is apparently too ghastly to be remembered at all. Mark Bauerlein's outstanding 2001 book on the riots, *Negrophobia*, gives an hour-by-hour playing out of the riots, which were more like lynchings than riots. For our purposes, the Atlanta riots of September, 1906 clearly delineate a sort of "third rail," an electrifying picture of what could have happened the night of August 13, 1906 in Texas had Mayor Ray Combe not have been so diligent in heading off confrontation, and had the black men in question not been heavily armed and well-organized. The Atlanta Riots also remove any curse that might linger over Texas from the Brownsville incident, demonstrating that violent racism was a condition across the American South, if not the American landscape as a whole.

## CHAPTER 22

# A Twitch on the Right Side

> John D. Weaver is an author known to his friends as a fanatical stickler for accurate details. Because of this, 167 black soldiers stand exonerated of a crime that had tarnished their names for 66 years.
>
> -- *Book review of The Brownsville Raid*

A DOCTOR IN ENGLAND JUST after World War I could not figure out why his patient kept twitching on his right side. He had examined the young man, a veteran of the war, over and over, and had found nothing that could explain the severe facial twitch, so pronounced that it prevented the patient from holding a job. He also experienced loss of memory, and a fractured sense of time. There was no damage to his torso or head, no lingering wound, no medical reason for these chronic symptoms.

Over long interviews with his patient, the doctor discovered that, during a horrific battle, the young soldier's best friend had been killed. The friend's face had been blown apart. The friend had been stationed on the patient's right side in the trenches.

Unable to process or absorb the shock of his friend's killing, the patient had suppressed the memory. It was too much for him to comprehend, so his mind buried it in the dungeons of memory. Yet the trauma (from the Greek word for "wound") was so vivid that it would not stay buried. This explosive memory forced itself into the patient's life through the unconscious and destructive act of repetitive twitching, a sort of dumb beacon to the existence of an unremembered horror. The doctor gradually retrieved the memory. The act of bringing the past trauma into the light helped purge the patient of his symptoms. As the memory returned, the twitch disappeared.

Since that landmark case, trauma has become increasingly useful as an explanatory model for human behavior. Theorizations of trauma have spread far beyond the fields of medicine and psychology into sociology and even into literature. "Literature of trauma" looks at literature which retrieves social or common wounds, events which were so profoundly disturbing that we collectively repressed them, pretending they didn't happen. We buried their memory. Yet, like the young British patient, we experience symptoms of pain and fragmentation as the memories refuse to stay buried. "Gradually, in a variety of ways, the trauma returns. We re-experience or reenact the traumatic event in dreams or in compulsive, repetitive actions. These symptomatic returns -- what psychologists call 'the acting out of trauma' - show that a person still is psychically immersed in the trauma."[1] Telling stories is a way for us to retrieve the traumas from our memory

## A Twitch on the Right Side

and assimilate the experience, whether the stories are in the form of novels, jokes, movies, histories, poems, plays, or folktales.

Under this model, a culture needs a witness figure to do its remembering – a witness who can bring the uncomfortable memories to the surface. Just as a random event will bring an individual's memory back (when he or she is ready to remember it), so does a witness jog our collective memory. Without this remembering process, the violent memory remains suppressed in the social body, where it acts as a sort of cancer. Toni Morrison is such a "witness" author: her novels *Beloved* and *Song of Solomon* are much-studied examples of how trauma literature has helped us deal with the "ghosts," or unresolved memories, of slavery. Holocaust survivor Elie Wiesel is another such author, as is the Russian moralist Alexander Solzhenitsyn. A recent study of trauma in literature deals with the recent swell in Germany of remembering of World War II, a public effort to come to terms with that traumatic period of history. Susanne Vees-Gulani's 2003 book *Trauma and Guilt: Literature of Wartime Bombing in Germany* is a study which seeks to reconcile issues of German aggression and German victim-hood which have been long been avoided.

The trauma field of literary theory has produced some of the most tortuous writing in the English language. Here is one small example:

> **Beloved** *does not recall the past as past and bring the past and the future into a continuous relation without always repeating the past and instating unpleasure together*

> with pleasure. Pleasure's unpleasure, if
> you will.²

Cornell University's Dominick LaCapra is a leading scholar in the trauma field, and a rare advocate for clear writing. In his 2001 book, *Writing History, Writing Trauma,* LaCapra identifies certain narratives which allow us to re-experience collective trauma, books like Elie Weisel's *Night* and Alexander Solzhenitsyn's *The Gulag Archipelago,* as invaluable to the common good. LaCapra suggests that the process of inquiry itself has value, as research leads the "inquirer" to find different aspects of past events, and to take new attitudes towards them. Every inquirer, he writes, brings a fresh perspective to the search, and develops new positions in representing figures and events of the past. "In discussing the Holocaust, for example, it makes a difference … whether the historian is a survivor, the child of survivors, a Jew, a Palestinian, a German, a child of perpetrators …"³

In the traumatic scenario as applied the Brownsville Raid saga, John Weaver is the fulcrum. He is the witness figure, a watcher, a storyteller who reminds his tribe of its history. LaCapra might point out that Weaver is connected to the original trauma through his father, who was a clerk at the original trial. It was John Weaver who gave shape and continuity to the overall story of the Brownsville Raid. While his attempt to present the "whodunit" aspect of that fateful night as a detective story ultimately fails, for lack of a clear resolution, his overall story, incorporating Roosevelt and Foraker, holds up well. And it is Weaver himself who plays the final part in the Brownsville drama: by instigating

# A Twitch on the Right Side

the small, mostly unnoticed 1972 apology ceremony, Weaver himself brought about what trauma scholars call the resolution phase, where the trauma is dredged up from the unconscious to the conscious mind permitting us to stop repeating it. If he is not the most skilled of writers,[4] he is among the most tenacious. Yet his quiet zeal and implacable hunt for accuracy retold the true story of the Brownsville Raid clearly and correctly. It is Weaver who narrativizes this fragmented tale, pulling the disparate, disjointed and distorted pieces together. He took the time to go through the Congressional record. He took the trouble to travel to Texas and stand in the alleyways. He found copies of fifty-year-old newspapers in small towns in Georgia and Nebraska. It is his act of telling the story that gives it meaning. Perhaps the incident's final and greatest meaning has come through John's own detective work.

In tracking down the original story, Weaver is demonstrating the American method of resolution: this is how we work through psychological knots, with patience, hard work, logical argument, passionate commitment, simmering outrage, and a little sarcasm. Weaver, the former *Kansas City Star* journalist, displays a reporter's ability to track down disparate sources and present them as parts of an integrated whole. "The trauma of racism is, for the racist and the victim, the severe fragmentation of the self …" writes trauma scholar Njabulo Ndebele.[5] Ndebele points out the importance of "the restoration of the narrative. In few countries do we have a living example of people's reinventing themselves through narrative." Weaver is one of the few: he restored an entire episode, once repressed, to the national "self." The fact that only he and a handful of colleagues seemed to be the only ones aware of this act greatly frustrated him. The same forces that "buried" the story of the 25th Infantry for so long have kept it at the margins of American history, not "in the textbooks," as Weaver hoped. It was always a bad story – it had no satisfactory ending, justice was not done, and it made a villain out of one of our most cherished and popular leaders. Weaver's difficulty in dislodging the official version stems from his doing battle with two hugely powerful foes: the myth of "TR"; and our idea of ourselves.

# EPILOGUE

# Centennial

> Eventually, when our textbooks have been written to reflect the black experience, schoolchildren will be as familiar with Brownsville as with San Juan Hill, and when that day comes, they will want to know, "How did the story come out in the end?"
>
> -- John D. Weaver in a letter to Gus Hawkins,<br>April 10, 1971

ONE DAY IN 1973, A woman walking on a hillside stopped to read the lettering on a stone marker by the side of the path. It read:

> "John Fox, U.S. Army Lieutenant,
> Dec. 26, 1944"

The path was on a very step hill, in the Serchio valley in northern Italy.

The woman was an American, a San Francisco landscape artist named Solace Wales. She and her husband, Bill Sheets, had bought a house in the tiny village of Sommocolonia for the spectacular views.

She did not know any American solders had served there. She asked a neighbor about the stone marker. The neighbor explained that John Fox was one of a squadron of black Americans who had bravely defended the village against the Germans in World War II. "They almost all died …"

Solace Wales Sheets looked into it. She interviewed other villagers who remembered the black soldiers. She tape-recorded their interviews. She uncovered the story of John Fox, the forward scout who had called artillery down on his own position in order to destroy the enemy. She could not understand why no one had ever heard of this.

Two decades later, in July of 2000, Lieutenant John Fox's sisters, daughter, son, and grandchildren made the trip from America to Sommocolonia to join Solace Wales Sheets and the Italian villagers to honor John Fox and the men of the 92$^{nd}$ Infantry.

"Lieutenant Fox's gallant and courageous actions," reads his Medal of Honor citation, "at the supreme sacrifice of his own life, contributed greatly to delaying the enemy advance until other infantry and artillery units could reorganize to repel the attack. His extraordinary valorous actions were in keeping with the most cherished traditions of military service, and reflect the utmost credit on him, his unit, and the United States Army."

On July 13, 2000, the *San Francisco Chronicle* ran a long article on the ceremony. Here is part of the article:

### Almost-Forgotten Heroes

**Italian town honors black GIs who were shunned by their own country**

Frank Viviano, Chronicle Staff Writer

# Centennial

**(07-13) 04:00 PST Sommocolonia, Italy**
*-- When a massive German assault was launched on this windswept mountain village in December 1944, a scant two platoons of American infantrymen were dug in here. Their own commanding officers expected them to throw down their guns and run.*

*But for 20 critical hours, the tiny complement of 70 GIs -- all of them black, from the U.S. Army's segregated 92nd Infantry Division -- held out against an offensive that might have changed the course of World War II.*

*Then they vanished, almost completely, from the war's official records.*

*It has taken five decades of stubborn efforts by the battle's few survivors, and 20 years of research by a Bay Area woman who accidentally stumbled onto their tale, to fill in the empty page in that history.*

*On Sunday, they will reassemble in Sommocolonia, northwest of Florence, to dedicate a "peace park" to the memory of their lost comrades in the presence of U.S. diplomats and Italian dignitaries.*

*Put bluntly, the park is also a monument to American racial bigotry at a moment when the U.S. Army was waging war against Adolf Hitler's racist ideology and dreams of world domination.*

### Black and Not Fully Soldiers

*A mile to the north of Sommocolonia was the forward encampment of the German 14th Army, which had been instructed not to take prisoners from the 92nd Division because its soldiers were black -- and, by official Nazi standards, not fully human.*

*Six miles to the south was the command post of the American Fifth Army, which refused to provide either reinforcements for the besieged troops in Sommocolonia or blood transfusions for their wounded. They were black, and by official U.S. Army standards in World War II, not fully soldiers.*

*"In those days, if you were not white, you had to fight on two fronts at once," says former Maj. Otis Zachary of Carson (Los Angeles County) a veteran of the battle. "One against the Nazis, and another against the mentality of your own superiors."*

*One black veteran of World War II combat operations in Italy welcomed the U.S. government's belated recognition of the "Buffalo Soldiers" -- the name given to the all-black 92nd Infantry Division.*

*"Anything that honors black American soldiers in Italy is important," said former Capt. Harry Cox of Mill Valley, who served with the 92nd.*

# Centennial

**January, 2003**

"Looks like war," said President George W. Bush to his Secretary of State, Colin Powell.

It was felt in January of 2003 that "the powers that border the Persian Gulf, Persia itself, Turkey, and some minor Arabian communities, are unable to give either the commercial or the military security that the situation will require."

So America intervened.

The two men whose decision it was to go to war in the Persian Gulf were seated in the Oval Office, four months after the 9/11 attack on the World Trade Center and the Pentagon had left almost three thousand Americans dead. The Iraqi tyrant Saddam Hussein was stockpiling weapons, possibly biological weapons, possibly even nuclear weapons.

The President knew that Powell did not want to go to war.

"Are you aware of the consequences?" the Secretary of State asked the President. His tone was chilly.[1]

This was far from an idle question. Ever since the 9/11 attack, Powell had been advising that the President make full use of all diplomatic channels before deciding on a military approach to the problem – a somewhat ironic position, since Powell was one of the few among the President and his close advisors who had served in combat. The State Department had done extensive studies showing that toppling the Iraqi dictator would lead to a host of complex nation-building challenges requiring an enormous, multi-year investment of time, money and manpower.

But among the President's top advisors, Powell was the odd man out. Vice President Dick Cheney and Secretary of Defense Donald Rumsfeld were determined to press forward with a bold plan to create a new democracy in the region Alfred Mahan had called the Middle East. Powell's position had lost ground as the correspondence of nations foundered.

The decision to go to war had been made several days earlier, without Powell's direct involvement. Two days prior to this meeting, Cheney and Rumsfeld had called in a key ally, Saudi Prince Bandar bin Sultan, to inform him of the plan for war.[2] "You know, you're going to be owning this place," said Powell, a brief statement that meant much, much more than it sounded like.

"I understand that," said the President.

"Will you be with me?" he asked.

"I'll do my best, Mr. President, I'll be with you."

It is important to note that Powell disavows this version of events, which is taken from Bob Woodward's 2004 book *Plan of Attack*. According to Powell, he had been briefed on a regular basis, and he has consistently underscored his support for Bush's actions.

In the months that followed that decision, the President's constitutional authorities were much debated. A Senate Republican would directly challenge President Bush's declaration that "I am the decision-maker" on issues of war. "I would suggest respectfully to the president that he is not the sole decider," Senator Arlen Specter, said during a 2006 hearing on Congress' war powers amid an increasingly harsh debate over

# Centennial

Iraq war policy. "The decider is a shared and joint responsibility," Specter said.

Sixty days after the conversation between the 43rd President and his Secretary of State, at the request of its country, the 10th Cavalry rode into the borderlands of the water has ever been there, or will ever come. This desolate section of the vast *Qal Gah Bekmhe* intershelf desert basin, land once conquered by Gilgamesh and the ancient armies of Babylon, seven hundred miles west of the Moroccan lands where the bandit *Mulai Ahmed el Raisuli* had kidnapped Ion Perdicaris a century earlier.

The cavalry's job is to lead the army into combat.

In March of 2003, the 1st Squadron, 10th Cavalry led the 4th Infantry Division north from Baghdad in support of Operation Iraqi Freedom.

The 1st Squadron crossed the border into Iraq in the early dawn hours of April 14, leading the 4th Infantry Division north from Kuwait.

When U.S. forces found 14 barrels of chemicals in a vast weapons storage area in north-central Iraq, it was the 10th Cavalry. Initial tests indicated that they contained a deadly mixture of cyclosarin nerve agent and mustard gas. The tan barrels were found in a three-square-mile storage area that also contained missiles, missile parts, gas masks, protective gear, a stripped mobile weapons laboratory and large storage containers covered by camouflage netting. The 10th Cavalry team used baling wire to remove a sample from one of the barrels.

In an interview with NBC News the following day, President Bush said that despite the lack of definitive evidence, he was convinced that Saddam Hussein did hide weapons of mass destruction.

The 1st Squadron led the 4th Division up Highway 1 through Baghdad, Taji, and on to Saddam Hussein's hometown of Tikrit, "destroying resistance from Iraqi forces. They secured and held multiple airfields and military complexes for later use by follow-on forces as far north as K2 Airfield near Bayji.

"In June, the Squadron conducted a grueling forced march of nearly 200 kilometers from K2 airfield to the Iran-Iraq border to stop Iranian infiltration into Iraq, demonstrating remarkable endurance. Cavalry troops occupied the border cities, destroying enemy resistance and conducted civil military operations, assuming responsibility for 336.5 km of the border, a Brigade sized area, with a third of the equipment and personnel. Over the next four months the Squadron stood up, trained, and equipped Iraq Border Police and other security forces, 1600 Iraqis in all. The 10th Cavalry troopers screened the inhospitable border region, providing medical care, food, and water to over 27,000 pilgrims in a massive humanitarian undertaking."[3] In October, the Squadron conducted air combat operations in support of divisional units during Operation Ivy Typhoon, patrolling Highway 1 from Taji to outside Tikrit.

The 1st Squadron, 10th Cavalry, was led by Lt. Col. Reginald Allen, the first African-American to command the 10th Cavalry in combat.

A CNN report from Tikrit under the headline "Buffalo Soldiers Serve Proudly in Iraq" reported in January, 2004, that

# Centennial

the 1st Squadron's job was to keep Iranian influences out of Iraq, guarding the "porous Iran-Iraq border."

"We go where we're told and we'll win when we fight," said Lt. Col. Allen.

About his predecessors, the men of the original Buffalo Soldiers, the young officer was quite clear. "The incredible thing about the Buffalo Soldiers, especially those who served early on, is that they loved this country enough that through the racism, through the bigotry, they still wanted to serve.

"They wanted to better themselves and serve the nation. They served with less than the best equipment and less than the best provisions at the farthest and most remote outposts in the United States. They served with pride and honor and professionalism. That is absolutely no different than what the Buffalo Soldiers today are doing "The squadron has a great history. It was formed as a Negro regiment in 1866 with white officers and I thought it would be kind of neat for a black officer to command that organization … It is a point of pride for me to be able to command [the 10th Cavalry]."[4]

## July 12, 2006

French President Jacques Chirac presided over a ceremony in the same cobblestone courtyard of L'Ecole Militaire where Captain Alfred Dreyfus had been stripped of his officer's rank.

Descendants of Captain Dreyfus and of the writer Emile Zola were present as Chirac spoke. In marking the anniversary of the

Dreyfus Affair, President Chirac warned that "the combat against the dark forces of intolerance and hate is never definitively won."[5]

## August 11, 2006

The flights to Brownsville depart from the old wing of the Houston airport. The air conditioning does not work so well here as it does in the ultra-modern United concourse next door.

I am waiting for the flight taking me to Brownsville to attend the Centennial celebration of the Brownsville Raid. A young black man, the same age John Hollomon was a century ago, mutters to himself as he walks down the broad empty airport corridor. Walking with command is difficult, since he is wearing blue jeans pulled down so low that his leg movements are constrained. The name "Ace Bang" decorates the jeans' back pocket. His light blue baseball cap is worn sideways across his head. He is part of a family of six, four girls, no father in attendance.

All of Theodore Roosevelt's worst fears about impending chaos and Armageddon were well-founded.

All hell did break loose.

The balance of power which preoccupied Roosevelt toppled. The new modern world he warned us about brought war and disease and depravity sweeping in successive waves across the world, even beyond Roosevelt's worst nightmares, starting in Turkey in 1904 and continuing to this writing. "The Twentieth Century is by a factor of over 100 the most murderous century in the history of mankind," writes Welsh historian Niall Ferguson in his 2006 book *The War of the World: Twentieth-Century Conflict*

# Centennial

*and the Descent of the West*. Ferguson details how, setting aside nuclear and high-technology weaponry, ethnic tribes of one kind or another have murdered other ethnic tribes all across Asia, Africa, Europe and the Americas with unprecedented savagery in the modern age. This ethnic unrest, he theorizes, is prone to break out during periods of economic volatility -- booms as well as busts. A contributing factor for Ferguson is the fall of empires, from the Ottoman to the French colonial, which have left vacuums often filled by volatility and violence.[6]

In the three decades since the publication of Weaver's *The Brownsville Raid*, a number of new perspectives have opened up on three questions: why did the Raid occur?; why did Roosevelt dismiss the soldiers before they had a fair trial?; and why did it take so long for the true story to be told? These ideas cast new light both on the original events and on Weaver's role in uncovering the full historical account.

Two scholars in particular, James Leiker of Kansas City and Garna L. Christian of Houston, have put forth a relativistic view of the social chaos that characterized the Rio Grande Valley in the years between the Civil War and World War I. Absorbing Weaver's correction of the record against the troops of the 25th, these historians have gone further, identifying multiple sources of the social dysfunction which gave rise to the shooting.

Leiker, in his 2002 book *Racial Borders: Black Soldiers Along the Rio Grande*, sets the Brownsville Raid in the context of a larger pattern of border conflicts. He points to "a blood feud" between black troops and Hispanic civilians in tows throughout the Rios grand Valley. "...An examination of Brownsville's many antecedents gives reason to challenge …the binary model of 'white and nonwhite …'"[7] In addition, he concludes that resentment against the military played a significant part of the incident. He writes that "race played a small role compared to the class stratification of lower valley society … Overall, the problems that black soldiers faced in Brownsville had less to do with regional racial mores, which can be characterized as "southern," than with the peculiarities of a militarized border area."[8] That is, it was the black men's uniforms more than it was the black men. He compares the Brownsville shooting to a similar incident in Rio Grande City. "By omitting the black-Hispanic relationship that had helped provoke the incident, national press coverage perpetuated ignorance of Brownsville's demography and culture."[9] Leiker urges historians to move beyond interpreting the affray "as another example of Jim Crow-style discrimination against African Americans, a testimony to the power of bipolar models."[10] Leiker goes on to directly criticize Weaver. "….In blaming 'white Texans' and white racism for the shooting, Weaver neglected to define just who, exactly, was 'white.' His writings refer often to the Mexican presence in Brownsville, but rather than analyze it as part of border culture, he categorized Hispanic participants as 'white' and 'southern' by virtue of their being 'nonblack' – an approach considered dubious by Chicano scholars."[11]

At a century's distance, it is clear that Theodore Roosevelt was a successful "triangulator." He showed one face to the Russians in public, and quite another in private, hoping to make progress by these two very different approaches. This served him well in the negotiations which ended the Russo-Japanese War. Roosevelt did the same with J.P. Morgan and the Rockefellers, alternately charming and derogatory, flattering and litigious. This served him and the country well: he moved the nation forward in breaking the monopolies and trusts, while still keeping Morgan "in the fold" as an unofficial Secretary of Treasury. Through the lawyer Cromwell, the President offered Morgan dramatic profits from the Panama Canal project, and Morgan in turn saved the country from financial crisis in late 1906.

These same tactics which served Roosevelt well in so many instances broke down in the Brownsville matter. He offered the men of the 25th Infantry only one face, or one side of the triangle.

J.P. Morgan's cameo appearances in the Brownsville narrative are not by accident. Roosevelt needed J.P. Morgan to build the Panama Canal. It is easy to see why, on the night at the Gridiron Dinner, Roosevelt started out with Morgan as the object of his wrath and then shifted his attention to Foraker. The hunter, Roosevelt, knew that the second prey had fewer resources to fight back. Roosevelt needed to curb the powers of the monopolies, and more importantly he needed to be seen as the enemy of the trusts -- yet he in no way envisioned America without them. To the contrary, he needed Morgan to help stabilize the economy, and to help build the Canal. Morgan would be rewarded for this understanding, and Rockefeller would be punished for his lack of understanding. "As Roosevelt turned the presidency into a ... broker between capital and labor, Morgan, unlike the more myopic Rockefeller, saw that Roosevelt stood ready to make concessions to cooperative businessmen."¹² The Panama Canal was just such a concession. "…Roosevelt treated the Morgan interests (U.S. Steel, International Harvester, et. al.) more leniently than he did Standard Oil."¹³

In the months and years that followed, Roosevelt rehashed his explanation of what had gone wrong in the Brownsville affair. "Owen Wister says Roosevelt admitted to him that at one point he had been badly advised by the War Department."¹⁴ "These revelations about Foraker are very ugly," Roosevelt confided to Henry Cabot Lodge in a letter of September 19, 1908. "They of course show what everyone on the inside knew, that Foraker was not really influenced in the least by any feeling for the Negro, but that he acted as the agent of the corporations. Of course this has been the real reason why he has fought us so bitterly …" In his reply, Cabot wondered if any one would "see what a cleverly managed and malicious fraud the Brownsville business was." Just before he left office, Roosevelt wrote to Senator Aldrich, "I have no question … that the bulk of Company B … are guilty to a degree that should rightly bar them from ever again reentering the American army. I am strongly inclined to believe, however, that the bulk of the members of Companies C and B had no such guilty knowledge."¹⁵

It should be no surprise to us that, in the decades after Roosevelt's presidency, we continue to discover the full range of the many actions he hid from view. As Edmund Morris comments, this was "… a commander in chief who accomplished much of his grand strategy in silence and secret."¹⁶ In Tyler Dennett's research into John Hays and the Perdicaris incident, in Weaver's

Brownsville book, in Espino's document of the Panama Canal machinations, in Edmund Morris' uncovering of the Venezuela treaty, we see more fully that Roosevelt's was an imperial presidency in two ways: that he acted above the law; and that he was building an empire. Just as building the Panama Canal and courting J.P. Morgan were key parts of that empire, so was the strict hand of punishment against insubordination in the imperial ranks (as it had been in past empires).

Roosevelt correctly pegged Congress as "indecisive and irresolute," and true to this characterization, the Senate and House did nothing but fume while he created the nation of Panama, built the Panama Canal, dismissed black troops, negotiated in secret wit foreign powers, and conducted all other manner of Presidential enterprise. The Brownsville matter followed the Panama blueprint: Foraker made excellent speeches in Congress while the President did as he pleased.

It is difficult at this distance to understand what Foraker was thinking. It seems that Foraker's mistake, or his missing ability, was in not measuring the room. Roosevelt certainly had done so. What was Foraker's plan? What did Julia Foraker, so shrewd in her memoirs, think would happen? Did she tell her husband to wait and hope that Roosevelt would simply change his mind? Did Foraker imagine that the rest of the Senate would suddenly come to their senses, or Taft? That black voters would throw all of Congress out of office on November 1?

Taft played a key part in the tantrum because he failed to stop it. Taft knew the President was wrong and told him so, in a telegram, quite clearly. Roosevelt rebuked him. Taft reconsidered. He tried only the one time, then stepped aside – actually, he did much more than step aside, he served as a willing accomplice in the attempt to hide the true facts of the case. So did his "co-workers," the men of the press, who knew as it was happening that Roosevelt was waging a concerted campaign to frame the black soldiers. "That was bully," Roosevelt told a cub reporter (Harold Howland) who had defended him in print. "You have done just what my cabinet members used to do for me in Washington. When a question arose that demanded action, I used to act. Then I would ask Root or Taft to find out and tell my why what I had done was legal and justified. Well done, co-worker."[17]

On board the plane for the short flight between Houston and Brownsville, I fold down the tray and set out the July 3 edition of *Time* magazine. It has Theodore Roosevelt on the cover. Inside is a collection of articles praising "Teddy the Great." Under a photo of Roosevelt posing beside a huge globe, the caption reads, "Roosevelt's energy and charm endeared him to the nation." It is still a good story, and still very much the story we want to hear about him, and about ourselves. The magazine text is varied, with nine authors and historians weighing in on various facets of Roosevelt the man, the president, and the legacy. The tone is largely adulatory:

> At home and abroad, Theodore Roosevelt was the locomotive President, the man who drew his flourishing nation into the future.

# Centennial

> *Presidents come and go, but monuments are always with us. There's a reason Theodore Roosevelt is the only 20th Century President whose face is carved in Mount Rushmore, the only one who could hold his own with Washington, Lincoln and Jefferson. Roosevelt not only remade America, but he also charmed the pants off everybody while he did it.*
>
> *He gave the nation a picture of itself as a place that could not fail to succeed, because it produced people who were vigorous and commanding – people like Teddy Roosevelt. It's not just that he was excited to be an American. He made it more exciting to be one.*

I look in vain for the Weaver paragraph, but there is no mention of Brownsville in the magazine. I find it in that night, prominent in the online version of the magazine, complete with display headline and a striking photo of the 25th Infantry posing in spiked helmets, white gloves and epaulettes, it is far more than a paragraph, and delivers almost all of Weaver's major points:

> *Five years [after Booker Washington's dinner at the White House], Roosevelt was involved in another racially charged incident, and in this one his behavior offered less to admire. On Aug. 13, 1906, a dozen or so gunmen went on a 10-minute shooting spree in the small town of Brownsville, Texas. They left a saloon bartender dead and a police officer seriously injured. Townspeople reported that*

*the attackers were soldiers from the all-black 25th Infantry Regiment, who had been stationed just a few weeks earlier at nearby Fort Brown. Tensions between the soldiers and the white citizenry had been brewing since the day the troops arrived.*

*An Army investigation eventually concluded that the soldiers were guilty. Townspeople produced shell casings, which they claimed to have found on the street, of the same kind used in the soldiers' new Springfield rifles. A number of eyewitnesses also claimed to have seen black soldiers in uniform on the streets during the shooting. But no evidence could link anyone to the incident, and subsequent investigations revealed the eyewitnesses to be unreliable—a nearly blind man claimed to have seen soldiers 150 ft. away on the moonless night—and heavily biased. "Citizens of Brownsville entertain race hatred to an extreme degree," said Major General F.C. Ainsworth, the Army commander in Texas at the time.*

*Even the investigators charged with looking into the matter were openly biased. When asked under oath, "Do you believe colored people, generally, are truthful?" Army Inspector General Ernest Garlington replied, "I do not." When no soldiers confessed, he called it a "conspiracy of silence." The President agreed, and with no trial ordered on Nov.*

*5 that 167 of the soldiers be discharged without honor, pension or benefits. "Some of those men were bloody butchers," he later remarked. "They ought to be hung."*

*Criticized as an "executive lynching," and a "despotic usurpation of power," the decision was widely unpopular among blacks and Northern whites. Even Roosevelt's ally Washington, who as a rule never spoke publicly against the president, opposed him. "Brownsville was an unforgettable shock. It erased any illusions about Roosevelt's benevolence created by the dinner at the White House," noted historian Louis Harlan in his 1983 biography of Washington. Roosevelt chafed at accusations that he dismissed the men because they were black and insisted that his decision was based solely on his "convictions." The Richmond Planet, a black newspaper, observed: "President Roosevelt may like Colored folks, but he has a devilish mean way of showing it."*

*The soldiers found a white ally in Ohio Senator Joseph Foraker, who managed to gather enough evidence of a flawed investigation to reopen the case in 1908, when he famously told the Senate, "They ask no favors because they are Negroes, but only for justice because they are men." The troops' white commander, Major Charles Penrose, testified before the Senate Military*

*Affairs Committee that, "my men had nothing whatever to do with it." But despite ample evidence of paid witnesses and biased investigators, a court of inquiry, consisting of five generals, concluded on April 6, 1910 that the soldiers were indeed guilty.*

*Forgotten for decades, the Brownsville affair got a fresh airing in 1972 with the publication of The Brownsville Raid by John Weaver, which revealed how even the telltale shell casings were probably planted on the streets as part of a frame-up. On Sept. 28, 1972, the Army announced that the soldiers would finally be granted an honorable discharge. Only one was still alive by then. Dorsie Willis, a former private, had spent some 60 years shining shoes in a Minneapolis bank building. When the arthritic 88-year-old received $25,000 in back pay in 1974, he told reporters, "You can't pay for a lifetime."*

Panamanian voters overwhelmingly approved the largest modernization plan in the history of the Canal. A multi-billion dollar expansion will allow the world's largest ships to pass through the locks which Theodore Roosevelt built, in a nation which he created. The plan also foresees raising the level of Gatun Lake, the main water source for the canal's locks, by a foot and a half.

# Centennial

According to the Associated Press, thousands of supporters wearing green "Yes" t-shirts cast ballots endorsing the $5.25 billion overhaul. The plan is to build a third set of locks on the Pacific and Atlantic ends by 2015. "We are gong to serve the world better and that means we are going to serve Panama better," according canal administrator Alberto Aleman Zubieta. One hundred and fourteen shipping routes currently pass through the canal.

"The expansion is necessary, but we all have to watch closely, make sure there isn't embezzlement and corruption," Igor Meneses, a 34-year-old advertising executive while waiting to vote in Panama City, would say. "With that kind of money," he would tell the Associated Press, "there is a lot to steal."

The AP article ends by explaining, "The United States arranged for Panamanian independence from Columbia to build the canal …"

I am in the borderlands of the southernmost tip of Texas.

The territory is flat and balmy, not nearly so lonely as west Texas, where the mountains seem to cut you off from the rest of the world. You can see shallow ravines where the river has switched back and forth across the valley. The Brownsville traffic lights are unusually long: drivers are aggressive, and several times I see muscle trucks swing recklessly into the broad middle lanes on the road leading from the airport into old Brownsville.

I stop to eat in Isabelle's Restaurant, which occupies the ground floor of an original building several blocks from the border crossing. Mingo might have eaten here.

## Teddy's Tantrum

"Brownsville is hardly the best of Texas, being at once tumultuous of motion and hangdog of manner. It reminds me of several other towns -- Port Said, Panama, Trieste -- where cultures are tossed against each other by history, now one pre-eminent, now another, but it somehow lacks the sting or fizz of confrontation," writes Jan Morris in her book *Journeys*. There is confrontation in Brownsville, if you ask me, but it seems to stay out of sight. The Treaty of Hidalgo is still a sore subject.

"In another city, 10 pounds of marijuana is a big deal."

James Mills is driving me around Brownsville in his pickup.

"Here, 500 and 1,000-lb. shipments of marijuana are not big news."

James, with a passion for south Texas history, teaches at the University of Texas at Brownsville. We have been corresponding since I made plans to attend the centennial, and James has graciously offered to show me around.

James is telling me that this has always been and is still a border town, where things happen. James tells me that early Brownsville was marked by high alcohol consumption because the water was so bad, also opium. He tells me about the huge fortunes made after the Civil War, about cotton barons and John Sherry's citrus empire. Jim refers darkly to "money that cannot be accounted for," money which influences events of all kinds in the region, both past and present. It is a phrase he repeats.

We tour sites from the original Raid. We drive past the old Miller Hotel at 13$^{th}$ and Elizabeth, then 14$^{th}$ and Elizabeth, the Lewis Cowan house. We turn left and drive west, towards Fred Combes' house, which is now a New Fashion store. The old part of town is compact, with catacombs of little streets and alleys jammed right next to one another. You can see a village within the modern city. James thinks that Weaver may have made a mistake about the location of John Hollomon's bar: 6th and Monroe seems too far from the barracks. He tells me that many fortunes were made, first in the cotton trade during the Civil War, then in citrus by men like John Sherry. As he shifts gears in his truck, he cites passages from Weaver's book from memory. We go back and drive it again: yes, it does seem far: but then, it seems unlikely that John D. Weaver made any mistakes.

I thank James for taking the time to show me around.

"Glad to do it," replies James. "I love history. Every time I bring it up around home, my wife and my mother just roll their eyes." He has endless questions about the Raid, and his quest is to solve the mystery. "We still don't know what happened that night. But someone out there does …"

Brownsville is a bustling town, with border traffic coming in and out of a busy commercial district. The fort's garrison wall is now International Boulevard, a flag-draped corridor that leads to and from the border crossing installation. On the other side is Matamoros, Mexico.

We walk through the community college. The handsome original pioneer architecture is still in place. We can see inside carpeted college offices along the brick breezeways with windows all the way to the ground. We stand at one of the buildings which housed the hospital where Gorgas and Finley worked to cure yellow fever.

Texas Southmost College was established in 1926 on the grounds of the military base, Fort Brown. In 1991, Texas Southernmost College joined the University of Texas system and is now known as TSC/UTB (University of Texas at Brownsville). It seeks "to be a community university which respects the dignity of each learner and addresses the needs of the entire community." Its classes are meant to be "affordable, accessible ... and to present programs of workforce training and continuing education, public service, and cultural value ... to the bi-national urban region it serves."

Conspiracy theories still float about the raid. One concerns a prominent south Texas political boss, Wells, who may have had his own reasons for starting a racial incident. Another has Mexican bandits crossing the border to shoot up the town, hoping to implicate the buffalo soldiers who inhibited their cattle rustling. If the soldiers themselves did the shooting, James thinks that Private Newton was the most likely candidate.

James points out that the town liked the income from then soldiers' fines. "Merchants would not be looking to lose those revenues," he says. He recommends I read Sam Rayburn's book about the Rio Grande Valley, *Century of Conflict*.

In Brownsville, the Raid is not ancient history. Sides are still being taken.

Two separate celebrations of the Raid took place on the Centennial weekend.

John Hawthorne, a dignified young man with a deep voice, is the Curator of the Brownsville Museum. He speaks at the Museum's centennial event, a small lecture and reception with a performance by high school students. Hawthorne says that notes from the doctor who treated Frank Natus show that the shots came from an angel two inches above Natus, meaning he was shot by someone on horseback (black soldiers were in the infantry and did not have access to horses). He points out that Natus was killed well away from the fort shootings. Hawthorne scoffs at the entire Cowan story – that the father was absent at midnight, that the children happened to be celebrating a birthday party (at 10:30 at night). The image of white children cowering under a table while bullets shatter glass around them is "to good to be true."

To him, it is a story intended to contrast wholesome white female innocence with the image of enraged dark-skinned marauders. Hawthorne casts the overall idea of random shots fired into houses as somewhat absurd: soldiers would aim at the men who abused them, as the soldiers in Houston and Atlanta did. As to the "attempted rape," he finds this dubious, "a total set-up" too typical of other spurious charges against black men to be credible. The whole affray "seems illogical."

Hawthorne points out an upside to the Affray – that there was no lynching, no extended retaliation, as there would be in similar incidents. Other Texas cities had it worse. The local investigation declined to indict, an action which surely have led to more violence.

At the second event marking the Raid's centennial, held the same afternoon as the Museum event, Jim Mills gives an effortless lecture recounting the events and characters of the shooting. Roosevelt is mentioned, but really the focus is almost entirely on the event as a local episode. The pattern of the shooting was the pattern of an Hispanic shooting, he points out, not the retaliation of soldiers experienced in combat. The ending of his speech is a call for whoever has that diary or that incriminating letter to come forward. The answer, James tells us, must be out there.

Just as Teddy Roosevelt and John Weaver told their stories with a slant, so have I. Ed Renehan, Roosevelt scholar and one of my early readers, feels I have overstated the degree to which the Brownsville episode was forgotten prior to Weaver. In particular, he points to the 1961 book *Power and Responsibility: The Life and Times of Theodore Roosevelt* by William Henry Harbaugh as one which explored Brownsville in detail. Renehan also wants to remind you that Roosevelt had only reports from Texas to rely on. That locals in Brownsville may have framed the black soldiers was, in retrospect for late 20th century scholars, much more clear than it could have been for TR. Far from acting hastily, Roosevelt put off any final decision as to the members of the 25th for as long as he could, then discharged the soldiers after considerable time had passed. An important point here is that there were those in Texas and elsewhere who lobbied for far more severe remedies.

The seven scholars in our third section have helped frame answers to the questions we posed at the beginning of this book. The men of the 25th infantry became embroiled in a dispute with locals because an unnamed bureacrat in Washington decided it was a good idea to transfer a black battalion to the Texas borderlands, where complex racial tensions created a cauldron. Roosevelt expelled the men of the 25th because he was impatient; because he could; because he believed them to be guilty and colluding against him; because he valued them less than a white

# Centennial

battalion; because it was politically expedient; because Foraker was not a worthy champion for the 25th; because Taft was too weak to stop him; because DuBois and Washington could not mount an effective campaign against it. Roosevelt persecuted them with private investigators because he could not stand to admit a mistake. Their story remained buried so long because Roosevelt's own story was too powerful and cherished to allow a contrary narrative. There was no conspiracy against the memory of the men of the $25^{th}$ Infantry; it was more that the collective marketplace would not support a retelling of the incident, even though it was widely publicized at the time. It was a story no one wanted to hear. Secondarily, we might conclude that the story remained buried because the black families who witnessed it had no access to its retelling, except in oral form. John D. Weaver dug it up because he saw a good story, one that involved righting an injustice. He pursued the soldiers' cause because he wanted everyone to know how badly they had been treated. The Army's apology came about because the efforts of Gus Hawkins and other individuals coincided with the Army's desire for justice (or, perhaps more cynically, a desire to mollify black soldiers at a time when minorities played an important part in the armed forces).

For me, three unanswered questions regarding the 100-year arc of the Brownsville Raid remain: what really happened on the night of August 6, 1906; what happened to the men of the $25^{th}$ Infantry; and where is the black Stephen Ambrose? We may never know the first two answers, but the third may yet emerge.

James Mills hopes and believes that one day, documents will surface which tell the truth about the original Raid. It would certainly make a difference to the story if we knew conclusively that Texas bandits had donned blackface and shot up the town in hopes of incriminating the black 25th, or if Privates John Holloman and Burt Conyers had in fact decided to take some revenge themselves.

The true protagonists of the Raid episode, the troops themselves, disappeared into society with little trace. While a handful of their histories have surfaced, most of them have not. John D. Weaver could not find where most of them moved, what jobs they took, and what became of their sons and daughters, who are the true legacies of Special Act 266, and neither could I.

My third unanswered question is this: Where is the black Stephen Ambrose? The narrative of the rise to honor of the American black soldier over the course of perhaps the most eventful military age in recorded history is a surely a grand one, and it is still largely untold. It is a most resonant story, one which contains thrilling episodes of heroism as well as incidents of infamy. It features a series of well-meaning Presidents who deliver the troops into the maw of rising and falling empire which has market the past two centuries. It includes not only tragedies like Brownsville and Sommocolonia and Dak To, but also little-noticed victories of advancement for generations of disenfranchised young black men in the integrated armed forces. Its jewel in the crown is Colin Powell, a black soldier who rises in the ranks to the highest military rank the nation can offer. It begins with young tribal warriors patrolling the borderlands of Benin in western Africa, and ends with their descendants, young black American soldiers patrolling the corridors of Northern Africa, wearing symbols on their uniforms to honor their many predecessors.

On Saturday, August 13, 2006, it is hot in Brownsville Texas. I am wearing a light cotton short-sleeved shirt I bought at a downtown store, and I am still hot.

The principal Centennial event is held at the University of Texas at Brownsville, the college which stands on the old fort's grounds. A breeze blows off International Boulevard, the main drag where Mingo Sanders and John Hollomon and Mayor Ray Combes all walked, not thirty yards away.

John Weaver's book, *The Brownsville Raid*, is displayed in a glass case in the reception hall, its red cover bright and visible. Planted in the sunny courtyard lawn outside, 167 small flags fly, one for each of the dismissed soldiers. Handsome full-color invitations and at least a dozen articles in the Brownsville *Herald* have anticipated today's event. Jeff Raymond, a smart young reporter, has not missed much in his exhaustive covering of the episode and its many tributary topics. The reporter has heard that an Army Captain who was privy to the behind-the-scenes machinations resulting in the 1972 apology is writing his memoirs, and hopes to fill in that missing piece of the Raid mosaic.

In a small outdoor ampitheatre outside the reception hall, the ceremony begins with the posting of the colors – the Texas flag, the American flag – and a rendition of the national anthem by a high school student. The teenaged boys in the color guard glance at one another to make sure they keep the proper spacing.

# Teddy's Tantrum

The University President speaks first, welcoming the audience. "It is an honorable event," she says, especially since it takes place on the footprint of Fort Brown.

Monroe Saulter of the Texas NAACP speaks next. He tries to establish a link between the Raid and the formation in 1910 of the NAACP by a group of liberal-minded white citizens in New York City. This seems a tenuous link at best: Mr. Saulter is looking for some benefit that derived from the Raid, something tangible which can balance the scales, but there may not be one.

Congressman Solomon Ortiz is the main speaker. An Army veteran, he is a member of the House Armed Forces Committee.

"Today, we take a hard look at our past," he begins.

Ortiz gives us his personal background. At age 16, Ortiz' father died and he dropped out of school to help his mother pay the bills for their family. Shortly after that, he joined the army because "It was the one place that would give me free room and board and let me send my check back home to my Mother." Ortiz received his basic training at Fort Hood, Texas

The army did right by him. And he is here to do right by those long-ago soldiers who faced adversity. Ortiz refers knowingly to "…smirks on the white faces" and "aspersions cast on an entire race of people just because of the color of their skin."

But bitterness and recrimination are not on today's agenda.

"The only way we can overcome the uglier incidents in our history is to face them," says Solomon Ortiz. *Dominick LaCapra would love to hear him say that*, I am thinking.

## Centennial

"When somebody repents," Ortiz tells the small crowd, "God is happy." Applause greets this comment, and almost every comment that follows.

"I am here to honor those 167 soldiers."

"That's right," says Monroe Saulter.

"Let us remember that the young soldiers lost everything," says Ortiz.

"Yes, they did," responds the crowd.

"We come together in love." Ortiz commends the university for the courage to talk about the imperfections in our past.

"When we acknowledge our mistakes, we become better citizens," he says, and I begin to think that there could not possibly be a better way to say all this.

"We reflect on the times and the individuals who went before us." Yes we do, answers the crowd.

"We are the result of what came before us." Yes, we are, agrees Monroe Saulter.

"We all live for the love of our brothers." He goes on to say that soldiers of all races have evolved into the premier fighting force in the world, the U.S. Army. "The only color that matters to them is the color of the uniform." I am looking at the young men of the color guard: they are paying careful attention to what Ortiz is saying. I am really, really wishing John Weaver was here to see this.

"How people are connected today is formed by generations past," Ortiz says, "and connected to generations yet to come.

"What we're doing today – in acknowledging these events – this is going to bless our community."

*Yes, it is,* I think.

Then a series of young men and women, students from the college history department, read the names, one by one, from Private James Allen to Sergeant Mingo Sanders to Private Dorsie Willis, until there is a name for each of the flags waving in the courtyard.

"Never forget," concludes Solomon Ortiz.

# Centennial

# Endnotes

## INTRODUCTION

1      Quentin and the spitballs anecdote from Looker, *The White House Gang*, pp.16-17

2      "a relentless and undying hatred…" Sarah Watts, *Rough Rider*, p. 157

3      Benjamin Cleavland "hanging and mutilating any Tories…"quoted in Watts p. 157

4      "… just and strong and brave." Quoted in Watts p. 157

5      Roosevelt describing cowboys who "become more furiously angry and excited than I do" quoted in Watts, p. 59

## PROLOGUE

1      There are many rules or principles of war, and many lists of them. The list I am using is taken from the list currently used in training the U.S. Armed Forces:

> 1. Objective (Mission). Define a decisive and attainable objective for every military operation.
> 2. Offensive. Always advance. Seize, retain and exploit the initiative.
> 3. Mass. Supply sufficient force to achieve the objective.
> 4. Economy of force. Focus the right amount of force on the key objective, without wasting force on secondary objectives.
> 5. Maneuver. Place the enemy in a position of disadvantage through the flexible application of combat power.
> 6. Unity of command. For every objective, there must be a unified effort and one person responsible for command decisions.

# Endnotes

7. Security. Never permit the enemy to acquire an unexpected advantage.
8. Surprise. Otherwise known as Audacity. Strike the enemy at a time and place and in a manner for which he is unprepared.
9. Simplicity. Prepare clear, uncomplicated commands and clear, concise orders.

2   Members of the U.S. Army high command were fighting the last war, which in this case was the Civil War. Military historian Richard Killblane comments in his article, "The Assault on San Juan Hill," (*Military History* magazine) that "the senior American officers had seen service in the Civil War. That conflict had taught them to await orders and follow them." By contrast, the "junior field grade officers had begin their careers fighting Indians" and were accustomed to action on their own initiative.

Leonard Wood, one of the officers who held back, went on to become Army Chief of Staff under Taft, despite his overly cautious decision-making on Kettle Hill that day. Wood, a career doctor, met Roosevelt while Wood was serving as White House Physician to Grover Cleveland.

3   Account of the Jules Ord charge in *"The Crowded Hour: The Charge at El Caney and San Juan Hills"* newspaper article by Richard Harding Davis.

4   *Ibid*

5   "Black troops can survive in the tropics...." The U.S. Army employed four black regiments to serve in the Spanish-American War, the 9th and 10th Cavalry along with the 24th and 25th Infantry. "Assumptions of racial immunity to disease pervade nineteenth-century medical and social theory," writes Warwich Anderson in his article "Immunities of Empire" in the *Bulletin of History of Medicine 70.1 (1996)*

## Teddy's Tantrum

94-118. The 7th, 8th, 9th and 10th U.S. Volunteer Infantry later came into existence in response to Congress' need for more soldiers, who might be "immune" to tropical diseases.

6     Steward, *The Colored Regulars in the U.S.Army*, p. 16.

7     Steward, p. 16. The heroic Lieutenant Jules Garesche Ord sparked the charge up the slope but did not survive it. He was shot minutes after his heroic call to arms, killed as he leapt over the Spanish trenches in front of the blockhouse at the crest of the hill. He had told a friend before the battle that he would emerge from combat either as colonel or a corpse.

8     "Wild and gallant soul ..." is taken from Roosevelt's own memoir of the battle, "Account for the Battle of San Juan and Kettle Hills." Excerpted from Roosevelt's *The Rough Riders* (Da Capo Paperback reprint version), New York: Charles Scribner's Sons, 1920.

9     "His carotid ..." *Ibid*. Just prior to this, Roosevelt's previous orderly ("a brave young Harvard boy, Sanders, from the quaint old Massachusetts town of Salem") had died from fever.

10    Gerstle, *American Crucible*

11    Eyewitness account from journalist Richard Harding Davis

12    Roosevelt, *The Rough Riders*, p. 116

### Chapter 1: Bonus March

1     Thomas R. Henry's description of the Bonus marchers in the *Star* newspaper

2     John D. Weaver in *As I Live and Breathe*, p.5

3     *As I Live and Breathe*, page 6

# Endnotes

4   *As I Live and Breathe,* page 11

5   *As I Live and Breathe,* page 17

6   John D. Weaver, "Bonus March" article, *American Heritage Magazine*

7   *Ibid*

8   *Ibid*

## CHAPTER 2: THE WORK OF THE WORLD

1   Boris Ananich, *Russian Military Expenditures in the Russo Japanese War* essay

2   Ananich, p. 451.

3   page 471 of *The Short Victorious War: The Russo-Japanese Conflict 1904-5.*, from Edward S. Miller, "Japan's Other Victory" essay.

4   description from Semenov's diaries

5   *Ibid*

6   *Path Between the Seas*, p. 445

7   *Path Between the Seas*, p. 423. This is taken from a letter from William Gorgas' wife Marie, describing her first impressions of Panama.

8   *Path*, p. 439.

9   *Path*, p. 440.

## CHAPTER 3: HARRIETT

1   "I had never seen someone so lovely or so shy." *As I Live and Breathe,* page 24

2    "They listened to Stravinsky records, discovered Joyce, devoured *The American Mercury* ..." *As I Live and Breathe*, page 17

3    "Two years later we were living on mustard greens and trying frantically to peddle the car." *As I Live and Breathe*

4    Arthur Miller's description of Untermeyer comes from Miller's 1987 autobiography, *Timebends -- A Life*

5    *As I Live and Breathe*, page 27

### CHAPTER 4: A QUASI BATTLEGROUND

1    John W. Bailey's essay "Civilization the Military Way: The Generals' View of the Plains Indians, 1866-91" in *The Military and Conflict between Civilizations*, Ed. James C. Bradford. College Station: Texas A & M University Press, 1997.

2    Custer died in 1876

3    "Heavy columns ..." Bailey essay in Bradford.

4    "Tomorrow's conventional war ..." *Ibid*

5    "stirring up the Indians..." *Ibid*

6    "Indian warfare was perceived as a fleeting irritant..." *Ibid*

7    "Victorio launched into a harangue ..." Frank N. Schubert, *Black Valor*. Wilmington, Delaware: Scholastic Resources (1997), page 51

8    "Black-whitemen! The Buffalo Soldiers!" Schubert, page 65.

9    "The Buffalo Soldiers also explored and mapped large areas of the southwest and strung thousands of miles of telegraph lines." Bradford, page 62.

# Endnotes

10   Wham's account of the payroll robbery, Schubert pp. 91-2. Sergeant Benjamin Brown and Corporal Isaiah Mays were awarded the Medal of Honor for their courage in this engagement.

11   "The physique of the black soldiers must be admired – great chests, broad-shouldered, upstanding fellows …" Frederic Remington quoted in Katz, *The Black West*. New York: Doubleday, revised edition 1973, p.224.

12   "…the material redemption of unimproved properties to the benefit of mankind at large." As phrased by Alfred Thayer Mahan in a letter to *The New York Times*.

13   "…to assimilate and profit by American or European ideas, the ideas of civilization and Christianity." From Roosevelt's 1910 speech to an Egyptian college audience

14   "The powers that border the Persian Gulf…" Alfred Thayer Mahan in a 1902 article.

15   "Endeavor to explain a statement of plain fact from any Egyptian…" Lord Cromer, writing in his book *Modern Egypt*, as quoted by Edward Said in *Orientalism*, p. 38.

16   "…barbaric black heathen or fanatical Mohammedans." Alfred Thayer Mahan in a 1902 article.

17   "In the Soudan, Mahdism during the ten years of its unchecked control was responsible for the death of over half the population and meant physical and moral ruin …" From Roosevelt's 1910 Egyptian speech.

18   "It is necessary 'to consider each of the several centres of interest as not separate, but having relations to the whole …" Roosevelt's 1910 Egyptian speech.

19    "The world took 'a step back on the ramp to war.'" Roosevelt's own description, in a letter to Henry Cabot Lodge.

20    Jews tired "of receiving blows and not protesting, of bending the spine, waiting for the storm to pass…" The French writer Bernard Lazare, quoted in Jean-Denis Bredin's book *The Affair: The Case of Alfred Dreyfus*, p. 137.

## CHAPTER 5: FORWARD OBSERVER

1    Lenny Spigelgass "considered it unpatriotic" for Cheever to be assigned to the infantry, *Glad Tidings*, page 3.

2    "The army is very big, and moves very slowly …" Cheever in a letter home, from *Glad Tidings*, page 2.

3    Description of the "massive German assault" from John Fox's Medal of Honor citation.

4    Houston, 1917 military incident taken from *The Invisible Soldier: The Experience of the Black Soldier, World War II*, Edited by Mary Penick Motley, p. 12

5    The WWI memo to French officers regarding black American troops was originated by General Pershing's office. *Invisible Soldier*, page 13.

6    black enlistees' letter to FDR taken from Gerstle, p. 212

7    from John Fox's Medal of Honor citation.

## CHAPTER 6: JUSTICE OR DEATH

1    In his library of literary enthusiasms, Roosevelt was also passionate about Kenneth Grahame's *The Wind in the Willows*, the story of the charismatic, chaotic poet-warrior Toad and his many adventures. Informed by the most noble causes, Toad is distracted, seduced and

# Endnotes

almost destroyed by his fascination with the devices of modern life (the thrilling "Poop-Poop!" sound of car engines is his siren call). Toad, like Roosevelt, struggles mightily to contain the wild urges within, urges which his loyal friend Badger calls "the poison in his system" and which the sensible Rat refers to as "these painful attacks." It does not take too much imagination to see Roosevelt as Toad, beset by well-meaning advisors like Elihu Root (Badger), Taft (Mole), and smart, steadfast John Hay (Rat). Here Toad emerges from a talking-to by Badger after stealing a car and crashing it:

> "There's only one thing more to be done," continued the gratified Badger. "Toad, I want you solemnly to repeat, before your friends here, what you fully admitted to me in the smoking-room just now. First, you are sorry for what you've done, and you see the folly of it all?"
>
> There was a long, long pause. Toad looked desperately this way and that, while the other animals waited in grave silence. At last he spoke.
>
> "No!" he said, a little sullenly, but stoutly; "I'm *not* sorry. And it wasn't folly at all! It was simply glorious!"

Here, Toad is walking down a country road after escaping from jail:

> "Ho, ho!" he said to himself as he marched along with his chin in the air, "what a clever Toad I am! There is surely no animal equal to me for cleverness in the whole world! My enemies shut me up in prison, encircled by sentries, watched night and day by warders; I walk out through them all, by sheer ability coupled with courage. They pursue me with engines, and policemen, and revolvers; I snap my fingers at them, and vanish, laughing, into space. I am, unfortunately, thrown into

a canal by a woman fat of body and very evil-minded. What of it? I swim ashore, I seize her horse, I ride off in triumph, and I sell the horse for a whole pocketful of money and an excellent breakfast! Ho, ho! I am The Toad, the handsome, the popular, the successful Toad!"

Buttressed by his friends and reminders of his own glorious past, Toad rallies against his own indolence and leads the forces of civilization into battle against the lazy stoats.

Roosevelt read the British edition of Grahame's book and wrote a note to Charles Scribner, urging him to publish an American edition. It became one of the bestselling children's books of all time, thriving in multiple editions a century later.

2   "Nor could they judge …" *Titan*, Ron Chernow, page 521

3   "During Brownsville's heyday…" Leiker, James N. *Racial Borders: Black Soldiers Along the Rio Grande*, page 132.

4   "…fewer than half a dozen black families." Weaver, *The Brownsville Raid*, p. 68

5   "King Fisher of Maverick County …" In his fine book, *Black Soldiers in Jim Crow Texas 1899-1917*, Garna L. Christian details the obstacles facing the black troops asked to patrol the gigantic hostile territories of Texas. His mention of "prominent rancher-rustlers such as King Fisher" comes on page 17.

6   "All were loud in their denunciation of negro soldiers …" Weaver, *The Brownsville Raid*, p. 21. He goes on to write: "When it was first announced that the garrison's white soldiers were to be replaced by Negro troops, the townspeople talked of little else and Mexican women crossed themselves in Christian resignation at the prospect of being raped by black heathen."

# Endnotes

7   "You look like an ape..." From *The Senator and the Sharecropper's Son*, page 71.

## Chapter 7: Studio 55

1   *Holiday Affair* ... Another short story of Weaver's which made its way onto film is the aptly- titled *A Matter of Principle*. It is a sort of hallucinogenic version of Weaver's own predicament: a man (Flagg Purdy) of great convictions finds himself deeply conflicted when his convictions threaten the home life of his wife and 11 children. By refusing to pay an 89-cent county tax on his phone bill, this stubborn West Virginian loses his family's phone service. Emotional turmoil ensues, followed by lessons in civics and family truths. Starring Alan Arkin and Barbara Dana, *A Matter of Principle* was produced in 1983 for the *American Playhouse* series.

2   "Not enough closet space ..." *As I Live and Breathe*, p. 41.

3   The long passage of Harriett meeting the Weaver clan from p. 62-3, *As I Live and Breathe*

4   Selznick anecdote from *Glad Tidings*, p.6.

5   "I felt like killing myself ..." *Glad Tidings*, page 55.

6   "Did you know publishers can ..." *Glad Tidings* p. 105

7   "I seem to have scored a victory ..." *Glad Tidings*, p. 53

8   David McCullough's biography, *Truman* (Simon & Schuster, 1992) p. 570. As archives from Communist-era Russia have been opened, the origins of the Korean War have increasingly been viewed as complex. Priscilla Roberts of The University of Hong Kong mentions the possibility that South Korea was equally eager to reunite the two Koreas, and that the United States ignored Chinese warning and was pro-active in crossing

the 38th parallel. Prof. William Stueck of Georgia points to a "gross lack of preparation" by the South Koreans. Stueck also lays responsibility for U.S. fortunes at the feet of Douglas MacArthur, whose Inchon landing cut off chances for effective diplomacy.

9   "three million deaths …" Priscilla Roberts, "New Light on a Forgotten War," *Organization of American Historians Magazine*, 1998.

10   *"the integration of the armed forces was political suicide [for Truman]"* … David McCullough, *Truman*, pages 569-71.

11   Charles Bussey quote, *"I watched the group of farmer-soldiers …" from Bussey, Firefight at Yechon: Courage and Racism in the Korean War.*

12   Quoted in Astor, Gerald. *The Right to Fight: A History of African Americans in the Military*, page 357.

13   Roy Edgar Appleton quote, "They abandoned weapons upon positions …" from the U.S. Army's official history of the Korean War, *South to the Naktong, North to the Yalu,* (1961) authored by Appleton.

14   "…no agreement could be reached" on black regiments' performance in Korea. Appleton's 1961 official version was corrected in a later study which gave a more balanced view of the performance of all-black regiments.

15   description of Untermeyer's firing from quiz show from Arthur Miller's *Timebends - A Life* (1987)

16   "Lie low …" from Untermeyer's March 16, 1951 letter to Weaver.

## Chapter 8: Einen Wilden Baren

1   "DuBois suspected greener was a spy … He was correct." Jean Strouse, *Morgan: American Financier,* p. 515. "In 1906 [Greener]

## Endnotes

attended a meeting of the pro-DuBois Niagara Movement at Harpers Ferry as a spy for Booker T. Washington..."

2   "while armed and angry men ... behind bolted doors" from

3   Captain Kelly quoting Brownsville citizen ... "That man had never been a soldier." *TBR*, p. 68.

4   "We got him ..." *TBR*, p. 73.

5   "I saw their – what do you call it? – bulk." Witness quote from TBR, p. 127.

6   Belle da Costa Greene's impromptu war dance from Strouse, p. 529

7   "small and slender ..." description of Belle da Costa Greene from Strouse, p. 531

8   "mute objects that speak with golden eloquence ... " Mrs. Schuyler Van Rensselaer, "Ancient Egypt in America." *The North American Review* 218, July 1923.

9   "every self-respecting bookcase" ... *Ibid*

10   "a sincere expression of the rational temper ..." *Ibid*

11   "Both of these lessons we need to learn ..." *New York Times* article on King Tut, quoted in Strouse, p. 177

12   "the militia of Egypt ..." Labib Habachi, "The Two Rock Stelae of Sethos I," *Le Bulletin de l'Institut Français d'Archéologie Orientale (BIFAO)* 73 (1973) p. 120

13   "conquered territories were annexed ..." *Ibid*

14   "mercenaries hired from the east and north ..." *Ibid*

15   "fleeing from Nubia ..." *Ibid*

16   "obedience not always assured..." *Ibid*

17   "Belle da Costa Greene's Portuguese/Dutch descent was pure fiction ... " Strouse, *Morgan American Financier*, p. 520

18   TR's kinship with the German people ... Dyer, p.2

19   TR and H.G. Wells anecdote from *Path Between the Seas*, p. 499

20   The description of the Atlanta race riots is from Walter White's autobiography, *Walter White, A Man Called White (1948; reprint, New York: Arno Press, 1969)*, pp. 5–12.

## Chapter 9: Fire in the Hills

1   "Let's move on to other business ..." The Weavers' encounter with the Los Angeles Fire Chief anecdote told by their friend Jim Perry.

2   "The deadwood literally explodes ..." Richard Reeves' profile of Southern California personalities (including Harriett Weaver) appeared in *The New Yorker* magazine in 1972 and was also republished in his book *Jet Lag*.

3   "[Harriett] turned her shapely back on the mink-and-chrome fetishes of Status and Society and goes her own quiet way," from *As I Live and Breathe* promotional text.

4   "John was brainy ..." a description by his friend of many years, Carl Reiner.

5   "I do not see how we are ever going to get out of it without getting in a major war with the Chinese and all of them down there in those rice paddies and jungles." LBJ quote from CNN article "Doubts Plagued LBJ on Vietnam early in the war" by Alan Duke, Feb. 15, 1997.

# Endnotes

6   "LBJ was great in domestic affairs," the American diplomat Averell Harriman put it. "If it hadn't been for ...Vietnam he'd have been the greatest President ever." From Doris Kearns Goodwin's biography *Lyndon Johnson and the American Dream*, p. 251.

7   "If I left that war and let the Communists take over South Vietnam ..." LBJ quote from Alan Duke CNN article.

8   "The neighbors had to pull a kicking and screaming Skip away from the fight ..." from the chapter on Dwight Johnson in Allen Mikaelian's 2002 book of profiles, *Medal of Honor.*

9   "A battalion-sized enemy force appeared from nowhere." *Ibid.*

10   "He pulled a barely recognizable but still breathing crew member from the turret and carried him to the ground." *Ibid.*

11   "Returning to his tank through a heavy volume of antitank rocket ... long passage describing Skip Johnsons's heroic act is taken from Mikaelian, pp. 241-2.

12   Westmoreland quote, "The enemy's return was nil," from William Westmoreland, *A Soldier Reports*. New York: Doubleday 1976 p. 282.

13   Marine Corps General John Chaisson questioned the numbers. "Is it a victory when you lose 362 friendlies in three weeks and by your own spurious body count you only get 1,200?" From *Terrence Maitland, Peter McInerny editors, A Contagion of War*. Boston: Boston Publishing Company, 1983, p. 168.

14   Dwight Johnson's psychiatrist, that "... He may have suppressed that anger, but he was aware of it. That's why he was afraid," from Mikaelian, p. 251.

15   "'I'm going to kill you.' I kept pulling the trigger until the gun was empty.'" Mikaelian, p. 253.

## Chapter 10: Special Order 266

1   "I have not been able to think out any solution of the terrible problem offered by the presence of the Negro on this continent, but of one thing I am sure, and that is that in as much as he is here and can neither be killed nor driven away, the only wise and honorable and Christian thing to do is to treat each black man and each white man strictly on his merits as a man." TR quoted in Gerstle, p.22.

2   "[Roosevelt] had appointed black officeholders in the face of white opposition ... and had given the impression that he meant to give a 'square deal' to each American. Photographs of Washington and Roosevelt together had become extremely popular wall decorations for black homes and were referred to as 'Social Equality' pictures." Lewis Wynne, "Brownsville: The Reaction of the Negro Press." *Phylon, The Atlanta University Review of Race and Culture,* Volume XXXIII, Number 2 Summer, 1992. (p. 154).

3   The grand jury "made a very thorough investigation, but failed to find an indictment against any of the parties under arrest." Joseph Foraker's autobiography, *Notes of a Busy Life*, p. 233.

4   Henry Weaver ... "a lawyer, a parliamentarian, and one of the fastest shorthand writers in the world." This is his son's description, from *As I Live and Breathe,* page 10.

5   "If the GOP could retain control of Congress, the party could claim a mandate for the presidential policies ..." The Congressional elections of 1906 were critical to Roosevelt for many reasons, among them his desire to shore up his support among southerners, particularly after the controversy over his White House dinner with Booker T. Washington.

# Endnotes

6   "So long as black brutes attempt to assault our white women, just so long as will they be unceremoniously dealt with." Atlanta mayor's quote from "Race Riots and Murders in Atlanta," *The Independent* 61, 27 September, 1906.

## Chapter 11: A Stray Remark

1   Weaver recounts the conversation which sparked his Brownsville odyssey in the Introduction to *The Senator and the Sharecropper's Son*.

## Chapter 12: The Aftermath

1   "No media coverage, black or white, doubted that the affray originated with former Confederates' disdain for armed blacks." Leiker, p. 141.

2   "The impact of the Brownsville incident on the black population was tremendous." Lewis Wynne, "Brownsville: The Reaction of the Negro Press." *Phylon, The Atlanta University Review of Race and Culture,* Volume XXXIII, Number 2 Summer, 1992. (p. 154).

3   "Reaction to Roosevelt's order came swiftly and bitterly in the Negro press." Wynne, p. 155.

4   "The hand of Ben Tillman nor Vardaman never struck humanity as savagely as did the iron hand of Theodore Roosevelt. His new dictum is lynch-law, bold and heartless." Quoted in Wynne, p. 155.

5   "The most notable silence was that of Booker T. Washington who, as Roosevelt's political referee, was unwilling to make any statement denouncing the President." Wynne, p. 157.

6   "... but he does not measure up to presidential timber." Wynne, p. 158.

7   Foraker "writing, wiring, sending men out to Texas to take sworn testimony, to secure exact details; spending hours and hours in a thickening jungle of newspapers, clippings, letters, and calf-bound books." Julia Foraker describes her husband's obsession with Brownsville in her autobiography, *I Would Live It Again*.

8   "Quietly they went their separate ways." *TBR*, page 109.

9   "I think Mother has really enjoyed it…" TR's letter to his children, written on the voyage back from Panama.

10   "It is a splendid thing to see one of these men-of-war, and it does really make one proud of one's country …" From TR's letter home, regarding the sea voyage from Panama.

11   Roosevelt read Gibbon constantly, taking volumes with him on a long train trip or on a hunting expedition. Morris, pp. 285-6.

12   He understood very well one of Gibbon's primary themes, that Rome fell from internal decline.

13   "…in the enjoyment of the peace and glory of his reign, forgave the cruelties by which it had been introduced." Septimus Severn quote, Gibbon Volume VIII, 195.

14   "Nor did Theodore Roosevelt ever forget the cruelties by which the nation had been introduced …" Cruelties which he then visited upon the men of the 25th Infantry.

15   "Gibbon also blamed Rome's soldiers for Rome's fall." Gibbon blamed everyone and everything. "In the first half of the Decline and Fall there are at least two dozen specific 'causes' given for the fall of Rome … they march across the pages of the Decline and Fall, seemingly without pattern, and seemingly unrelated to each other." David P. Jordan,

# Endnotes

*Gibbon and His Roman Empire*. Urbana: University of Illinois Press, 1971 (p. 213).

16  "With bloody hands, savage manners, and desperate resolutions, they sometimes guarded, but much oftener subverted, the throne of emperors." Gibbon, Volume VI, 147.

17  "At the age of twelve years, he embraced the rigid system of the Stoics, which taught him to submit his body to his mind, his passions to his reason; to consider virtue as the only good, vice as the only evil, all things external as things indifferent." Gibbon, Chapter 3.

18  "Whatever evils either reason or declamation have imputed to extensive empire, the power of Rome was attended with some beneficial consequences to mankind …" Gibbon, Chapter 2.

19  "The emperor of the West, if his ministers disturbed his amusements by the news of the impending danger, was satisfied with being the occasion and the spectator of the war." Gibbon, Chapter 30.

20  "John Milholland, the wealthy white sponsor of the Constitution League, wanted her to go over to the War Department" *TBR*, p. 105.

21  "Much agitation on the subject," he advised Roosevelt, "it may be well to convince people of fairness of hearing by granting rehearing." Taft telegram quoted in *TBR*, p. 106.

22  Long description of TR in Panama, *Path Between the Seas*, pages 494-97.

23  "Roosevelt was obsessed with the idea that someone was trying to hide something from him because of the Erie Canal." During Roosevelt's first term as Governor of New York, "… a special investigative committee had reported on the 'improper expenditures' of at least a million dollars

in the state's Erie canal Improvement project." Edmund Morris, *The Rise of Theodore Roosevelt*, p. 666.

24   Roosevelt admitted there was a "conflict of evidence" regarding the exact chain of events, but he dismissed the contradictions as a "wholly unimportant matter."

25   "I did my utmost to prevent his taking the action he did. I feel that I did my full duty in the matter which the enclosed copy of a letter from him will show." TR in a letter to a friend, quoted in Emma Lou Thornbrough's article, "The Brownsville Episode and the Negro Vote," *The Mississippi Valley Historical Review*, December 1957, p.474

26   "It has been a year of excesses," he began ... *The Senator and the Sharecropper's Son*, p. 66.

27   "Newspapermen and their guests leaped up, cheering, crowding around the Senator and offering their congratulations" ... *Ibid*

28   "The papers are still full of the Foraker row and I am glad you are not here to be wounded by it," wrote Nellie. "I fear it will be injurious to your chances." Judith Icke Anderson, *William Howard Taft: An Intimate History* p. 94.

29   TR quote, "I don't go so far as to think that the only good Indians are the dead Indians, but I believe nine out of every ten are, and I shouldn't like to inquire too closely into the case of the tenth." General Philip Sheridan has repeatedly been named as its originator of the hateful phrase, *The only good Indian is a dead Indian.*

30   Foraker ... "I have shown that the testimony first submitted by Major Blocksom, although only loose-jointed, unsworn, inconsistent and contradictory statements, was regarded by the President as 'conclusive'..." Foraker, p 316.

# Endnotes

31   The stock market lost 8.3% of its value when a speculator named Augustus Heinze bought the Knickerbocker Trust bank and began speculating aggressively, trying to corner on United Copper. Morgan's role in the 1907 Wall Street rescue package from John Steel Gordon's *The Great Game*.

32   The pair interviewed various members of the scattered battalion and returned with dramatic results, giving for the first time "the true secret history of the Brownsville raid."

33   "President Roosevelt gave an interview of such hostile character, and President Taft assumed such an attitude of opposition, if not of hostility … the tide turned against me."   Foraker, p. 333.

34   Booker T. Washington … worked "to minimize the effect of Brownsville on Negro voting habits …"Rather than offend Roosevelt by pushing harder for a reconsideration of the decision, Washington quietly acquiesced. Roosevelt rewarded this passive attitude by granting Washington patronage." Wynne, p. 157.

35   "Black leaders … consistently failed to take major issues to the grass roots level." Wynne, p. 159.

36   "Black leaders have too often been guilty of dealing with issues on an intellectual plane and have tended to ignore the practical aspects … It is this failure … that has consistently hurt Negroes." Wynne, p. 159, paraphrasing Henry Lee Moon's argument in his 1949 book *Balance of Power*.

37   Ironically, the Atlanta riot got in the way of a unified black response to Brownsville. Coming so close on the heels of the raid, this "cataclysmic event … made Brownsville seem pale in comparison." From Wynne, pp. 159-160.

### Chapter 13: Weaver Investigates

1   "Roosevelt, like Lincoln, was in a true sense a preserver of our National unity. Lincoln saved us from section cleavage, Roosevelt saved us from class cleavage. He pointed out the road of straight Americanism where all could walk in amity towards the same goal." Calvin Coolidge in an Introduction to a Roosevelt biography.

2   the violence that night in Brownsville caused "as a result of the deeds of the black troops ..." Lewis Gould in his Introduction to *TBR*.

3   "Oh, I think if only I could taste a little success!" John Cheever in a letter to the Weavers, *Glad Tidings*, page 53.

4   They assured Roosevelt and Taft that "the guilty men would be unmasked before the voters went to the polls in November."

5   "I suppose you noted the fact that the President has sent Secret Service men down to Brownsville ..." Weaver found a letter from a Cleveland correspondent to Foraker regarding Roosevelt's misuse of federal resources. Weaver, *The Senator and The Sharecropper's Son*, p. 145.

6   "...Not only had young Elkins recognized these ... raiders as Negro soldiers at a distance from thirty to forty paces, he had even been able to idenify the color of their trousers (yellow khaki) and, in one instance, a summer Army shirt (blue)." *TBR*, page 77.

7   "Taft was even more apathetic about black rights than was Roosevelt, and he consistently and openly declared that the dismissals were justified." *Ibid.*

8   "If possible," Roosevelt urged Taft, "you should give Foraker a mauling." Anderson, p.121.

# Endnotes

9     "They just roared through town shooting wildly, mostly at lighted rooms in houses. A couple of people just accidentally got in the way of bullets." JDW in the Gladwyn Hill article, *New York Times*.

10    *Ibid*

11    He calls the Browne-Baldwin report "shameless forgery." He decries "the so-called 'confession' of Boyd Conyers and "the Administration sleuths with their threats and misrepresentations," who made up their "own version of a Company B conspiracy and put it forth as a 'confession' by this likeable, hard-working happily-married young Negro."

Weaver portrays Foraker in the light of Atticus Finch, as played by Gregory Peck (not surprisingly, there are letters in Weaver's files referring to Weaver and Carl Foreman visiting Gregory Peck at his Los Angeles home to discuss Peck playing the role of Foraker in the never-produced Brownsville film). Where Edmund Morris sees Foraker as "a negative influence," Weaver casts him in the same light as the protagonist in Harper Lee's *To Kill a Mockingbird*, a beleaguered lawyer defending the rights of innocent black men who are in peril from unjust persecution. Weaver does not, however, shy away from his protagonist's flaws, and documents all of Foraker's ties to Standard Oil as thoroughly as he documents everything else.

12    "Oh, shame upon a Government that will employ all its power ... every power that it commands, not for the purpose of protection of men in their right to be presumed innocent until they are proven guilty, but to prove men, who claim they are innocent, to be guilty of a heinous crime, and to do it behind the door and in the dark." *TBR*, p. 206.

13    "Alive, they were denied the equity of the white man's justice and, dead, the vindication of his Jim Crow history." *TBR*, page 212.

14  [Brown and Baldwin] had offered him money, confronted him with what they knew to be perjured testimony, promised him protection and tried to frighten him with the prospect of Texas noose." *TBR*, p. 206.

15  "The interplay among local events in Brownsville, the politics of the army, and the national scene is one of the strongest parts of his story." Lewis Gould, in his introduction to *TBR*.

## Chapter 14: A Reputation Cleared

1  "Three men took seats in a narrow triangle in the White House Situation Room." Scene as described in the excellent book on Kissinger, *The Flawed Architect* by Jussi Hanhimäki.

2  "Overdue," said Haldeman. "Long overdue." *Ibid*.

3  "By the end of 1971, almost 1 million men served in the ARVN ..." April, 1972 article "Thiet Gap! The Battle of An Loc," by James H. Millbanks *Combat Studies Institute* Leavenworth, Kansas (1993)

4  The 25th Infantry – now re-formed and fully integrated – "participated in Allied thrusts deep into enemy sanctuaries located in Cambodia." Eric Bergerud. *Red Thunder, Tropic Lightning: The World of the 25th Infantry Combat Division in Vietnam*. Boulder: Westview Press, 1993.

5  "Where were the other scholars to follow in his footsteps?" From interview with Simon Elliot, UCLA librarian who spent time with Weaver during the decades after his Brownsville book appeared.

6  "Weaver tracked down third and fourth generations of the Combe, Fernandez, and Hollomon families." Some of his correspondence with them is given in *The Senator and the Sharecropper's Son*.

# Endnotes

7    "They were two wonderful people," he said of Captain Lyons and his wife, as Weaver describes it, "tears came to his eyes as his crippled hand slowly and painfully forced his name, letter by letter, onto the title page." Dorsie Willis quoted in *The Senator and the Sharecropper's Son*, p. 200.

8    "The only reason that the Army acted today was that I spent nearly three years studying the records and discovering that injustice had been done," Weaver said. From the Gladwyn Hill article, *New York Times*.

9    "My father's experience at Brownsville and my personal experience in World War II convinced me that the U.S. was unable or unwilling to defend the rights of the black people who go forth to defend it." Robert Hollomon wrote this in a letter to Gus Hawkins' committee, declining to attend the ceremony.

10    Acting Attorney General Richard Kleindienst noted that the Army had missed the point: no one wanted a new investigation, but "to rectify the gross injustice involved in the mass discharge of 167 soldiers."

11    "John D. Weaver is an author known to his friends as a fanatical stickler for accurate details," began the article. "Because of this, 167 black soldiers stand exonerated of a crime that had tarnished their names for 66 years." From Jack Jones,"167 Blacks Cleared by Army in 1906 'Brownsville Affray' Mass Punishment Held Unjust." *Los Angeles Times*, Friday, September 29, 1972.

12    "It's wonderful," said Mr. Willis, "It's wonderful. It's wonderful." *Ibid.*

## Chapter 15: Jalester Lincoln

1   He called the body-count metrics of how the war was being won "nonsense" and "flabby thinking" and worse. From Colin Powell's autobiography, *An American Life*, p. 103.

2   He worried that "a corrosive careerism had infected the Army," and that he was part of it. *An American Life*, p.146 "Readiness and training reports in the Vietnam era were routinely inflated to please and conceal rather than to evaluate and correct … The powers that be seemed to believe that by manipulating words, we could change the truth."

3   He became convinced that "War should be the politics of last resort. And when we go to war, we should have a purpose that our people understand and support…you do not squander courage and lives without clear purpose, without the country's backing, and without full commitment." *An American Life*, p. 148.

4   Their attitude seemed to be 'Take that,' whereas the white offender's attitude was 'Who? Little me, sir?'" *An American Life*, p. 192.

5   While he had been patrolling the A Shau Valley for Viet Cong, he found out later, his father had been sitting up all night on the porch of his Birmingham, Alabama home, a shotgun across his lap, protecting Powell's pregnant wife. Martin Luther King had marched on the Birmingham city hall. *An American Life*, p. 93.

6   The Jalester Lincoln story is recounted in *An American Life* pp. 274-276.

## Chapter 16: A Second Book

1   description of the scene at the ceremony from the preface to Tom Willard's 1996 novel *Buffalo Soldiers*, New York: Forge.

# Endnotes

2   "A new strength. A new tomorrow." Powell's speech is a clever and appropriate combination of the ethic struggle with the imperial mission. Powell shows Rooseveltian qualities in his stress of progress and togetherness, perhaps explaining why he went so far in an organization where others are often mired by obstructions.

3   "...the Bonus March remains one of the most controversial and grotesquely distorted episodes of recent American history." From Weaver's *American Heritage* article on the Bonus March.

4   "As a result of the radiation therapy, the bones in Harriett's hip have deteriorated to such an extent that she moves about on a cane with some difficulty and ... considerable pain." From JDW letter to Pamela Fiore.

5   "One friend saw relief in John's face at her funeral ... Harriett was the one who loved to entertain, cooking dinners for their circle of friends," recalls David Zeidberg, who was a UCLA librarian during the years Weaver researched there. Zeidberg also remembers John seeming relieved at the funeral, perhaps (he thought) both because Harriett's suffering was over and his own burden of caretaking had been lifted.

6   "Living in Encino, he seemed to friends to be adrift ..." Jim Perry interview.

7   "He was due royalties in Russia, but he would not travel to collect them." Chica Weaver interview.

## Chapter 17: More Lost Stories

1   "Did you know that your country was conceived in Room 1162 of the Astoria Hotel?" From Espino's Introduction.

2    That he "had the outlines of a story hidden for almost a century." *Ibid.*

3    "My father ... warned me that my book diminished not only the Americans, but our own patriots, and begged me to suppress the truth about the corruption and the Wall Street ties." *Ibid.*

4    "...bought the shares of the bankrupt French Canal company and sold it to Roosevelt for $40 million, far above its worth." Espino pp. 3-4. The Espino book helps explain why Roosevelt was so nervous about "someone trying to hide something from him" during the construction of the Isthmian Canal. Deception was how he won the Canal, and he must have worried that he himself was not exempt from it. Cromwell, it is estimated, profited at least $6,000,000 – and that is only for legal fees. Ovidio Espino implies that gigantic sums of money went unaccounted for in the transfer of funds from the U.S. government to France, to the stockholders, and the many subcontractors. Whatever his level of detailed understanding of the *Nouvelle Compagnie,* Roosevelt was too intelligent not to know that he was allowing fortunes to pass through the hands of Cromwell and his many associates with little supervision, in exchange for the Canal getting built.

5    "Cromwell's "law offices at No. 41 Wall Street were ... regarded by many as the real executive offices of the Panama Canal." The October 6 *World* story as quoted on p. 3, Espino.

6    "Loyal to his commander, he tried to explain to an interviewer." The interviewer was P.J. O'Rourke, the profile appeared in the *Atlantic Monthly*, August 2, 2004.

7    "[Powell] said State Department officials were working during the weekend to find out how the mistakes occurred, and he said he would

# Endnotes

meet Monday with officials from those agencies to discuss the errors." As reported by CNN.

## Chapter 18: The Anger of the Legions

1   One of the first black cadets, Johnson C. Whittaker, after two years of academic success at the Academy, was found tied to his bed on April 6, 1880, his ears slashed and his hair cut. He was court-martialed after being charged with inflicting the injuries on himself. Katz, p. 219.

2   "...represented an ethos of discipline and manly virtue superior to the easygoing values of civilian society." From Lasswell, *Essays on the Garrison State*. Piscataway, NJ: Transaction Publishers, 1997.

3   "Desertions were common. Non-Russian soldiers needed little incentive to desert the cause, and were often quick to surrender." From Geoffrey Jukes, *The Russo-Japanese War of 1904-1905*. Oxford: Osprey Publishing, 2002 (p. 82).

4   "The Zulu army in the field was like a spring that had been wound to breaking point by days of psychological preparation, and it required only the presence of the enemy for it to snap." Ludwig Alberti in his book *Account of the Tribal Life and Customs of the Xhosa in 1807*.

5   "...Many came to refer to themselves by their regimental, rather than their clan, names." *Ibid*.

6   "The common soldier very often was recruited territorially ..." James Utley's essay in Bradford's *Crucible of Empire* (p. 93).

7   "[Roosevelt] was not prepared for the opportunity that the victory at Kettle Hill and San Juan Hills had handed him." Gerstle, *American Crucible*, p. 17.

## Chapter 19: Mosaic

1   "The trend toward accepting Roosevelt's heroic interpretation of his own life has not abated in our own time." Kathleen Dalton, *Theodore Roosevelt: A Strenuous Life,* p. 8

2   "To see TR anew ... we have to look beneath the heroics." Dalton, p. 8.

3   "Family and friends edited or destroyed embarrassing letters and hid family secrets in order to keep the story of Roosevelt's life and times presentable." Dalton, page 6

4   "Roosevelt was the first president to articulate the shared anxieties of his generation," Watts writes, "and he provided its first seemingly coherent response to the cultural dislocations of modern society." Sarah Watts, *Rough Rider,* page 2.

5   "Thus locked together, race, manhood and nation stood in polar opposition to all elements of modern life." Watts, page 33.

6   "...You were a masculine sort of a person with extremely masculine virtues and palpably masculine faults." William Allen White letter to TR., quoted in Watts 25.

7   'Sinister opposition,' those congressmen who voted against naval appropriations." Watts, p. 8

8   "Treason, like adultery, ranks as one the worst of all possible crimes." Watts, p. 35.

9   Rubenzer and Thomas Faschingbauer assembled a panel of over 100 experts in presidential history to give a psychological profile of each of the presidents. The experts on the panel were instructed to look only at the five-year period before their respective subject became president

# Endnotes

to avoid the influence that life in the White House might have had on their behavior.

10   "Candidates with a solid character--straightforward, dutiful and disciplined--often run into trouble being an effective president." Thomas Rubenzer, a Houston-based clinical psychologist and co-founder of the Foundation for the Study of Personality in History.

11   "The narcissist 'has a grandiose sense of self-importance ...'" Rubenzer, p.211.

12   As quoted *Narcissism Revisited*. Ed. Sam Varkim. Prague: Narcissus Publication, 1991.

13   From *Winning the West*, quoted in *American Crucible*, p. 20.

14   "Theodore Roosevelt's moment of reckoning had come early in his life, sometime in 1872." His father's challenge, to remake himself into a stronger person or die, is described in Edmund Morris' *The Rise of Theodore Roosevelt*, p. 60.

15   "Nothing seemed to relieve him from its strangling grip." Kathleen Dalton gives a detailed account of Roosevelt's childhood illness. Dalton, pp. 35-37.

16   A neurologist diagnosed Theodore as suffering from "the handicap of riches ... excessive upper-class refinement." From Dalton, p. 37.

17   From that point, Theodore began to transform himself, both in body and in identity, from a "nervous and timid child" and "foreordained and predestined victim" into a mighty man of valor. Morris, *The Rise of Theodore Roosevelt*, pp. 59-63.

## Chapter 20: Imperial Grunts

1   "Like the ancient Egyptian ..." *Colossus*, p.14.

2   "Actual annexation of territory..." *Colossus*, page 15

3   "Great reputations were made and destroyed..." *Path Between the Seas*

4   "The Orient has helped to define Europe (or the West) as its contrasting image, idea, personality, experience." Introduction, *Orientalism*

5   "He spoke for and represented her." *Ibid*

6   Because the French writer was wealthy, and from the West, and male, he was able to "speak for her and tell his readers in what way she was 'typically Oriental.'" *Ibid*

7   "The power to narrate, or to block other narratives from forming and emerging ... " Edward Said's Introduction to *Culture and Imperialism*.

## Chapter 21: Tribal Loyalties

1   Roosevelt held the "dream of war as the crucible for forging a superior white race." Gerstle, *American Crucible*, p. 18.

2   "These Teutons possessed the intelligence, the independence, the love of liberty and order, and the intense tribal loyalty (patriotism) necessary to push civilization forward." *Ibid*.

3   "Roosevelt said and wrote much about racial theory and racial beliefs that helped to set the tone for the American understanding of the concept." Dyer, Chapter 1.

# Endnotes

4   "In the intellectual ambience of the late nineteenth century, it would have been remarkable if any individual with Roosevelt's interests and inclinations had not developed a fondness for the discussion of race and race theory." *Ibid*

## CHAPTER 22: A TWITCH ON THE RIGHT SIDE

1   "...what psychologists call 'the acting out of trauma' - show that a person still is psychically immersed in the trauma." From James Berger's essay, *War of Ghosts*. *Contemporary Literature Magazine*. Madison: Fall 1997. Vol. 38, Iss.3

2   "*Beloved* does not recall the past as past and bring the past and the future into a continuous relation without always repeating the past and instating unpleasure together with pleasure. Pleasure's unpleasure, if you will." This example is from an otherwise excellent and insightful essay by Petar Ramadanovic, "In the Future ...:On Trauma and Literature," in *Topologies of Trauma*, ed. Belau and Ramadonovic, New York:Other Press (2002).

3   "In discussing the Holocaust, for example, it makes a difference ... whether the historian is a survivor, the child of survivors, a Jew, a Palestinian, a German, a child of perpetrators ..." LaCapra, *Writing History, Writing Trauma*, p. 40.

4   "If [Weaver] is not the most skilled of writers..." Weaver's truncated 26-page film treatment of *TBR* suggests that his narrative skills lack the scope of his Herculean researching skills.

5   "The trauma of racism is, for the racist and the victim, the severe fragmentation of the self ..." writes trauma scholar Njabulo Ndebele. In his 1998 essay, "Memory, Metaphor, and the Triumph of Narrative," anthologized in *Negotiating the Past The Making of Memory in South Africa*, Editors S. Nuttall and C. Coetzee, (pp.21 - 28).

## Epilogue: Centennial

1   "Are you aware of the consequences?" the Secretary of State asked the President. From Bob Woodward's 2004 book *Plan of Attack* (New York: Simon & Schuster).

2   "Two days prior to this meeting, Cheney and Rumsfeld had called in a key ally, Saudi Prince Bandar bin Sultan, to inform him of the plan for war." *Ibid.*

3   "In June, the Squadron conducted a grueling forced march of nearly 200 kilometers …providing medical care, food, and water to over 27,000 pilgrims in a massive humanitarian undertaking." Long paragraph description from Knight Ridder article, *Barrels Found in Iraq May Contain Chemical Weapons,* by John Sullivan, Knight Ridder, European edition, Sunday, April 27, 2003.

4   "It is a point of pride for me to be able to command [the 10th Cavalry]." CNN, "Buffalo Soldiers Serve Proudly in Iraq" reported in January, 2004.

5   President Chirac warned that "the combat against the dark forces of intolerance and hate is never definitively won." From the *New York Times* article on anniversary of Dreyfus exoneration.

6   " …vacuums often filled by volatility and violence." Niall Ferguson explains this fully in his book *Empire: The Rise and Demise of the British World Order.*

7   "…An examination of Brownsville's many antecedents gives reason to challenge …the binary model of 'white and nonwhite …'" Leiker, p. 119.

# Endnotes

8   "...The problems that black soldiers faced in Brownsville had less to do with regional racial mores, which can be characterized as "southern," than with the peculiarities of a militarized border area." Leiker, p. 132.

9   "By omitting the black-Hispanic relationship that had helped provoke the incident, national press coverage perpetuated ignorance of Brownsville's demography and culture." Leiker, p. 141.

10   "...to move beyond interpreting the affray "as another example of Jim Crow-style discrimination against African Americans, a testimony to the power of bipolar models." Leiker, p. 143.

11   "....In blaming 'white Texans' and white racism for the shooting ..." Leiker, p. 143.

12   "Morgan, unlike the more myopic Rockefeller, saw that Roosevelt stood ready to make concessions ..." Chernow in *Titan* p. 433.

13   "Roosevelt treated the Morgan interests (U.S. Steel, International Harvester, et. al.) more leniently than he did Standard Oil." *Titan* p. 538

14   "Owen Wister says Roosevelt admitted to him that at one point he had been badly advised by the War Department." Wagenknecht, p. 235.

15   "... I am strongly inclined to believe, however, that the bulk of the members of Companies C and B had no such guilty knowledge." TR letter to Aldrich quoted in Wagenknecht, p.235.

16   "... a commander in chief who accomplished much of his grand strategy in silence and secret." Edmund Morris, "A Matter of Extreme Urgency: Theodore Roosevelt, Wilhelm II, and the Venezuelan Crisis of 1902" *Naval War College Review*, Spring 2002, Vol. LV, No.2.

17   "...well done, co-worker." Howland, *Theodore Roosevelt and His Times*, p.p 18-19

# Teddy's Tantrum

# Select Bibliography

Abshire, David M. *Triumphs and Tragedies of the Modern Presidency: Seventy-Six Case Studies in Presidential Leadership*. New York: Praeger Publishers, 2001.

Alberti, Ludwig. *Account of the Tribal Life and Customs of the Xhosa in 1807*. Rotterdam: A.A. Balkema Publishers, 1968.

Alexander, Jeffrey C. ed. *Cultural Trauma and Collective Identity*. Berkeley: University of California Press, 2003.

Anderson, Judith Icke. *William Howard Taft: An Intimate Biography*. New York: W.W. Norton & Company, 1981.

Astor, Gerald. *The Right to Fight: A History of African Americans in the Military*. Novato, California: Presidio Press, 1998.

Bauerlein, Mark. *Negrophobia: A Race Riot in Atlanta, 1906*. San Francisco: Encounter Books, 2001.

Bederman, Gail. *Manliness and Civilization: A Cultural History of Gender of Race in the United States 1880-1917*. Chicago: University of Chicago Press, 1995.

Berger, James. "Book Review: War of Ghosts." *Contemporary Literature Magazine*. Madison: Fall 1997. Vol. 38, Iss.3

Bergerud, Eric. *Red Thunder, Tropic Lightning: The World of the 25th Infantry Combat Division in Vietnam*. Boulder: Westview Press, 1993.

Boot, Max. *The Savage Wars of Peace: Small Wars and the Rise of American Power*. New York: Basic Books, 2003.0

Bradford James C., Editor. *Crucible of Empire: The Spanish American War and Its Aftermath.* Annapolis, Maryland: Naval Institute Press, 1993.

Bradford James C., Editor. *The Military and Conflict Between Cultures: Soldiers at the Interface.* College Station, Tex.: Texas A&M University Press, 1997.

Brands, H. W. *T.R. The Last Romantic.* New York: Basic Books, 1998.

Bredin, Jean-Denis. *The Affair: The Case of Alfred Dreyfus.* New York: George Braziller. 1986.

Buckley, Gail. *American Patriots: The Story of Blacks in the Military from the Revolution to Desert Storm.* New York: Random House, 2001.

Burton, David Henry. Theodore Roosevelt, American Politician: An Assessment. Teaneck: Fairleigh Dickinson University Press, 1997.

*Bussey, Charles M. Firefight at Yechon: Courage and Racism in the Korean War. Lincoln, Nebraska:University of Nebraska Press. 2002.*

Carroll, John M., ed. *The Black Military Experience in the American West.* New York: Liveright Press, 1971.

Chace, James M. *1912: Wilson, Roosevelt, Taft, Debs -- The Election that Changed the Country.* New York: Simon & Schuster, 2004.

Chernow, Ron. *Titan : The Life of John D. Rockefeller, Sr.* New York: Random House, 1988.

Christian, Garna L. *Black Soldiers in Jim Crow Texas 1899-1917.* College Station: Texas A&M University Press, 1995.

Collier, Peter. *The Rockefellers: An American Dynasty.* New York: Henry Holt, 1976.

# Select Bibliography

Cooper, John Milton. *The Warrior and the Priest: Woodrow Wilson and Theodore Roosevelt.* Cambridge: Belknap Press, 2004

Dalton, Kathleen "Theodore Roosevelt and the Idea of War." *Theodore Roosevelt Association Journal* 7 (1981).

Dalton, Kathleen "Why America Loved Teddy Roosevelt: Or, Charisma Is In the Eye of the Beholders." Pp. 269-91 in *Our Selves/Our Past: Psychological Approaches to American History* ed. Robert J. Brugger. Baltimore: Johns Hopkins University Press, 1981.

Dalton, Kathleen. *Theodore Roosevelt: A Strenuous Life.* New York: Alfred A. Knopf, 2002.

Dallek, Robert. *Hail to the Chief: The Making and Unmaking of American Presidents.* New York: Oxford University Press, 2001.

Denson, John V., ed. *Reassessing the Presidency: The Rise of the Executive State and the Decline of Freedom.* Auburn: Mises Institute (June, 2001).

Dyer, Thomas G. *Theodore Roosevelt and the Idea of Race.* Baton Rouge: Louisiana State University Press, 1980.

Edgerton, Robert B. *Hidden Heroism: Black Soldiers in America's Wars.* Boulder, Colorado: Westview Press, 2001.

Elmes, Michael and Barry, David. "Deliverance, Denial and the Death Zone: A Study of Narcissism and Regression in the May 1996 Everest Climbing Disaster." *The Journal of Applied Behavioral Science*, Vol. 35, No.2, June 1999.

Espino, Ovidio Diaz. *How Wall Street Created a Nation.* New York: Four Walls Eight Windows, 2001.

Esthus, Raymond A. *Theodore Roosevelt and the International Rivalries.* Waltham, MA: Ginn–Blaisdell, 1970.

Eyerman, Ron. *Cultural Trauma: Slavery and the Formation of African American Identity.* Cambridge, New York: Cambridge University Press, 2001.

Farrell, Kirby. *Post-Traumatic Culture.* Baltimore and London: The Johns Hopkins University Press, 1998.

Foraker, Joseph. *Notes of a Busy Life.* Reprint Services Corp., 1917

Foraker, Julia. *I Would Live it Again Memories of a Vivid Life.* New York: Harper Brothers, 1932.

Freidel, Frank. *The Splendid Little War.* Boston: Little Brown, 1958.

Gerstle, Gary. *American Crucible: Race and Nation in the Twentieth Century.* Princeton: Princeton University Press, 2002.

Gibbon, Edward. *The History of the Decline and Fall of the Roman Empire.*

Gronk and Feaver, editors. *Soldiers and Civilians.* Cambridge: MIT Press, 2001.

Gould, Lewis L. *The Presidency of Theodore Roosevelt.* Lawrence: Kansas University of Kansas Press, 1991.

Hare, James H., editor. *A Photographic Record of the Russo-Japanese War.* New York: PF Collier & Son, 1999.

Harbaugh, William. *Power and Responsibility: The Life and Times of Theodore Roosevelt.* New York: Octagon Books, 1975.

Hanhimäki Jussi M. *The Flawed Architect.* Oxford: Oxford University Press, 2004.

# Select Bibliography

Hofstadter, Richard. *American Political Tradition*. New York: Vintage, 1984.

Hofstadter, Richard *The Age of Reform*. New York: Vintage, 1988.

Howard, Allen Howard. "Veteran Celebrated in Italy: Lt. John Fox Received Medal of

Honor for Defending Village." *The Cincinnati Enquirer*, Monday, July 10, 2000.

Howell, J. & Shamir, B. "The role of followers in the charismatic leadership process." *Academy of Management Review*, 2005, 30, 96-112.

Howland, Harold. *Theodore Roosevelt and His Times*. Yale University Press New Haven 1921

Iglehart, Ferdinand Cowle. *Theodore Roosevelt: The Man As I Knew Him*. New York: The Christian Herald, 1919.

Jacobson, Matthew Frye. *Barbarian Virtues: The United States Encounters Foreign Peoples at Home and Abroad, 1876-1917*. New York: Hill and Wang, 2001.

Jordan David P. *Gibbon and His Roman Empire*. Urbana: University of Illinois Press, 1971.

Jukes, Geoffrey. *The Russo-Japanese War of 1904-1905*. Oxford:Osprey Publishing, 2002.

Katz, William Loren. *The Black West*. Anchor Books Doubleday New York revised edition 1973.

Keegan, John. *The Face of Battle*. New York: Penguin, 1984.

Keegan, John. *The Mask of Command.* New York: Penguin, 1988.

Keller, Morton, editor. *Theodore Roosevelt: A Profile.* New York: Hill & Wang, 1967.

Kernis, M.H. & Sun, C.-R. "Narcissism and Reactions to Interpersonal Feedback." *Journal of Research in Personality*, 1994, 28, 4-13.

Killblane, Richard E. "The Assault on San Juan Hill," *Military History* (1992).

Kissinger, Henry. *Ending the Vietnam War.* New York: Simon & Schuster, 2003.

Knight, Ian. *The Anatomy of the Zulu Soldier: From Shaka to Cetshwayo.* London: Stackpole Books, 1999.

LaCapra, Dominick. *History and Criticism.* Ithaca:Cornell University Press, 1984.

LaCapra, Dominick. *Writing History, Writing Trauma.* Baltimore: The Johns Hopkins University Press, 2001.

Lane, Ann. *The Brownsville Affair: National Crisis and Black Reaction.* New York: Kennikat Press, 1971.

Lasswell, *Essays on the Garrison State.* Piscataway, NJ: Transaction Publishers, 1997.

Leiker, James N. *Racial Borders: Black Soldiers Along the Rio Grande.* College Station, Texas: Texas A&M University Press, 2002.

Leys, Ruth. *Trauma: A Geneology.* Chicago:University of Chicago Press, 2000.

# Select Bibliography

Lodge, Henry Cabot. *Selections from the Correspondence of Theodore Roosevelt and Henry Cabot Lodge, 1884-1919*. New York: Scribner's, 1925.

Looker, Earle. *The White House Gang*. New York: Fleming H. Revell Co., 1929

Maccoby, M. "Narcissistic leaders: The incredible pros, the inevitable cons." *Harvard Business Review*, 2000, 78(1), 68-78.

Mahan, A.T. *The Influence of Sea Power Upon World History, 1660-1783*. New York: Dover Publications (reprint).

McCullough, David. *Mornings on Horseback* New York: Simon & Schuster, 1982.

McCullough, David. *Path Between the Seas*. New York: Simon & Schuster, 1977.

Means, Howard. *Colin Powell*. New York: Donald I Fine, 1992.

Mikaelian, Allen. *Medal of Honor: Profiles of America's Military Heroes*. New York: Hyperion, 2002.

Millard, Candice. *River of Doubt: Theodore Roosevelt's Darkest Journey*. New York: Doubleday, 2005.

Milton, George Fort. *The Use of Presidential Power 1789-1943*. Boston: Little Brown and Company, 1944.

Morris, Edmund. *The Rise of Theodore Roosevelt*. New York: Coward McCann and Geoghegan, 1979

Morris, Edmund *Theodore Rex*. New York: Coward McCann and Geoghegan, 2001.

Morris, Edmund. *"A Matter of Extreme Urgency": Theodore Roosevelt, Wilhelm II, and the Venezuela Crisis of 1902*. Naval War College Review, Spring, 2002

Motley Mary Penick. *The Invisible Soldier: The Experience of the Black Soldier*. Wayne State University Press Detroit 1975

Nalty, Bernard C. *Strength for the Fight: A History of Black Americans in the Military*. New York: Free Press, 1986.

Neustadt, Richard E. *Presidential Power and the Modern Presidents*. New York: Free Press, 1991.

Oshinsky, David M. *A Conspiracy So Immense: The World of Joe McCarthy*. New York: The Free Press, 1983.

O'Toole, Patricia. *When Trumpets Call*. New York: Simon & Schuster, 2005.

Ponder, Stephen. *Managing the Press: Origins of the Media Presidency, 1897-1933*. New York: St. Martins Press, 1998.

Powell, Colin L. *My American Journey*. New York: Random House. 1995

Raskin, R.N. & Hall, C.S. "A narcissistic personality inventory." *Psychological Reports*, 1979, 45, 590. *Journal of Personality Assessment*, 1981, 45, 159-162.

Rauchway, Eric. *Murdering McKinley: The Making of Theodore Roosevelt's America*. New York: Hill & Wang, 2002.

Renehan, Edward J. *The Lion's Pride: Theodore Roosevelt and His Family in Peace and War*. New York: Oxford University Press, 1999.

Reeves, Richard. *Jet Lag*. New Yorker 199__. (essay on the Weavers' involvement in Los Angeles Fire Department)

# Select Bibliography

Riis, Jacob A. *Theodore Roosevelt the Citizen*. New York: The Outlook Company, 1903.

Roosevelt, Theodore. *The Rough Riders*. New York: Charles Scribner's Sons, 1920 (a reprint of the original 1902 edition).

Roosevelt, Theodore. *Theodore Roosevelt An Autobiography*. New York: The MacMillan Company, 1913.

Roosevelt, Theodore. *The Works of Theodore Roosevelt*. New York: Charles Scribner's Sons 1923-26.

Rubenzer, Fashingbauer and Ones. *Personality, Character and Leadership in the White House: Psychologists Assess the Presidents*. Dulles, Virginia: Brasseys, 2003.

Rubenzer, Fashingbauer and Ones "Psychological Scaling Among U.S. Presidents." Research paper presented to the American Psychological Association, 2000.

Rudalevige, Andrew *The New Imperial Presidency : Renewing Presidential Power after Watergate*. Ann Arbor: University of Michigan Press, 2005.

Said, Edward. *Orientalism*. New York: Vintage, 1979.

Said, Edward. *Culture and Imperialism*. New York:Vintage, 1994.

Said, Edward. *The Edward Said Reader*. New York: Vintage, 2001.

Sankowsky, D. "The charismatic leader as narcissist: Understanding the abuse of power." *Organizational Dynamics*, 1995, 23(4), 57-72.

Schubert, Frank N. *Black Valor: Buffalo Soldiers and the Medal of Honor 1870-1898*. Wilmington, Delaware: Scholarly Resources, 1997.

Smith, Gene. *Until the Last Trumpet Sounds: The Life of General of the Armies John J,. Pershing.* New York: John Wiley & Sons, 1998.

Steward T.G. *The Colored Regulars in the U.S.Army.* New York: Arno Press, 196_.

Stoler, Ann. *Race and the Education of Desire: Foucalt's History of Sexuality and the Colonial Order of Things.* Durham, N.C: Duke University Press, 1995.

Strouse, Jean. *Morgan: American Financier.* New York: Random House, 1999.

Tal, Kali. *Worlds of Hurt: Reading the Literatures of Trauma.* Cambridge, MA and Cambridge, UK: Cambridge Studies in American Literature and Culture, 1996.

Thornbrough, Emma Lou. "The Brownsville Episode and the Black Vote." *The Mississippi Valley Historical Review: A Journal of American History.* Vol XLIV, No.3, December, 1957.

Vickroy, Laurie. *Trauma and Survival in Contemporary Fiction.* University of Virginia Press, 2002.

Viviano, Frank. "Almost-Forgotten Heroes: Italian Town Honors Black GIs." *San Francisco Chronicle,* Thursday, July 13, 2000.

Wagenknecht, Edward. *The Seven Worlds of Theodore Roosevelt.* New York: Longmans, Green & Co., 1958.

Walder, David. *The Short Victorious War: The Russo-Japanese Conflict 1904-5.* New York: Harper & Row, 1973.

Ward Geoffrey C. *A First-Class Temperament: The Emergence of Franklin Roosevelt.* HarperCollins New York 1989

# Select Bibliography

Watts, Sarah. *Rough Rider in the White House: Theodore Roosevelt and the Politics of Desire*. Chicago: University of Chicago Press, 2003.

Weaver, John D. *The Brownsville Raid*. New York: W. W. Norton & Company, 1970.

Weaver, John D. *The Senator and the Sharecropper's Son: Exoneration of the Brownsville Soldiers*. College Station: Texas A & M University Press, 1997.

Weaver John D. *Glad Tidings, A Friendship in Letters: The Correspondence of John Cheever and John D. Weaver, 1945-1982*. New York: HarperCollins, 1992.

Weaver, John D. *As I Live and Breathe*. New York: Rinehart & Company, 1959.

Weaver, John D. *Earl Warren: The Man, The Court, The Era*. Boston: Little Brown, 1967.

Willard, Tom. *Buffalo Soldiers*. New York: Forge 1996.

Wilson, Robert A., editor. *Power and the Presidency*. New York: Public Affairs/Perseus Books 1999.

Wister, Owen. *Roosevelt – The Story of a Friendship, 1880-1919*. Macmillan, 1930.

Wood, Fred S., editor. *Roosevelt As We Knew Him: Personal Recollections of 150 Friends*. Philadelphia: The John C. Winston Co., 1927

Woodward, Bob. *Plan of Attack* New York: Simon & Schuster, 2004.

Wynne, Lewis N. "Brownsville: The Reaction of the Negro Press." *Phylon, The Atlanta University Review of Race and Culture*, Volume XXXIII, Number 2 Summer, 1992.

Explore the history of *Teddy's Tantrum*. Extensive interactive content and media is available online at:
https://view.genial.ly/5fa63a1e89da530d018cdf7d/presentation-tt-intro

www.ingramcontent.com/pod-product-compliance
Lightning Source LLC
Chambersburg PA
CBHW022006120526
44592CB00032B/131